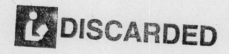

Hungary

HUNGARY

a short History

C. A. MACARTNEY D. LITT.

EDINBURGH
at the University Press

EDINBURGH UNIVERSITY PRESS
22 George Square, Edinburgh
North America
Aldine Publishing Company
529 South Wabash Avenue, Chicago

ISBN 0 85224 035 X

Library of Congress
Catalog Card Number 62-19084

Reprinted 1966, 1968, 1974

Printed in Great Britain by
Lewis Reprints Ltd.
(member of the Brown Knight & Truscott Group)
London & Tonbridge

PREFACE

MY warm thanks are due to my two alleged pupils – sed plus docuerunt, quam didicerunt – Mr J. Bak and Mr L. Péter, for their criticisms and suggestions on respectively the earlier and later chapters of this book. They are, of course, blameless for any errors of fact which have escaped their scrutiny, and for interpretations and judgments which reflect a view of Hungarian history, and of many persons and processes in it, with which they must not be held to agree.

C. A. MACARTNEY
All Souls College, Oxford
November, 1961

CONTENTS

ILLUSTRATIONS

MAPS

The Publisher is much indebted to various organisations and individuals for help in obtaining photographs for reproduction: in particular the Hungarian Legation, Radio Times Hulton Picture Library, and Dr Macartney. None of these are responsible for weaknesses in the quality of reproduction of certain plates, which are due to prevailing difficulties in obtaining new photographs of certain historical material.

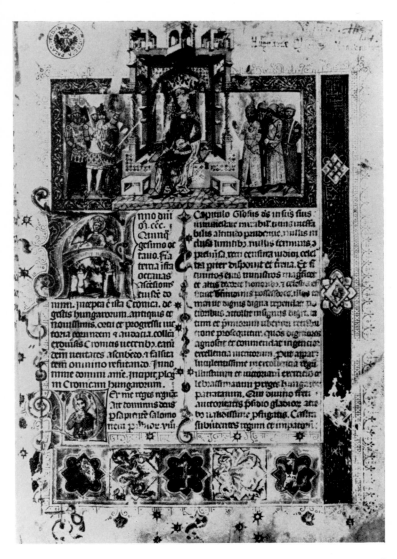

1. *Title page of the National Chronicle of Hungary written in the reign of Louis the Great, c. 1370: ref. p. 43*

2 and 3. *The Alföld at Hortobágy '. . . an open, featureless expanse, a true steppe-land': ref. p. 3*

I

THE BEGINNINGS

No STATE in European history has a beginning so precisely definable as Hungary. It was brought into being well-nigh full-panoplied, by a single act, when the Magyars, until then a people without fixed abode, entered the basin of the middle Danube, a place at that juncture as good as masterless, and made it their home. This was in the last years of the ninth century A.D.

Many writers, not Hungarians alone, have dilated on the 'natural unity' of the Middle Danube Basin, which now became Hungary. The parts of it seem, indeed, designed by nature to form one harmonious whole. Through the heart of it the great river itself runs a course of nearly 600 miles, most of it through flat or flattish lands which form an oval plain, about 100,000 square miles in extent, 400 miles at its greatest width from west to east, 300 from north to south. This plain is surrounded by a ring of mountains, whose valleys converge on the central plain; of the rivers of Historic Hungary, only one flows north, to join the Vistula; one, like the Danube itself, cuts its own way through the Transylvanian Alps; all the rest join the Danube on its central course. The mountains, which in the north and east form an almost continuous wall, rarely broken, with the dense forests which up to recent times covered their slopes, form a natural defence for the plain, especially towards the east. The products of plain and mountain are mutually complementary, linking their inhabitants in a natural community of destiny.

But if there is to be unity here, it can never derive from uniformity, but only from a synthesis of mutually disparate

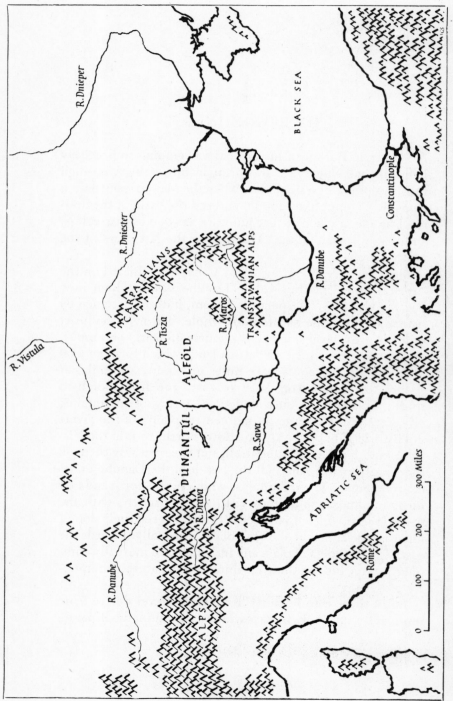

Map 1. The Middle Danube Basin

components. And this disparity is not only between plain and mountain. The vast plain itself consists of two parts which differ in important respects, both in their own characters and in their natural connections and relationships with the outer world. The smaller, western portion, which is contained within the crook of the Danube, the Pannonia of the Romans, called by the Hungarians the Dunántúl – the land beyond the Danube – hardly deserves the name of plain: it contains some large flat spaces, but most of it is a pleasant, undulating country of hills and valleys, the geographical continuation of the outliers of the Eastern Alps and the Balkans, from which, and from their hinterlands, it is easily accessible. On the other hand, what lies between the left bank of the Danube and the Transylvanian foothills – the Alföld, or lowland proper – is an open, featureless expanse, a true steppe-land, a sort of outpost of the vaster Pontic and Caspian steppes, from which only the Carpathian wall separates it; and in that wall, solid as most of it is, there are breaches at least one of which was in the older days easier to force than the crossing of the mighty Danube itself.

Even if we disregard the high mountains and Transylvania, which usually lived its own life, the fates of the two parts of the plain in early times and the Dark Ages were often very different, sometimes sharply opposed. The western half was usually peopled and intermittently controlled from its immediate or remoter central European, or Italian, hinterlands; for several centuries it belonged to Rome. By contrast, the Great Plain was recurrently occupied by waves of nomadic horsemen, the overspill from the seemingly inexhaustible reservoir of these peoples which then filled the Pontic, Caspian and central Asiatic steppes. Scythians, Sarmatians, Huns (with their Germanic subjects), Bulgars and Avars all successively sought in it a refuge from more powerful neighbours, and a home.

These two elements – Europe and Asia – strove for mastery, and neither ever achieved it quite completely. The horsemen, when they arrived, were usually the stronger in the field and some of them carried their conquests across the Danube and as far as the western forests, but in time they always weakened, their empires collapsed and Europe reasserted itself. On the other hand, the Europeans seldom ventured beyond what was for them the greatest of natural defensive lines, the Danube; the Romans themselves, who for a while held Transylvania as well as the west, left the Great Plain alone, even during a long period when its nomadic population was exceptionally weak. There were other times when neither Asia nor Europe was present in force, and when the whole Basin was little more than a no-man's land, and the end of the ninth century A.D was one of these times. The Avars, the last invaders to enter the Basin in force, had ruled the whole of it for the unprecedented span of over two centuries, but their power, too, had decayed with time, and at the opening of the century Charlemagne had destroyed it utterly. The German Empire had, however, limited its subsequent extension of its political frontiers to the old Pannonia and the areas flanking it north and south, and even there it had done no more than set up a series of dependencies, governed by Slavonic 'dukes', whose allegiance was often insecure. One of these vassal states, Croatia, had made itself fully independent in 869, and Sviatopluk, Duke of Moravia, which then included the area between the Danube and the Gran, had been in open defiance of his overlord for as long.

The East Roman Empire, of which the Serbia of the day was a loose dependency, disputed Syrmia with the Western Empire, but did not look across the Danube-Drave line. Bulgaria may have exercised suzerainty over the Alföld, and perhaps Transylvania, but its rule over either area was at best shadowy. Thus a number of Powers claimed rule over parts of the Basin, but all of them were peripheral to it, their own centres far distant from it. The native populations ruled by these Powers were as various as they. There were Moravian Slavs in the north-west, Slovenes in Pannonia; in the north, and along the banks of the Tisza, some more Slav settlements, and roaming the plains of the Alföld, a nomadic people of Eastern origin, perhaps akin to the Magyars themselves: the Szekels. The ethnic appurtenance of the then inhabitants of Transylvania is acrimoniously disputed between Roumanian and Hungarian historians, the former maintaining that a Roman, or alternatively, Romanised Dacian, population had survived the Dark Ages, the latter pointing to the fact that all the pre-Magyar place-names of Transylvania are Slav, except four river-names, which are not Latin; also that the first mention of 'Vlachs' in Hungarian documents comes in the thirteenth century, when they figure only as roving shepherds, and not numerous.

In any case, all these populations were sparse. The most densely populated area was probably the foothills and open valleys of the north-west. The upper valleys and mountains of the Carpathians were practically uninhabited. There were only one or two places larger than hamlets in Pannonia, or in the Alföld. Transylvania, too, whatever the ethnic appurtenance of such inhabitants as it possessed, consisted at that time mostly of unpenetrated forest.

Such was the situation in the Basin when the Magyars appeared on the further side of the Carpathian Gate.

To all appearance, the Magyars were just such another horde of Asiatic strangers as their predecessors – the Huns (with whom their victims, and later, their own national legend, mistakenly identified them), the Avars and the rest. The travellers, Arabs and Greeks alike, who first came into contact with them, described them as 'a race of Turks'. Ethnologically, this was incorrect. The linguistic evidence shows that the Magyars' remoter ancestors belonged to the Finno-Ugrian family of peoples whose habitats in olden days extended from the Baltic to the middle Urals. In their original homes, which were densely forested, these peoples lived a primitive existence as hunters and fishers, hardly acquainted even with agriculture and possessed only of the most primitive political and social organisation. But early in the Christian era some causes unknown to us seem to have driven the Magyars' direct ancestors, who were the easternmost of these peoples, across the Urals, and thence southward into the steppes, and here, under the influence of geography and, presumably, of the Turki and Iranian peoples with whom they came into contact (how far, if at all, this contact took the form of conquest it is now impossible to say), they exchanged their former way of life for the nomadic herdsmen's existence appropriate to their new environment.

They now also became exposed to the fate of all the steppe-dwellers, attack by a stronger neighbour – nearly always on their east – forcing them to change their feeding grounds; an easy matter for nomads provided that their western neighbours, in their turn, were weaker than they. The Magyars' moves west seem to have begun in the fifth century A.D. Recent research has thrown doubts on what had been the accepted version of their movements during the next four centuries, and we may omit a conjectural account of it here. We reach firmer ground about A.D. 830, when we find them established – by all evidence, newly so – above the Maeotis, on the right bank of the Don. This body of them consisted of seven hordes, or tribes, but they had certainly shed some parts of the nation on the way: some 'Magyars' are attested as still living in the Ural steppes in the ninth century, others, a century later, in the Caucasus. The name of 'On Ogur' or Ten Arrows (the word 'Hungarian' is a Slavicised form of this Turkish term) by which their neighbours knew them may enshrine a memory of their earlier condition, or may refer to their organisation in the ninth century, for on the Maeotis they

were joined by three dissident hordes – known as Kavars –
of the Khazars, the powerful Turki nation, famous for its
conversion to the Israelite faith, which at that time held
the mouths of the Volga.

By this time the Magyars were indeed 'a race of Turks'
to all outward appearance. They subsisted by pasturing
their herds in summer over the grasslands round their base,
retiring in winter to the shores of the Maeotis and the
banks of the Don. Although they now practised a little
agriculture, their chief sustenance was meat, mare's milk
and fish. Much of their lives was spent in the saddle, and
their raids and campaigns, too, were conducted on horse-
back. Their favoured arm was the bow and arrow.

If any earlier conquest of the primitive Finno-Ugrians
by a more warlike Turki people had ever taken place, all
memory, and all trace, of it had vanished. Except for the
penal slaves, the Magyars were 'all free men'; elaborate
social differentiation between them was unnecessary, for
they supplied themselves adequately with slaves by raiding
the neighbouring Slavs. They supplemented their incomes
by selling the surplus in the Crimean markets.

The basic social unit was the clan, the members of
which acknowledged a real or imagined common ancestry.
A varying number of clans went to the tribe. The authority
of the tribal chiefs seems to have been hereditary, but
when we first hear of them, the tribes were united only in
a loose federation, owning no single supreme authority.
They were at one time in an alliance, which may not have
been quite an equal one, with the Khazars, and according
to one source the Khazar Khagan tried to unite them by
marrying his daughter to the most powerful of their chiefs,
but the marriage proved barren, and with it, the attempt.

The same source ascribes to the Khagan a second, and this
time successful attempt with another chief. The Magyar
national tradition, ignoring the Khazar element, says that,
having decided to migrate, the seven chieftains elected the

most powerful of their number, Árpád, son of Almus, to
lead them, swearing with ritual drinking of mingled blood
to accept him and his male issue in perpetuity as heads of
the nation. (Almus was then still alive, but presumably too
old to be an effective leader.) According to this tradition,
the decision to migrate was motivated by pressure of population on the feeding grounds; foreign sources reveal that
in fact the Magyars had suffered defeat at the hands of a
nation newly arrived from the East, the Petchenegs, who
had evicted them from their feeding grounds. This was in
A.D. 889, and Árpád now led his people westward in quest
of a new home. The Kavars came with them, as did half a
dozen small hordes of Turki or Ugrian origin.[1] Their journey brought them to the outer slopes of the Carpathians,
and by the favour of fortune, to a new life beyond them.

For had the passes been held strongly against them, this
would have been the end of their national existence; those
not destroyed by the Petchenegs would gradually have lost
their national identity, as refugees in foreign lands and
mercenaries in foreign armies. But far from finding their
road barred, they were actually invited to enter on it. In
892 the Emperor Arnulf enlisted a contingent of them to
help him against his rebellious vassal, Sviatopluk. The weakness of the land was revealed to them. In 894 they were
back, raiding Pannonia on their own account, and in the
autumn of 895 or the spring of 896 the entire nation, with

[1] These smaller hordes figure in the central Hungarian narrative
chronicles under the generic name of 'Kuns'. The 'Anonymus'
translates this term as 'Cumani'. Hungarian historians have fallen
into confusion by identifying Anonymus' Cumans with the Kavars
and by regarding the tribes enumerated by Constantine Porphyro-
genetos, with the Kavars and the Magyars themselves, as tribes of the
Magyars. But the truth is that the cortège consisted of (1) the
Magyar nation, subdivided into seven tribes, all calling themselves
Magyars; (2) six or seven minor 'Kun' hordes; (3) three Khazar
tribes, collectively known as 'Kavars'. The Kavars were so independent that the national tradition retains no memory of them.

4. 'The seven chieftains elected Árpád to lead them': ref. p. 8

5. Silver-gilt pouch-covers of Migration-period Magyars

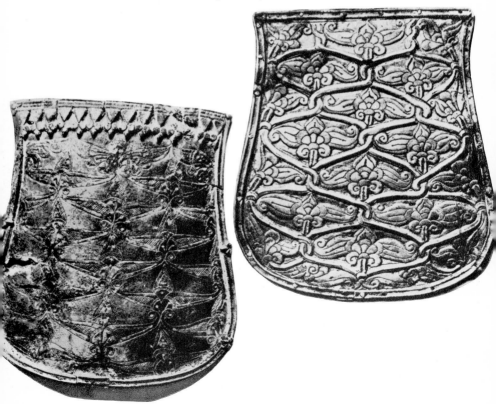

6. *An Árpád dynasty fortress at Esztergom : ref. p. 11*

7. *Ruins of an early castle at Diósgyör*

their auxiliaries, crossed the mountains for good. A little fighting left them in possession of the Alföld (where the Szekels submitted themselves voluntarily) and put an end to any resistance from Transylvania. The Germans and Moravians patched up their differences in view of the common danger, but by A.D. 900 Frankish rule in Pannonia had vanished. The final destruction of Moravian rule in the north-west came in 906. In 907 a Bavarian army was annihilated at Ennsburg and the Magyars' rule extended up to the Avars' old frontier where the Enns runs into the Danube.

The Magyars had thus entered on possession of their new homes speedily and completely, far more so than, as far as we know, any of their predecessors. It is important to emphasise that what had been done was indeed to establish a nation in a new home, not, as the Normans did in England or Russia, to impose the rule of a relatively small band of conquerors on a subject people. The invaders did not, of course, exterminate the indigenous populations, and may even have admitted some of their chieftains into their own ranks, with their status unimpaired; but most usually, they were allotted as subjects or tributaries to one or another of the Magyar tribal chiefs, or at best, given a semi-free status. The polity was exclusively that of the Magyars and their confederates.

We have no certainty as to the invaders' numbers; one of their chroniclers gives the number of the Magyar clans at 108, which reads like genuine tradition, but his statement that each of the 108 could produce 2,000 armed men seems more dubious. The Magyars and their allies were, however, numerous enough to occupy in sufficient force all the then habitable parts of their new home, viz. the plain, using the term in its widest sense. Árpád's own horde settled in the Dunántúl, between Székesfehérvár, on the site of which, or near it, he made his headquarters, and Buda. Of the six other Magyar hordes, three settled respectively north-west,

west and south-west of the leading tribe, one on the middle
Tisza and one on the upper. The seventh, the tribe of Gyula,
after first settling in the west, moved to the approaches of
Transylvania. The plain of the lower Tisza and its tributaries was allotted to the Kavars, while the 'Kuns' took the
northern fringes of the Great Plain.

The invaders did not then attempt to occupy the mountains, which were not adapted to their economy. These,
and certain marshlands, were deliberately left as an un-
cultivated and impenetrable belt, known as 'gyepü', the
passages across which were watched by permanent guards,
a service to which most of the Szekels were assigned.
Beyond this again, there were perhaps isolated outposts.

For the next half-century the Magyars were the scourge
of Europe, which they raided far and wide, striking terror
into the hearts of their victims with the suddenness of
their descents – for their little, lithe horses outdistanced
any news of their coming – the ferocity of their attacks,
their outlandish and, to Western eyes, hideous appearance,
their blood-curdling battle-yells. Historians have counted
thirty-three expeditions between 898 and 955, some of
them to places as far afield as Bremen, Cambrai, Orléans,
Nîmes, Otranto and Constantinople, and there must have
been innumerable smaller enterprises of which no record
has survived. Most of these raids were simple profit-
making expeditions, in which cities and churches were
ransacked and gold and treasure carried off, with captives
for domestic use, re-export or re-sale in return for ransom.
Alternatively, Danegeld was exacted. In addition, the
Magyars often hired out their services to one or another
warring prince, against his neighbours.

In this half-century they inflicted dreadful damage on
Europe, but even for themselves this mode of life was not
invariably profitable. Arnulf of Bavaria almost annihilated
one of their armies in 917. In 933 Henry the Fowler gave

them a frightful beating near Merseburg. Finally in 955 Otto the Great inflicted a terrible defeat on them outside Augsburg. Their leaders were taken and shamefully hanged and according to legend only seven of the whole host escaped, to beg their way round Hungary, disgraced men for ever.

By now the west had organised its defences, and the Hungarian nation itself was changing. The flower of it had perished in the barren fighting, and among the survivors, miscegenation must have thinned out the old, fiery 'Scythian' blood. Possibly, too, the natural increase of home-bred slaves was enough to make the acquisition of new ones unnecessary.

Another influence was that of Christianity. It was the age when Rome and Byzantium were competing for the souls of the east European peoples. The Eastern church had secured the allegiance of the Bulgars, the Serbs, the Russians and, for a while, the Moravians. Rome had then wrested the Moravians from it and had gained the Slovenes, the Croats and, of course, all the Germans. Both churches were anxious to add the Hungarians to their bag. In the middle of the century the Eastern church gained the adhesion of two important Hungarian chieftains, but the advantage lay with its Western rival. Not only was its faith that of the Hungarians' own Moravian and Slovene subjects, but it was also being vigorously propagated from Bavaria, with which Hungary had drifted into a not unfriendly relationship. The decisive step came about A.D. 970. Árpád's grandson, Taksony or Toxun, died and was succeeded by his son Géza, who, breaking with his father's policy, sent ambassadors to Otto's court and established friendly relations with him. The raids in the west ceased. A great missionary activity set in under the auspices of the Bavarians Wolfgang and Pilgrim of Passau, later reinforced by Adalbert of Prague. Géza moved his capital to Esztergom and surrounded himself with a bodyguard of Bavarian knights, on whom he bestowed large estates. Progress was delayed by conflicts in Germany, but when Henry II recovered the dukedom of Bavaria in 985, he renewed the old alliance with Hungary. His successor, Henry III, consented to the marriage of his sister, Gisella, to Géza's son Vajk, who had already been baptised under the name of Stephen (István). The marriage took place in 996. A year later, Géza died.

Under St Stephen (he was proclaimed Saint in 1083), the best-beloved, most famous and perhaps the most important figure in Hungarian history, and largely through his personal genius, the transition begun under Géza was completed.

Stephen's own position depended on the success of the new trend, for he was still a young man when his father died[1] and there were elder members of his family alive. One of these, a certain Koppány, claimed the succession under the principle of *senioratus*, and it was only the help of his father's and his wife's heavy cavalry from Bavaria that brought Stephen the victory, after a severe struggle. Then, in A.D. 1000, he applied to Rome for recognition as a king.

He was uniquely fortunate in the moment of his application. Other aspiring rulers before him had made the same request. Sometimes the Pope had rejected it (legend has it that the Duke of Poland applied almost simultaneously with Stephen, and was refused); sometimes he had granted it and the kingdom failed to maintain itself, owing to the Emperor's hostility. Some crowns the Emperor granted, and the absence of Papal endorsement allowed rivals to question their validity. But precisely in A.D. 1000 both the Pope and the Emperor of the day were remarkable figures, and an unique relationship existed between the young Otto III, who dreamed of 'renewing the Empire', and Sylvester II,

---

[1] The date of Stephen's birth is uncertain. Some chronicles give it as early as 967, but the older of his legends describes him as 'still a child' when he succeeded his father.

who had been Otto's tutor, was still his friend and mentor, and was able to make him see the Empire rather as an oecumenical community of Christian nations than as a Germanic temporal dominion. So it came about that with Otto's agreement, Sylvester sent back Stephen's emissary bearing, if the legend is true[1], the gifts of a crown and an Apostolic cross, joint tokens of Stephen's royal dignity and status and of his authority to establish a national church. The coronation and unction took place on Christmas Day, A.D. 1000.

It is impossible to over-emphasise the importance of these ceremonies. By them both Stephen's own status and that of his people were transformed. The act of conversion changed the Hungarian people from an outlaw horde against whom a Christian Prince was not only free, but bound by duty, to take up arms, into a member of the Christian family of nations, and their prince into one of those rulers by the Grace of God whose legitimate rights his fellow-princes could not infringe without sin. The royal crown made its wearer a true sovereign, not indeed the Emperor's equal in status, but in no respect subject to his overlordship, while the Apostolic insignia made the Hungarian church free of any other authority save that of Rome alone – an enormous reinforcement of the country's real independence.

Coronation also transformed Stephen's position *vis-à-vis*

---

[1] Some modern historians doubt whether these physical emblems were really sent, and it is certainly impossible to accept without qualification the national tradition which long identified the famous Holy Crown of Hungary, still in existence, with Sylvester's gift, for the circlet which forms the lower part of the crown is demonstrably Byzantine work of the eleventh century; it seems to have been sent, in or about A.D. 1075, to the Hungarian King Géza I by the Byzantine Emperor Michael Dukas VII. There are, however, no technical grounds against assigning an earlier date to the closed upper part with which the circlet has been united (probably under Béla IV), and foreign sources, as well as the Hungarian legend, attest the sending of a crown. The Cross is mentioned only in the Hungarian legend.

his own people, for the political philosophy of the day conceded to a crowned king practically unlimited powers, subject only to the precept of Christian morality that he should
exercise those powers with justice and mercy. Hungary was
again fortunate in that Stephen had the capacity to attack
his new task seriously, and was granted length of years (he
died only in 1038) to consolidate it, at home and abroad.
The maintenance of Hungary's international status gave him
no serious trouble. He easily repelled a single attack, which
seems to have been quite unjustified, launched on him in
1030 by the Emperor Conrad; apart from this, and from
some minor brushes with Poland and Bulgaria, his reign
was untroubled by international conflict. At home, he had
one more struggle against a malcontent relative, this time
his maternal uncle, who had established a quasi-independent
principality in Transylvania, and another against a certain
'very powerful prince' in south-eastern Hungary, named
Ohtum or Ajtony, who was probably the last of the Kavars;
at any rate, they are not heard of again, as a unit. With the
defeat of these two men the royal authority became unchallenged through all Hungary.

By that authority, Stephen seems to have claimed and
exercised all the recognised prerogatives of mediaeval
kingship: the conduct of international relations, with the
jus belli et pacis, the *jus legis ferendae*, the right to appoint
any man of his choice to any office, the right to dispense
justice. In the book of precepts which he had compiled
for the guidance of his son, he advises him to take council
with elders and to defer to their advice, and his laws
mention a 'Senatus', but in a context which suggests that
this was a purely advisory body. One document records,
in rather obscure language, that a wider body, the 'tota
communitas', was consulted on a question of nation-wide
importance and its decision accepted, but there is no
evidence of a general, institutionalised national assembly.

On the other hand, Stephen believed in law and held that

the laws of every country and people should be appropriate
to themselves. He did not, therefore, touch the traditional
national structure more than was necessary to adapt it to
the new situation. The body of freemen – i.e., the descendants in the male line of the old conquerors, in so far as
they had not forfeited their status by rebellion or individual
crime, together with any new elements admitted to the
same status – retained their special position. They were not
merely a privileged class of subjects: they were the sole
positive element among them; if not the king's partner in
the polity, then at least his counterpart. They, and only
they, were entitled to participate in such consultations on
policy as took place and to hold public office: they and they
alone had direct access to the king's justice. Stephen imposed on them the obligation of paying tithes to the church,
but they paid no other taxation; their obligation towards
the polity was discharged by military service, which it was
their duty and their prerogative to perform whenever required. Lands held by them *jure primae occupationis* were
truly their own, and Stephen laid down that they should be
free to bequeath them to any member of their families, or
to the church. Otherwise, the national tradition had it that
a man's land, failing traceable heir, reverted to his clan (it
must be remembered that the bulk of the Magyars were
then still living in clan communities).

Stephen did not interfere with the institution of slavery,
although he set his people an example, which some of
them followed, by liberating his own slaves. Manumission
did not, of course, confer admission to the national community, but to an intermediate condition of personal freedom, not accompanied by political status. The proportion
of the population so situated was, already in his day, considerable, for, besides freed slaves, it included also 'guests'
or voluntary immigrants, some of whom were able to contract for relatively favourable terms. Generally speaking,
these men of this class, answering to the Saxon geneats and

geburs or villeins, paid dues to their lord – the king or another – for their lands.

The soil of Hungary now fell into three categories. There were the lands held by the clans, communally or individually, *jure primae occupationis*. In principle all the rest – and this amounted to a full half of the whole, for besides Stephen's own patrimony and land confiscated from rebels, it included the gyepü and what lay beyond it, as well as unoccupied areas within the belt of settlement – now became formally king's land. Some of this, however, Stephen bestowed in the form of donations, to the church or to private individuals, whose titles now ranked equally with those of the original freemen; and so far as is known, they owed no obligation in return for them except that of personal military service, although the big concessionaries, like their native counterparts, must have been required to bring followers to war. The land retained by the king for his own was divided for administrative purposes into units known by the Slavonic name of 'Megye' (county), each under a king's official, the 'Ispán' (another Slavonic term), who administered the unfree population living on it and collected from them the taxation which formed the royal revenue, national and local. Each Ispán maintained at his 'vár' (fortress) or headquarters an armed force composed of freemen who took service under him, or of persons freed by the king. In Stephen's day there were forty-two such counties. It does not appear that the Ispáns of the day had any jurisdiction over the clan lands near their várs, and the scarcity of várs recorded in the Kun area suggests that Stephen did not introduce the system at all where large masses of freemen were living together. But it was at the várs that the king or his deputy, the 'Comes Palatii', administered justice between the local freemen when they went on circuit, and it is reasonable to suppose that smaller bodies of clansmen followed the local Ispán in battle.

8. *The Holy Crown: ref. p.* 13

9. *The Seal of King Géza II*

10. *St Ladislas I: 'a true paladin and gentle knight': ref. p. 20*

Géza's Christianity had been assumed for purely political purposes, and had not even involved complete renunciation of the old beliefs. He is said to have declared himself 'rich enough to afford two Gods'. Stephen, on the other hand, had been brought up in the new faith, receiving instruction, amongst others, from St Adalbert of Prague, and although he was certainly not blind to the political connection between kingship and Christianity, he was a sincere believer. In his Admonitions to his son, he names the Faith first among the props of the royal power; the church second, and the priesthood third; and it was, in fact, far rather on the ecclesiastical than on the lay arm that he rested his authority. The conversion of the people, which he carried through (principally, perforce, through the agency of foreign missionaries) went hand in hand with the establishment of a complete ecclesiastical organisation. When he died, Hungary was divided into two archiepiscopal and eight episcopal sees; there was one parish church to every ten villages. The sees and some of the numerous monasteries founded during his reign were among the largest landowners in the country.

2

THE NATIONAL KINGDOM

AFTER Stephen's death in 1038 Hungary experienced a long period of fluctuating fortunes, for which disputes for the crown were chiefly responsible. There was still no recognised law of succession: the Árpád family tradition, following the national usage, recognised the principle of *senioratus*, while the natural affection of kings caused them repeatedly to seek to pass over a brother or an uncle in favour of a son. While rebellion against a king recognised as legitimately crowned was rare, there were frequent disputes between rival pretenders to the crown, these civil wars being greatly facilitated by the custom of assigning one third of the country as his appanage to the king's next of kin, known as the 'dux' or 'herceg', who was thus able to raise an army from among his own followers.

The disputes began almost immediately after Stephen's death. All his sons had died in infancy except one, Imre, and he, too, had predeceased his father. Stephen bequeathed his throne to a nephew, Peter, son of his sister and the Doge Otto Orseolo. Peter was an overbearing youth who disliked his subjects and soon had them in arms against him. In 1041 they rebelled, driving him to take refuge at the court of the Emperor Henry III, and in his place elected Samuel Aba, a 'Kun' who had married another of Stephen's sisters. Aba proved as violent, in other directions, as Peter, who came back, assisted by Henry, in 1046; Aba, fleeing, was strangled by 'Hungarians whom he had harmed during his reign'. Peter was reinstated, but his rule was more unpopular than ever, and the Hungarians now bethought them of the surviving members of the House of Árpád – three brothers, Andrew, Béla and Levente, the sons of Stephen's nephew, Vászoly, who had been living in exile in Poland since their father had committed some offence which had caused Stephen to throw him into prison and put out his eyes. The brothers were called back; Peter was killed in flight, and Andrew became king (1047). He lived peaceably with his brothers until he tried to secure the succession for his seven-year-old son, Salamon, whom he had married as an infant to the Emperor Henry III's child daughter, Judith. Levente had renounced his rights rather than accept Christianity, but when Andrew actually had Salamon crowned, Béla revolted. Andrew was killed in the fighting, Salamon took refuge with his father-in-law and Béla mounted the throne (1060). When he died in 1063, his two sons, Géza and Ladislas, who were mutually devoted, at first accepted Salamon as the lawful king, but in 1074 the cousins quarrelled and Salamon was evicted. Géza ruled for three years (1074–7) and Ladislas after him for eighteen (1077–95). Ladislas had only a daughter, and designated as his successor Almus, the younger of Géza's two sons, the elder, Kálmán, having been destined for the church; but Kálmán seized the throne on his uncle's death, and although Almus at first accepted the situation, the brothers ended by quarrelling and Kálmán had both Almus and his infant son, Béla, blinded. Kálmán then finished his rule (1095–1116) unchallenged, as did his son Stephen II (1116–31) after him. Dying childless, Stephen was succeeded by the blind Béla II, who had been brought up in secrecy by his father's friends. Under Béla (1131–41) and his son Géza II (1141–62) there was no important internal discord, but the succession of Géza's son, Stephen III (1162–72) was disputed, first by his eldest uncle, Ladislas II, who seized the throne in 1162, and after Ladislas' death, in January 1163, by his younger brother, Stephen IV. Stephen IV's death in the spring of 1165 happily exhausted the sum of

Stephen III's uncles, and he had no sons. His brother and successor, Béla III (1173–96) had no domestic rivals to his throne, but the short reign of his elder son, Imre (1196–1204) was spent largely in strife with his younger brother, Andrew, who on Imre's death expelled his infant son, Ladislas IV (who, fortunately for his country, died the next year) before beginning his own long reign (1205–35).

This endemic dynastic warfare did Hungary much harm. Not only did the fighting which accompanied it bring with it loss of blood and material devastation, but many claimants to the throne called in foreign help – German, Polish and, in the twelfth century, Byzantine – thus opening the way to foreign interference in the country's internal affairs and sometimes bringing political degradation and temporary or permanent losses of territory. Both Peter and Salamon sacrificed the independent status which St Stephen had won for Hungary by doing homage for their thrones to the Emperor. Stephen III's uncles were clients of Byzantium. Aba's wars against Peter's protectors lost Hungary her territory west of the Leitha, which thereafter became the Austro-Hungarian frontier until 1918. Syrmium and Dalmatia, acquired earlier, were temporarily lost in the twelfth century.

For all this, it must be said that Hungary was, on the whole, lucky in its kings. Quarrelsome as they were, they were generally able, and often attractive. Ladislas I, who, like Stephen and his son, Imre, was canonised after his death, was the outstanding personality among them: a true paladin and gentle knight, a protector of his faith and his people, and of the poor and defenceless. Kálmán, nicknamed 'the Bookman', was, in spite of his atrocious crime against his brother and nephew, an exceptionally shrewd and enlightened ruler (it was he who enacted a famous Law forbidding trials of witches (strigae) *quia non sunt*). Several other of the Árpáds were men of ability and of endearing nature. Of them all, only Stephen II was almost entirely bad, and Andrew II, irremediably silly.

There were several factors favourable to Hungary's development in the eleventh and twelfth centuries; chief among them, perhaps, the unusually peaceful conditions prevailing during this period in the steppes. The Petchenegs, who had driven the Magyars into Hungary, were themselves pushed into the Balkans in the eleventh century by the Cumans, whose main power was based further east. Hungary suffered only two severe inroads from them, in 1068 and 1091 respectively, and both were incursions of raiding parties which returned to the steppes with their booty. After Austria grew big at the expense of Germany, most of Hungary's other neighbours were approximately her equals in strength, and Hungary contrived to live with most of them on reasonably friendly terms, particularly since all the smaller countries soon came to be linked by a network of dynastic marriages. The wars which did take place were usually family affairs, waged in support of some claimant to a throne and not with the idea of expansion, for the local nations, including the Hungarians, did not think in terms of national imperialism. 'Who', wrote a chronicler once, 'ever heard of Hungarians ruling Czechs, or Czechs, Hungarians?' One of the great virtues of the Árpáds as rulers was that, in the main, they accepted this outlook.

In these relatively peaceful conditions, the population of Hungary increased rapidly, the natural growth being reinforced by a steady flow of immigration. By the end of the twelfth century the cultivable parts of the Dunántúl carried a reasonably dense population, and the Great Plain, too, was beginning to fill up, although more slowly. The valleys of the Vág and Nyitra, the political appurtenance of which had perhaps been doubtful in the tenth century, now came definitively under Hungarian rule, and Transylvania was effectively occupied (probably in several stages) and incorporated. The frontier now ran along the crest of the western Carpathians, through the Tatra, across the upper Poprad

valley, and thence along the watershed of the eastern Carpathians and the Transylvanian Alps. Here, too, there was
growth. The valleys debouching from these mountains into
the plain filled up, while the upper valleys and the basins
behind the passes were settled with semi-military communities. Hungarian expansion did not reach into the Austrian
Alps, which were now being recolonised and consolidated
by the Babenbergs, nor across the Save and Danube in the
south, but Syrmium was conquered and colonised about
1060, and in 1089–90 Ladislas I occupied (or perhaps re-
occupied) 'Slavonia', between the middle courses of the
Save and the Drave. In addition, Kálmán in 1097 took possession of the former kingdom of Croatia, of which he was
crowned king in 1102, having meanwhile secured possession also of the northern Dalmatian coast through a complex transaction which included the betrothal of his cousin,
Piroska, to John Comnenus, then heir to the Byzantine
throne.

Croatia was a dynastic acquisition. How far the Hungaro-
Croat union was real (in later phraseology), and how far
only personal, is a question which the historians of the two
countries argue and can never resolve, since they are talking in terms to which the Middle Ages assigned no precise
and immutable meaning. It is certain that Croatia was never
treated as an integral part of Hungary. The royal title ran
'King of Hungary and Croatia' and Croatia was administered
by a viceroy ('Ban') through its own institutions.

But there were close links, even here; for instance, the
Croat privileged classes seem to have enjoyed automatically
the status of their Hungarian counterparts. And the advance
to the frontiers in the north and east was a process of or-
ganic expansion from the earlier nucleus. The normal procedure was to advance the gyepü when conditions allowed,
incorporating the former gyepü land into the county system, and forming a new gyepü beyond it. Eventually, when
the frontiers became clearly fixed, counties came into being

along the whole line. Transylvania was a partial exception. Here the colonisation was exceptionally extensive, and carried through largely with non-Magyar elements. First a screen of Szekels was set in front of the Magyar settlements in the west of the country, and then the Szekels were moved forward into the valleys behind the main eastern passes, the Magyars following behind them. Then 'Saxons' (really Germans from the Rhineland) were settled in the gaps in the line, round Sibiu, Brassó and Beszterce. Both the Saxons and the Szekels enjoyed extensive self-government, the former directly under the king, the latter under a 'Count of the Szekels' representing him; and the whole area, Saxon and Szekel districts and Hungarian counties, was, in view of its dangerous and exposed situation and its remoteness from the capital, placed under a local governor, the 'Voivode of Transylvania'. Unlike Croatia, however, Transylvania was not a separate Land of the Hungarian Crown, but simply an administratively distinct part of the kingdom of Hungary.

Thus even if we leave Croatia out of the account, the effective area of Hungary had by 1200 almost doubled since the original occupation and its population had risen to the big figure (for the time) of some two millions.

The political unity which had been the first of Stephen's great gifts to his country had survived, and so had his second gift of Christianity. His death had, indeed, been followed by a powerful reaction in which attachment to the old beliefs had been inflamed by resentment against both the discipline and the economic burdens (especially that of tithe) imposed by the new faith, and by its foreign associations, as personified in the German and Italian clerics. The second revolt against Peter had been led by the pagan party, who had expected the sons of Vászoly to restore the old religion. In this outburst many monks and clerics had perished, including the saintly St Gerard, martyred on the hill overlooking Buda which still

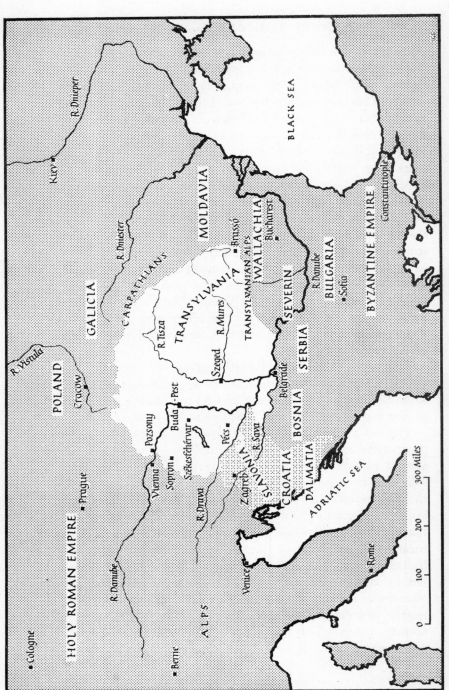

Map 2. Central and S.E. Europe showing the area of Hungary during the National Kingdom

bears his name. A second outbreak had occurred in 1063.

After this had been put down, however, Christianity had not again been in danger. None of Stephen's successors had rested their power on the church quite so explicitly as he, but several of them, notably Ladislas I, had been powerful protectors and generous patrons of it. The ecclesiastical organisation of the country had been extended *pari passu* with its political expansion, and the network of monasteries covering the country had grown denser.

Many of the monks were foreigners, chiefly Germans, but some of them Italians or Frenchmen. Their presence had helped to raise the cultural standards of the country, and had also assisted it to make important progress in other fields. By the middle of the twelfth century, agriculture was beginning to go over from stock-breeding to arable farming and viticulture. There were already some towns. The gold, silver and salt-mines were coming into fuller production, to the especial benefit of the king's treasury, into which their yield went. Hungarian coins, and also some Hungarian products, found their way far afield.

All this growth was, of course, gradual, but it soon enabled Hungary to meet any of her neighbours on at least equal terms. In fàct, after the accession of Ladislas I, nothing was heard for a long time of German claims to overlordship. Later, the Emperor Manuel Comnenus made pertinacious efforts to establish suzerainty over Hungary, which he invaded no less than ten times in twenty-two years; but although vexatious, his attempts never seriously threatened Hungarian independence. After 1100, indeed, it was more often the Hungarian kings who intervened in their neighbours' affairs, than the converse. Both Kálmán and Stephen II intervened repeatedly in various Russian principalities. Béla III, who had been brought up at the Byzantine court and destined by Manuel, before his marriage, for his heir, ended by turning the tables, and although he did not succeed in acquiring the imperial crown, the lustre of his own easily outshone that of Manuel's successors. He largely dominated the Balkans and also, for a while, exercised sovereignty over Halics.[1] Hungary in his day was almost, or quite, the leading power in south-eastern Europe. Symbolic of this was the fact that while his predecessors' consorts had most often been the daughters of Polish, Russian or Balkan prince-lets, Béla's father-in-law was the king of France himself. An interesting document – the statement of his revenues – sent by Béla to his prospective father-in-law during the marriage negotiations, shows that these were equal to those of his English and French contemporaries and inferior only to those of the two Emperors.

The political form of the country during the period re-mained that of the absolutist patrimonial kingship. On the very few occasions on which a revision of the laws was undertaken, the *optimates*, as well as the chief prelates, were consulted, and the king's Council seems to have evolved into a recognised permanent institution. Never-theless, up to the reign of Andrew II, the field of the king's prerogatives was not restricted and his authority in matters falling within it remained as absolute.

Otto of Freising, writing in the twelfth century, notes that if any grandee committed, or was even suspected of, an offence against the king's majesty, the king could send from his court a servant, of however low degree, who could, single-handed, throw the offender into chains before his own adherents and carry him off to torture. It was only Andrew's follies and extravagances that produced a revolt, in consequence of which he was forced, in the famous Golden Bull of 1222, to submit to certain restrictions on his freedom of action (e.g., not to appoint foreigners to office without the consent of the Council), and to concede that if he or any of his successors violated these promises, the prelates and other dignitaries and nobles of the realm

[1] Roughly equivalent to the later Galicia.

should be free to 'resist and withstand' such violation without imputation of high treason. This *jus resistendi* remained a treasured, although seldom invoked, right of the Hungarian nation for more than four centuries thereafter.[1]

Other clauses of this famous charter dealt with the position of the freemen – that body which later usage knew as the 'Hungarian nation'.[2] Since St Stephen's day the composition in terms of ancestry of this class must have changed largely, for the limitation of 'noble' status (the term 'noble' was just coming into usage, but may conveniently be used here) to the male line must of itself already have greatly diminished the number of families able to claim it *jure descensus a Scythia*; not to mention the high mortality rate in a class which by definition was military. Other former freemen had lost their status through rebellion or personal crime, had had it filched from them by powerful neighbours, or had been driven by need to take employment out of their class. On the other

---

[1] In a second edition of the Bull this clause was whittled down to recognition by the King that the Primate-Archbishop was entitled to excommunicate him if he violated his oath.

[2] In the following paragraphs I have adopted an old-fashioned and probably somewhat over-simplified view of the processes described. Many modern Hungarian historians postulate an almost total decay of the old free class and the rise of a totally new one, the *servientes regis*, with a status originally inferior to that of the old freemen. Under this interpretation, the privileges granted in the Golden Bull to the '*servientes regis*' apply only to this new class, while the older freemen are not mentioned in the Bull at all. Those holding it explain the omission by saying that the privileges of the older class were so obvious as to need no reaffirmation. I find this interpretation contrary to common sense, to Hungarian psychology, and also to a number of texts. In any case, even if a distinction existed in 1222 between the freemen by hereditary right and the *servientes regis*, it disappeared soon after it. A decree issued by Béla IV in 1247 speaks specifically of '*nobiles Hungariae universi qui et servientes regis dicunter*', who approach Béla with the request '*ut ipsos in libertate a S. Stephano rege statuta et obtenta dignaremus conservare*'.

hand, successive kings had repeatedly carried through the necessary replenishment of the national defence forces by promoting unfree elements or importing foreigners.

The relative measure (it had, of course, never been more than relative) of economic homogeneity which steppe economy had enabled the old class to preserve had also naturally vanished apace under the new conditions, and especially with the transition to private property in land. Foolish kings or pretendents to the Crown had accelerated the process by buying, or rewarding, supporters with grants of land, sometimes very large, and even in the twelfth century we find here and there magnates who own vast estates and demean themselves on them in almost regal fashion. At the other extreme, many 'nobles' sank into real poverty, while preserving their political status. These 'sandalled nobles', as later generations called them, may already have outnumbered the more prosperous members of the 'nation'.

The wiser kings had, however, fought against the development of a magnate class – so Kálmán had enacted that all donations made since St Stephen's day should revert to the Crown on the extinction of the beneficiaries' direct heirs – and had refused to make offices of state hereditary. The class had thus never become institutionalised, and it had, incidentally, accelerated its own metabolism by the frequent commission of offences which entailed confiscation of its estates. The 'nation' had thus never developed along the hierarchical lines which characterised the societies of the contemporary western and central Europe. The most serious threat, to date, to the freedom of its weaker members, had come during Andrew's reign – he had been a notable offender in the matter of lavish bestowal of estates on supporters – and they had then revolted in defence of their old liberties. The most important clauses of the Golden Bull were those which restored their original status, making the 'nation' once more a legally undifferentiated class, the body politic – under and with the king – of Hungary, all of whose members had the same duty of bearing arms when required[1] and the same privilege of paying no taxation to the civic power.

The passage of time had, indeed, altered the social and political function of the 'nation' in another important respect. As we have said, the warriors who followed Árpád across the Carpathians were probably nearly, if not quite as numerous as their domestic slaves and the autochthonous populations put together: they could not unreasonably claim to be Hungary incorporate. But the promotions to their ranks, which in any case grew much rarer in the twelfth century,[2] probably did not even make good the wastage; they certainly did not keep pace with the growth of the unfree population. They dwindled to an oligarchy numbering only a comparatively small fraction of the total population. Further, the transition to private ownership of land, which gathered pace with the spread of arable farming, and took place equally on clan and crown land, combined with the effects of two centuries of donation, confiscation and migration, had altered the geographical distribution of the class. The old relatively clear-cut division into clan and crown lands was gone. There were still substantial areas of purely crown land, still pockets of clan land held by communities of small nobles, but by and large, the nobles were in the thirteenth century developing into a landlord class, spread fairly evenly over the entire country.

This change brought with it a modification of the political organisation. The county system now covered the whole country, except for the royal free boroughs and the specially exempted areas, such as those donated to the Transylvanian Saxons; and whatever the position may have been

[1] A novelty in the Bull was that foreign service had to be paid.

[2] This was due partly to the opposition of the existing nobles to further dilution of their privileges, partly to the introduction as principal arm of heavy cavalry, which made it useless to ennoble men who could not afford the new equipment.

before, the nobles of each county now had to recognise the authority of the local Ispán. In the year after Andrew II's death the nobles of one county initiated the practice, which was later generalised and institutionalised, of electing four of their own members – in practice, naturally, respected and influential men – as 'assessors' to represent their interests against encroachments by tyrannous Ispáns or lawless magnates. By 1267 this identification of the administration with the local nobility had gone so far that Béla IV ordered that two or three nobles from each county should attend the Court which he promised to hold annually for the airing of grievances.

Among the other classes of the population, slavery was on its way out. Still fairly common at the beginning of the thirteenth century, it had almost disappeared by the end of it, except for a few non-Christian slaves. The rest of the unfree population, although still politically non-existent, were now no longer chattels and enjoyed a measure of security in law. Some were farm-hands or craftsmen, employed on the big estates, lay or ecclesiastical; others in practice tenant farmers, paying a rent in labour or kind for their holdings. Their obligations were at any rate not onerous enough to deter a steady flow of immigrants from entering the country, and their right of free migration was, at this period, not questioned. Some communities, such as the Transylvanian Saxons, were personally free and paid only a nominal rent for their land.

Both the extension of the frontiers, and the immigration, had, of course, brought large new numbers of non-Magyars into Hungary. Croatia was purely Slavonic, with an Italian element in the sea-board towns. The political consolidation of the north-west added a fairly substantial Slovak population, later reinforced by immigration from Moravia. Russians filtered over the north-eastern Carpathians; Vlachs were found in, or entered, Transylvania. There was a big organised immigration of Germans: besides the

Transylvanian Saxons, already mentioned, another large body of 'Saxons' was brought in to develop the mines of the Szepes east of the Tatra. The towns throughout Hungary were, as throughout most of eastern Europe, mainly German. Considerable numbers of Petchenegs and kindred peoples entered Hungary from the east as refugees. Other, smaller, groups included Jews, Walloon vintners, and 'Ishmaelites' (Bulgars from the Kama), men skilled in the minting of money.

But this did not alter the essentially Magyar national character of the state. The Kuns were no longer distinguishable from Magyars. The recruits to the noble class, at least in the interior of the country, usually became completely Magyarised within a generation or so.[1] But neither was the picture of a 'ruling race' dominating 'subject peoples' any more generally true. The peasants of the Slovak mountains, the Saxons behind their barrier of jealously-guarded privileges, the German burghers of the towns, and the Vlachs and Jews, with their alien religions and outlandish modes of life, kept their distinct national identities, but the Szekels and all the eastern immigrants, with the smaller diasporae, melted in the Magyar flood, which was also now swollen by great numbers of déclassé Magyars. Documents show that except in the peripheral areas and the towns, the majority of the unfree populations now bore Magyar names.

When in 1235 death ended Andrew II's long and ill-fated reign, his son, Béla IV, did what he could to re-establish the royal authority. Several truculent aristocrats were thrown into prison, and commissioners sent out to check the legi-

---

[1] This generalisation does not apply to the remote peasant communities on the periphery who were 'ennobled' en masse, i.e., relieved of taxation in return for guarding the frontiers. But it is true of practically all families for whom ennoblement meant real advance in the social scale.

timacy of recent donations, a number of which were rescinded. But before Béla could complete his reforms, they were interrupted by the heaviest calamity which Hungary had experienced since the foundation of the state: the terrible Mongol invasion.

The Mongols, or Tatars, had been threatening eastern Europe for half a generation. As early as 1223 they had inflicted a terrible defeat on the combined Cuman and Russian armies on the Kalka. This battle had not, however, decisively broken the power of the Cumans, who continued to hold up the Tatar expansion for a long decade, but in 1239 they were crushingly defeated again, near the mouth of the Volga. In December 1240 Kiev was laid in ashes, and now the way to Poland and Hungary lay open.

Béla – almost the only man in his country who took the danger at its full value – had organised a system of defences on the passes and had tried to collect an army inside Hungary. But when the Tatars moved again, in the spring of 1241, they easily overran the frontier posts, and on 11 April outmanoeuvered the Hungarian army which met them at Mohi, on the Sajó, and almost destroyed it. Béla himself barely escaped with his life to the Austrian frontier, where Frederick of Austria could find nothing better to do than to blackmail him for an indemnity, extort three counties from him as security for the payment of it, and even invade them himself. The Tatars ravaged central Hungary at their leisure all summer and autumn, then, the Danube having frozen hard, crossed it on Christmas Day and spread destruction in the Dunántúl, while Béla, pursued by their light cavalry, fled ingloriously enough to an island off the Dalmatian coast. Hungary was saved from complete destruction only by the death of the Great Khan Ogotai in far-away Karakorum. Batu Khan, commander of the Tatar armies in the west, led them back to take part in the contest for the succession, and in March

11. *Szeged. The Demeter Tower (13th century)*

1242 the Tatars quitted Hungary as suddenly as they had entered it just a year before.

But they left total devastation behind them. Even of Hungary's walled places, not all had escaped. Székesfehérvár had been saved by the marshes round it, and the citadel of Esztergom had held out. But the town had fallen, as had Buda and many another. When they took a town the Tatars commonly reduced it to ashes and slaughtered all its inhabitants. In the countryside they had spared the peasants until the harvest was reaped, promising them that they would not be molested; but the harvest in, had butchered them. Finally, while leaving the country, they had beaten it for slaves: years after, the missionaries Plan Carpini and Rubruquis found Magyar slaves still in bondage in Tartary.

Those who survived had done so because they had escaped in time into forests or marshes. That year, with the plague and starvation which followed it, cost Hungary something like half its total population, the losses ranging from 60 per cent in the Alföld (100 per cent in certain parts of it) to 20 per cent in the Dunántúl. Only the north-west and the Szekel areas of Transylvania had come off fairly lightly.

To the sheer physical destruction of man and his works were added, of course, political and social disintegration and the threat of further assaults from greedy neighbours, headed by Frederick of Austria.

King Béla, whom his country not unjustly dubbed its second founder, set himself with courage, intelligence and tact to repair something of this damage. Drawing from experience the lesson that only walled places ensured safety, he organised a complete new defensive system, based on chains of fortresses. He reorganised the army, replacing the old light archers by a small force of heavy cavalry. He repopulated the country by calling in great new numbers of colonists from all available quarters,

12. *Ják Abbey, built before* A.D. 1256

paying especial attention to the foundation of new towns, which were equipped with generous charters. In a few years Hungary was well on the way to internal recovery and its international position seemed more potent than ever. In the west, the counties seized by Frederick were recovered and, for a short time, Béla even took Styria away from the Austrian. In the south and east, Hungary was surrounded by a ring of 'Bánáts' or client states embracing Bosnia and north Serbia, Severin, Cumania (in the later Wallachia) and Galicia.

Some of this work was of permanent advantage to Hungary; in particular, the multiplication of the towns lastingly benefited its economic structure. But many of Béla's improvisations, although unavoidable, had dangerous consequences. To get the fortresses built quickly he had been obliged, willy-nilly, to give great territorial magnates, new or old, practically a free hand on their domains. Half a dozen of these families – the Köszegis on the Austrian frontier, the Csáks on the Moravian, the Abas and Borsas in the north, the Káns in Transylvania, the Subiches in Croatia, made meteoric rises to near-sovereign state; a state of things which was particularly dangerous because with the extinction in Austria, of the Babenberg line in 1246, a scramble for its inheritance had begun, opening up golden prospects for a powerful local magnate to rise higher still, if he did not take his loyalty to his own monarch too seriously.

A danger of a different sort threatened from the Cumans. After the Battle of the Volga the Great Khan of the Cumans, a certain Kötöny or Kuthen, had sought asylum in Hungary with the broken survivors of his nation, still a large host. Béla had received them, seeing in them a force which could defend him against the Tatars and also help him against disloyal subjects of his own. But his hospitality had had disastrous consequences. It had given the Tatar Khan his pretext to attack Hungary, for 'harbouring his rebellious slaves'; meanwhile the Hungarians, for good reasons and for ill, had violently resented the presence of the wild newcomers, and just as the Tatars were crossing the mountain passes, had murdered Kuthen. Thereupon the enraged Cumans had left Hungary for the Balkans, murdering and pillaging as they went, so that Béla had not even had their help at the crucial moment.

Afterwards he called them back, with the smaller people of the Jazyges, and settled them on empty lands on the two banks of the Tisza, and to ensure their loyalty, married his elder son, Stephen, to a Cuman princess. The Cumans proved in fact a valuable fighting force, but they were detested by the Hungarians, whose villages they pillaged and whose women they raped. They were, moreover, mostly still pagans, for missionary work in which heroic friars had engaged among them for a generation previously had so far borne little fruit.

When Béla died, in 1270, the weak points in his work soon made themselves felt. Stephen, who incidentally had done much to embitter his father's last years and to undermine his work, died after a reign of only two years; no loss in himself, but his heir, Ladislas, was only ten years old. The 'Cumanian woman', his mother, who assumed the regency, was hated by the Hungarians, and although some of the magnates tried loyally enough to keep the state together, others, especially a few great west Hungarian and Croat families, made themselves into 'kinglets', who fought each other, and the king, for control of the state or for their own independence, allying themselves without scruple with foreign rulers. In the confusion, many of Béla IV's foreign acquisitions were lost again. When Ladislas came to man's estate, things were no better. He had grown up into a wild, undisciplined youth, far more of a Cuman than a Magyar. He favoured his mother's people so much that there seemed a danger that Hungary might revert to paganism; in the course of repeated exchanges, one Pope laid the country under interdict and another authorised the bishops to preach a crusade against the king. It took all the efforts of the Christian barons to mediate a settlement under which the Cumans, in return for the retention of their liberties and of certain national customs, undertook to accept Christianity, to exchange their tents for fixed abodes and 'to abstain from killing Christians and from shedding their blood'. Meanwhile, Ladislas himself neglected his wife and took pleasure only among Cuman women. At last, in 1290, he was murdered 'by those same Cumans whom he had loved'.

From the loyal Hungarians' point of view the most serious aspect of Ladislas' refusal to have commerce with his wife had been the danger that this might involve the extinction of the dynasty; for Ladislas' only brother had predeceased him, dying unmarried, as had his only paternal uncle. One Árpád of the blood was still alive, for Andrew II's third wife, Beatrice d'Este, had been delivered of a boy soon after her husband's death (on which she had returned to her father's people), and this boy had in due course married into a family of rich Venetian bankers and although himself dying young, had left a son, another Andrew. A party in Hungary had been supporting the claim of this boy to be regarded as heir presumptive to Ladislas, and meanwhile, 'Duke of Slavonia'. Since a few months before Ladislas' death Andrew had, however, been a prisoner at the court of Albrecht of Habsburg, now installed in Vienna. Meanwhile his rivals had been impugning his father's parentage, and when Ladislas died, claims to the succession were put forward by, or on behalf of, three descendants of the house of Árpád in the female line: the Angevin Charles Martell of Naples, son of Ladislas' sister Maria (the candidature supported by the Pope), the Bavarian Otto of Wittelsbach, son of Stephen V's sister Elizabeth, and the Bohemian Wenceslas II, grandson of Béla IV's sister Anne. In addition, the German King Rudolph of Habsburg recalled that Béla IV, in his extremity, had done him homage and invested his son Albrecht with Hungary.

The question was resolved by the prompt action of the Archbishop of Esztergom, Ladomer, who got Andrew smuggled out of Vienna, disguised as a friar, and brought to Hungary, where he was crowned amid the jubilation of by far the greater part of the country. It was a coup which might have proved a great blessing to the country, for true Árpád or not, Andrew showed himself to be one of the best of the Hungarian kings. He defended his position against the foreign claimants. Leaning on the smaller nobles, he succeeded in making headway against the unruly magnates, incidentally sanctioning a number of valuable constitutional institutions (for the idea of constitutional rule was not strange to his Venice-trained mind). On coronation he swore to respect the country's liberties; he repeated and extended Andrew II's pledge to make no appointments to higher office without the consent of the Royal Council, and even agreed to the institution of a permanent salaried Council, its membership to include representatives of their 'prelates, barons and nobles', whose consent was required for any major decision. 'All the barons and nobles of the realm'[1] were to meet annually to enquire into the state of the kingdom and the conduct of the high officials. Unhappily, he died on 14 January 1301, leaving only an infant daughter, and thus 'the last golden twig of the generation, blood and lineage of St Stephen, the first Hungarian king', was broken.

[1] This does not, of course, mean a general assembly of all the 'nobles' of Hungary, but of their representatives, the class from which the county 'assessors' were drawn.

3

THE FOREIGN KINGS

THE extinction of the old national dynasty with Andrew III's death altered its conditions of existence for the Hungarian state. Under its own interpretation of the position, the right of electing its new king had now reverted to the nation, whose freedom of choice was in theory unlimited; there was no theoretical bar to its setting one of its own members over it. But a firmly-implanted European usage had by this time come to limit the enjoyment of royal dignity to those who could show some hereditary title to it, most of these persons belonging to a small clique – into which the Árpáds themselves had levered themselves – of interrelated families of, as it were, professional royalties. It would have required a strong man, with a united nation behind him, to defy a well-supported claim from a member of one of these families, and the Hungarians, too, admitted the compulsive virtue of the blood-tie. They themselves confined their search to persons in whose veins the blood of the Árpáds ran, at least through some maternal forbear, who could continue the line – the line, not an individual, for the choice once made, the principle of legitimacy came into operation again; it was the singular misfortune of the country that for over two centuries after 1301, only one king died leaving behind him legitimate male issue. This meant that except in the one case in question, and in the two others where peculiar circumstances resulted, after all, in the election of a national king, their chosen ruler always came from some foreign, and foreign-based, dynasty. In fact, until the sixteenth century, when the Crown became permanently vested in the Habsburg dynasty, it was worn (transitory and disputed cases apart) by two Angevins, one Luxemburger, one Habsburg and three Jagiellos; with, intervening, two national kings, one of whom ruled only in part of the country.

To have a foreign king was by no means always an unmixed disadvantage for Hungary. Fresh ideas and institutions were sometimes brought in which fructified and enriched the political, social, cultural and economic life of the country, and without which it might well have failed to keep pace with the general advance of the contemporary Europe towards a higher level of civilisation. It is true that the Hungarians did not always relish these innovations, and often bound the monarch of their choice by strict capitulations to respect their own hardly-won and cherished national institutions. Their ability to do this – an outcome, strictly speaking, of the electoral nature of the Crown, not of the fact that the candidate was usually a foreigner – was a main reason why, for good or ill (and the advantages did not lie all on one side), Hungary throughout her history was able to preserve her native features in a larger degree than most other European countries. But the central issue was nearly always that of power, in relation to the international situation. A monarch disposing of resources of his own could be hoped to use them for the country's benefit, and especially for its defence; it was this calculation which more than once determined the national choice. On the other hand, a too powerful monarch, the centre of whose power and interests alike lay outside Hungary, might too easily use those resources, not to develop the country's national life, but to crush it, and to squander its own resources in the pursuit of his private, extra-Hungarian, objectives. The balance of advantage and disadvantage, in this respect, swayed uneasily throughout the centuries with the fluctuations of the international power-position and the personality of the ruler. Under many of its foreign rulers, and almost continuously after the Crown became stabilised

in the house of Habsburg, the central problem of the country's whole political life was whether the benefits brought
by foreign rule outweighed its disadvantages; and on this
question opinion in the country was eternally divided, up
to the last day of Habsburg rule.

These considerations were not yet apparent in the first
years after Andrew's death. What happened then was
simply that the dynastic rivalry of ten years before broke
out again in modernised form, the Angevin candidate,
whom the Pope supported, being now Charles Martell's
son, the boy, Charles Robert; the Czech, another boy,
Wenceslas III, for whom his father stood sponsor. This
time Albrecht of Habsburg did not claim the throne for
himself, contenting himself with supporting Charles
Robert. Charles Robert, Wenceslas and Otto of Bavaria
all had their partisans inside Hungary, and at first Charles
Robert's party was the weakest of all. Both Wenceslas and
Otto were in turn crowned, and Charles Robert's supporters could only give him a symbolic coronation, with a
substitute crown.[1] But in a few years his rivals gave up the
struggle in disgust. On 20 August 1310 he was crowned
again, this time in due form, and thereafter his rule was
not seriously opposed from abroad. He still, indeed, had
many opponents among the 'kinglets', but he was able to
win most of them over by diplomacy, and in 1312 won a
crushing victory at Rozgony over the chief of the remaining malcontents, the Amadés and the Csáks. This victory
re-established the royal authority on a firm footing; the
only internal trouble which he had to face thereafter was
in reality only half internal, fomented by Venice.

Charles Robert was undoubtedly favoured by the international situation, which, with Germany distraught by the
conflict between Empire and Papacy, the Tatars grown

[1] By this time the tradition had grown up that coronation was
invalid unless performed with the Holy Crown.

passive in the east and the power of Byzantium in full decay, was more favourable than ever before or since to the independent development of the states of east-central Europe; it is no accident that Poland, Bohemia, Hungary and Serbia should all look back on the fourteenth century as the age of their greatest glory. As these conditions favoured Hungary's neighbours, as well as herself, Charles Robert's attempts at expansion were only moderately successful. He made Bosnia his friend and client, but Venice snatched South Dalmatia from him, Serbia, the Bánát of Macsó, and the newly-founded 'Voivody' of Wallachia disputed Szörény with him and in 1330 inflicted a heavy defeat on his arms. Against this, he drove the Austrian and Czech marauders out of his land, and, on the whole, preserved friendly relations with Poland, Bohemia and Austria.

The latter part of his reign was in the main peaceful and marked by a steadily increasing prosperity, the lion's share of which accrued to the king himself.

One of the chief props of his power was the wealth which he derived from the gold mines of Transylvania and north Hungary, the production of which he stimulated by a number of sensible devices. Eventually it reached the remarkable figure of 3,000 lb. of gold annually – one third of the total production of the world as then known, and five times as much as that of any other European state. Some 35–40 per cent of this accrued to the Crown as revenue and enabled Charles Robert, first of all Hungarian kings, to introduce a systematic fiscal policy. He renounced the *lucrum camerae*, or profit on the coinage, on which many of his predecessors had largely depended, introduced a stable currency based on gold, and reformed the system of direct taxation, basing it on a house-tax levied on every *porta* or peasant household.[1] He still had enough to maintain a

---

[1] Strictly, the *porta* was the gate through which a peasant's waggon passed into his yard. It was thus not an exact measure, since two or three peasants might share one yard.

sumptuous and refined court, the cultural influences at which were, incidentally, French rather than German.

Not the least of the benefits conferred by Charles Robert on Hungary was to leave behind him, in the person of his son Louis (Lajos) an heir whose succession (*jure legitimo*) was not questioned either inside or outside Hungary. Conventional historians reckon the reign of Louis (the only one of its kings on whom the nation has conferred the name of 'Great') as marking the apogee of Hungarian history. Louis was, of course, fortunate in that the favourable European constellation continued to prevail, and, at home, he could build on the foundations laid firmly by his father; but in addition, he was a man of remarkable qualities of both head and heart. Charles Robert had been more respected than loved, especially after one curious incident in which he took an extraordinarily barbarous revenge on the family of a man who had tried to assassinate him; Louis was generally loved. 'I call God to witness', the Venetian envoy wrote of him, 'that I never saw a monarch more majestic or more powerful, nor one who desires peace and calm so much as he.' 'There was no other', wrote another contemporary, 'so kind and noble, so virtuous and magnanimous, so friendly and straightforward.' He was indeed a true paladin, distinguished not least for his extraordinary physical courage in battle.

It was chiefly his international triumphs that earned him the name of 'Great'. Keeping the peace with his western neighbours, he resumed Béla III's policy of expansion in the south and east. Venice was forced to re-cede Dalmatia. The Bánáts in the northern Balkans were restored. The Ban of Bosnia and the Voivodes of Wallachia and Moldavia (where a second Vlach principality had come into being when the Tatars were driven out of it) acknowledged him as their suzerain, as did, for shorter periods and more formally, the rulers of Serbia, northern Bulgaria and, for a few

years, Venice itself. Galicia and Lodomeria were recovered
in 1354. Over this ring of dependencies, Hungary presided
as *Archiregnum*. The climax of Louis' glory came in 1370,
when, by virtue of a dynastic compact concluded in 1354
with Casimir of Poland, he ascended the Polish throne.

At home, the gold flowed in an undiminished stream into
Louis' coffers, enabling him to keep a court even more
splendid than his father's. And the whole country, spared
for two generations from serious invasion or civil war,
blossomed with a material prosperity which it had never
before known. By the end of Louis' reign its total population had risen to some three millions, and it contained
49 royal boroughs, over 500 market towns and more than
26,000 villages. The economy was still predominantly
agricultural, but as these figures show, the towns, which
the Angevins favoured especially, granting many of them
extensive charters of self-government, prospered. Craftsmen began to practise their trades and to organise themselves in guilds. International commerce, favoured by the
continued stability and high repute of the currency, began
to make headway.

The arts, too, flourished. A university, one of the earliest
in Europe, was founded in Pécs in 1367 (it is true that
it proved short-lived). The first comprehensive national
chronicle, one copy of which is one of the most magnificent
illuminated codices in Europe, dates from about the same
period.

This prosperity, and not less the order which the two
Angevins were able to enforce, allowed the nation to accept, without serious resentment, the fact that their reigns
constituted what to modern eyes would appear a period of
political reaction. Even the memory of Andrew III's constitutional innovations (which had, indeed, never been put
into practice) vanished, it seems, even from memory, under
their rules. They made appointments according to their
pleasure, legislated as they pleased, and when (occasion-

ally) they convoked a Diet, it was simply to inform it of
decisions taken. Their absolutism was, however, not the
old patrimonial absolutism of St Stephen and his successors,
which was foreign to their eyes, but a much more hierarchical structure which embodies many features of west
European feudalism. Even after Charles Robert had broken
the power of the kinglets, he did not attempt to destroy
the magnates as a class, but bestowed a large part of the
confiscated estates on a new set of great families. Louis
continued this policy, and by the end of his reign about
fifty of these families owned between them one-third of the
soil of Hungary. The status and importance of the magnates
was enhanced by the new military system introduced by
the Angevins. Military service was still the obligation of all
noblemen, who, when their services were required, were
mustered under the 'banners' of the king, the queen, or
one of the great officials (the Voivode of Transylvania, etc.),
smaller contingents following the Ispáns of their counties.
But the lords were now required to bring contingents of
heavily-armed cavalry from among their own followers; if
a force numbered fifty men, it served under its lord's banner, and was known as his *banderium*. Many small nobles
took service in these private *banderia*. It was at this time,
and largely through this innovation, that the class of *familiares* – small nobles who took service, military or other,
under a magnate, becoming his henchmen and retainers,
while he in practice, although not in theory, was their
feudal superior, became numerous.

This growth of the magnates' power was, indeed, partially compensated by another development, in the opposite direction. It was not everywhere that a magnate's
authority quite eclipsed that of the county in which he had
his estates, and under the Angevins' system of delegating
power, rather than exercising it directly through their own
officials (they were no bureaucrats) the control of the administration and justice in each county passed during their

reigns increasingly into the hands of the *universitates* of the local nobles, who exercised it through their own elected representatives. These 'noble counties', which now began to replace the old 'royal counties', were from the first the special preserve and stronghold of the richer common nobles. They were, of course, still subject to the ultimate control of the king's representative, the Ispán, and the most common effect of the development, at least during its early stages, was to strengthen the king's authority by providing him, in the lesser nobles, with a counterweight against the magnates, such as the rulers of economically more developed countries found in the burgesses of their towns. This consideration led several of the kings to allow the counties to develop a very extensive autonomy, which at a later stage, when the magnate class had allied itself with the Crown, became the defence of the smaller men and, the crown being worn by foreign rulers, the defence also of the national cause, which they came to represent against both the other forces.

In 1351 Louis also confirmed the Golden Bull, adding an explicit declaration that all nobles enjoyed 'one and the same liberty', a provision which, it appears, besides reaffirming the rights of the noble class as a whole, including the *familiares*, also enlarged its ranks by bringing full noble privileges to a further class of border-line cases. Other provisions of the law stabilised land tenure by universalising the system of *aviticitas* under which all land was entailed in the male line of the owner's family, collaterals succeeding in default of direct heirs; if the line died out completely, the estate reverted to the Crown. The daughters of a deceased noble were entitled to a quarter of the assessed value of his property, but this had to be paid them in cash.

At the same time, Louis standardised the obligations of the peasant to his lord at one-ninth of his produce – neither more nor less. As he also had to pay the tithe to the

church and the *porta* to the state, the peasant's obligations
were thus not inconsiderable, but do not appear to have
been crushing in this age of prosperity; his right of free
migration was specifically re-affirmed.

Some Hungarian historians do not count the two Angevins as foreign kings at all, and it is true that both of them,
especially Louis, who was born and bred in Hungary,
regarded themselves completely as Hungarians. Charles
Robert had no other throne, and did not try to acquire
another for himself. Louis treated all his acquisitions,
except perhaps that of Poland, as appendices to Hungary,
and even Poland he ruled through Hungarians. But it is
easily arguable that his Balkan enterprises brought Hungary,
on balance, more loss than profit, even if the large expense
of them be left out of account, for few of the vassals proved
loyal when a crisis came. Rather they regarded Hungary
as an oppressor and hastened to make common cause with
her enemies.[1] She certainly got nothing at all, except a
little reflected glory, out of Louis' acquisition of Poland.
In south Italy Louis and his mother, carrying out plans laid
by Charles Robert, embarked on purely dynastic enterprises which brought positive and real damage to Hungary.
The object was to secure the throne of Naples for Charles'
younger son, Andrew, who, under a compact between
Charles and Robert of Sicily, had married Robert's granddaughter, Joanna, on the understanding that he should succeed to the throne on Robert's death (her father, Charles,
having predeceased Robert). But Andrew's accession was
unpopular in Naples. To get him recognised at all cost enormous sums of money in bribes, and, after a short and insecure reign, he was murdered. Louis undertook two campaigns in Italy to avenge his brother and secure the throne

[1] The resentment was particularly strong where religious considerations reinforced purely political ones, as among the Bogumils
of Bosnia.

for the latter's little son. Both were unsuccessful, and cost
Hungary money which, spent in the country, would have
transformed the face of it.

Matters took a sharp turn for the worse when Louis died
in 1382. He had left no son, but two daughters, of whom
he had destined the elder, Maria, then a girl of eleven,
and betrothed to Sigismund, younger son of the Emperor
Charles IV and himself Marquis of Brandenburg, to succeed
him on both his thrones. The Poles refused to continue the
union with Hungary, and although they ended by accept-
ing Maria's younger sister, Hedwig or Jadwiga, as queen,
they married her to Jagiello of Lithuania, under whom
Poland's ways diverged from Hungary's. The Hungarians
themselves were divided on the question of the female
succession, and a party of them crowned the girls' cousin,
Charles of Durazzo, only to see him assassinated a month
later. Another party had already crowned Maria, but her
rule was only nominal: Sigismund, after marrying his bride,
got himself crowned as her consort in 1387 and, after her
death in 1395, ruled alone until his own death in 1437.

Sigismund was at first extremely unpopular, not only for
the cruelty with which, in breach of his pledged word, he
put Charles' leading supporters to the sword, but also as
an intruder and a foreigner. 'By God', one of his victims
flung in his teeth, 'I am no servant of thine, thou Czech
swine.' In 1401 a group of nobles actually held him in
prison for several weeks, and two years later malcontents
called in another anti-king, who, however, failed to establish himself, although he retained possession of Dalmatia,
which he then sold to Venice. Later, passions cooled somewhat, but when Sigismund was elected German king in
1410, and still more when he succeeded his brother in
Bohemia in 1420, the nation complained with acerbity
that he neglected its affairs.

His reign had its redeeming features. The momentum

imported by the Angevins was still carrying the country forward, economically and culturally, and Sigismund himself, although extravagant and – at least in his youth – silly, was an intelligent enough man, with a European outlook. He introduced a number of useful administrative and military reforms, the latter including the institution of a *militia portalis*, or second-line army of peasant soldiers, and not the Angevins themselves did more than he to promote the prosperity of the towns and to raise their status. He encouraged maunfacture, and was the true father of Hungary's international trade, which he advanced by abolishing internal duties, regulating tariffs on foreign goods and standardising weights and measures throughout the country. Records show that Hungary in his day was importing cloth, linen, velvet, silks and spices and southern delicacies; her chief exports were linen goods, cloth, metal and iron goods, livestock, skins and honey. The memory of this well-being survives in the many fine buildings, dating from his reign, still to be seen in Hungary's towns. An unintentional benefit conferred by him on his country was that his repeated and prolonged absences from Hungary, and his extravagances, both enabled and compelled his subjects to recover some of the constitutional ground which they had lost to his predecessors. He found himself obliged to consult Diets, if not regularly, at least frequently, and to defer to the principle, then generally recognised in central Europe, that their consent was necessary when a subsidy, or new taxation, was required. It was during his reign that the office of the Palatine, who was head of the administration during the king's absence, developed (this was, indeed, formally legalised only under his successor) from that of the king's representative to that of intermediary between the king and the nation, whose function and duty it was to 'represent law and justice for the inhabitants of the country *vis-à-vis* the king's majesty, and for the king's majesty *vis-à-vis* them'.

13. *Sopron: Benedictine church, 14th century*

14 János Hunyadi:
ref. p. 52

15. Mátyás Hunyadi:
ref. p. 54

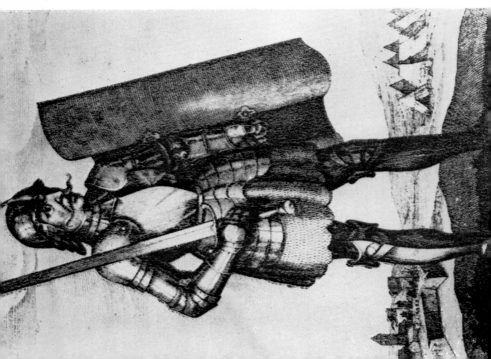

Under the same influences there now began to emerge the famous and peculiar mystic doctrine, formulated in classical form in the sixteenth century by the jurist Werböczy, of the Holy Crown: to wit, that the true political being of Hungary resided in the mystical entity (of which the physical crown was the incorporate symbol) of the Holy Crown, of which the king was the head and the nation, or corporate aggregate of nobles, the body; each member being incomplete without the other, and complementary to it, in that the king was the fount of nobility and the nobles, in virtue of their right to elect their king, the fount of kingship.

But the debit side of Sigismund's all too long reign was also very heavy. He never succeeded in recovering Dalmatia, and in his efforts to do so, he pledged the valuable counties of Szepes, a main source of the king's wealth, to Poland. The nation was perfectly justified in its complaints over his long absences, and by reason of them, and for other causes, partly personal, he was never truly master in the country. The new big families whom the Angevins had promoted had on the whole remained loyal to their benefactors, but they had yet acquired an unhealthy predominance in the country, and an excess of power in their own preserves, and towards Sigismund, as we have seen, they showed no such loyalty. He did not willingly promote their power, but in fact he increased it by the lavish sale, to meet his extravagant expenditure, of crown lands, which by the end of his reign were reduced to 5 per cent of the area of Hungary. Unable to cope with his most powerful subjects as a class, he could do no more than play off some of them against the rest. This he did by organising a group of them in a chivalric league, known as 'the Order of the Dragon', of which he was himself President. Offices and favours were shared out among the members of this group, but even they were not always reliable; cases occurred when the Order itself defied the king.

The smaller men suffered, especially the peasants, whose condition deteriorated substantially, less owing to any aggravation of their legal burdens (peasants serving in the *militia portalis* were exempt from the *porta* tax) than from increases in the tax itself, illegal exactions, and perhaps most of all, under the increasingly rapid transition to a money economy, with which they could not easily cope. The consequent unrest was fanned by the spread from Bohemia of Hussite doctrines, which took hold especially in north Hungary, and was embittered by the cruelty with which the heretics were persecuted. The first serious specifically peasant revolt which Hungary had ever known broke out in the very last months of Sigismund's reign, as the result of the action of a bishop in Transylvania in claiming the tithe in money. It spread over much of Transylvania, and gained considerable temporary successes before it was put down. A consequence of this revolt was the birth of an institution destined later to become important, the 'Union of the Three Nations', under which the Hungarian nobles of the Transylvanian counties, the Saxons and the Szekels formed a league for the mutual defence of their interests against all parties, save only the king.

This grievous event occurred at a moment when Hungary was most sorely in need of all her strength and all her unity, for her old unthreatened state was over. In 1352 the Osmanli Turks had crossed the Straits and established themselves in Gallipoli. In 1362 they took Adrianople. In 1388 they made Sisman's Bulgaria tributary; in 1389 they annihilated the power of Serbia on the field of Kossovo.

Sigismund, to do him justice, had early recognised the reality of the Turkish danger (to which Louis had been curiously blind) and in 1395 had led an expedition into the Balkans which had met with some success. He had followed this up the next year with a larger expedition in which crusading contingents from many European countries had taken part; but this time the Christian armies had been disastrously defeated at Nicopolis in north Bulgaria (22 September 1396), the Hungarian contingent, which had formed the bulk of the army, being annihilated, and Sigismund himself barely escaping with his life. Hungary, and all central Europe, lay open to the invaders, and were only respited, not by their own efforts, but by the intervention of Timur's Mongols, who were now threatening the Turks' rear and in 1402 actually took the Sultan Bayazid himself prisoner, after a pitched battle outside Ankara. For some time after this the Turks' operations on their European front were on a reduced scale, but they recommenced in 1415. The Voivode of Wallachia submitted, Bosnia repudiated Hungary's suzerainty, and her only remaining Balkan client was a fragmentary Serbia under the 'Despot', George Branković. South Hungary itself and Transylvania suffered repeated raids.

In 1437 the Sultan Murad was preparing for a grand attack on Hungary itself, and at this most inauspicious juncture Sigismund died, having crowned his disservices to Hungary by leaving no son, but only a girl, Elizabeth, the issue of his second marriage, with the daughter of the Count of Cilli, who was married to Albrecht, head of the Albertinian line of the Habsburgs and ruler of Austria Above and Below the Enns. Sigismund had designated Albrecht to succeed him in both Hungary and Bohemia, and the Hungarians duly elected him, while stipulating that he should defend the country with all his forces (also, that he should not accept the Imperial crown). All might have turned out well, for Albrecht, who was both conscientious and able, was prepared to fulfil his promise and in fact set about organising an army for a campaign against the Turks; but dysentery carried him off before he had reigned two full years and another dynastic crisis broke out. Elizabeth was big with child, and claimed at least the regency, but a majority of the Hungarians were unwilling to wait for the birth of a child who might not even be a boy, and in any case to endure a long regency under a woman. They elected the young king of Poland, Wladislaus III. Immediately after, Elizabeth was delivered of a boy, whom she succeeded in getting crowned, calling in to support her the Czech war-lord, Giskra, who occupied north-western Hungary. The position of the young Ulászló (as the Hungarians called him) was thus threatened from the rear at the moment when he most needed security.

In this most critical hour Hungary was saved principally by the genius of a single man, János (John) Hunyadi, one of the most interesting and attractive figures in the national history. He had risen from small beginnings; son of a lesser noble of Vlach origin (it is true that his ascent to position and wealth had been so meteoric as to give rise to rumours that he was Sigismund's own natural son), he had begun life as a professional condottiere, but had shown such extraordinary talent in that capacity that Sigismund had given him high command, and Albrecht even higher, appointing him Ban of Szörény. Ulászló, whose cause he had supported, promoted him to Captain-General of Belgrade and Voivode of Transylvania. He was now the most important man in Hungary, after the young king himself, and also in a fair way to becoming the richest, for he was as great a money-maker as he was soldier; by not long after this, his private estates were estimated to have covered nearly six million acres. In Transylvania, in 1442, Hunyadi brilliantly defeated a Turkish army, then in 1443 persuaded Ulászló to undertake a campaign in the Balkans, this being the first time for many years that the Turks had had the offensive taken against them on that front. This was so signally succcessful that the Sultan agreed to a peace which liberated all Serbia from his rule. Unhappily, the Papal Legate, who had been organising a crusade which was frustrated by Hunyadi's action in concluding the peace, persuaded Ulászló that a word given to an infidel need not be kept. The next year he and Hunyadi accordingly led a new army into the Balkans, where the enraged Sultan, meeting them outside Varna on 10 November, defeated them disastrously. The young king himself perished, with the flower of his army, while Hunyadi barely escaped with his life.

He managed, however, to get back to Hungary, where he performed a service hardly less valuable than his feats in the field, in mediating a solution of the dynastic question. For Elizabeth had meanwhile died, leaving her little boy, Ladislas (known as Ladislas Postumus), with the Holy Crown, in the charge of his uncle, the Emperor Frederick, and the easy-going Frederick was content to leave Hunyadi in charge of Hungary as 'governor' or 'regent' until the child should have grown up.

During the next years Hunyadi was by no means always successful; Giskra defeated him in 1447 and had to be left master of north-western Hungary, and in the same year he suffered another heavy defeat at the hands of the Turks in Serbia. He did, however, succeed in holding them back as no European had done before him. His crowning achievement came in 1456, when he so heavily routed a Turkish army which was besieging Belgrade that it was seventy years before the danger recurred in so acute a form.

The relief of Belgrade, for which the Pope ordered all the church-bells of catholic Europe to ring daily at noon, that the faithful might pray in unison for it, was also Hunyadi's last victory, for he died a few weeks later of a fever contracted in the camp. And at first it seemed as though he was to be ill repaid. In 1452 the Austrian and Bohemian Estates had forced Frederick to release Ladislas from tutelage, and the next year he was solemnly reinstated as King of Hungary. The boy-king allowed Hunyadi to remain *de facto* regent, but himself fell under the influence of his maternal uncle, the Count of Cilli, who distrusted the Hunyadi family, a feeling reciprocated by Hunyadi's brother-in-law, Mihály (Michael) Szilágyi. On Hunyadi's death, Ladislas nominated his uncle as the new Captain-General of Hungary, passing over Hunyadi's elder son, another Ladislas. Soon after, the king and his uncle visited Belgrade, then in Szilágyi's hands, and Szilágyi's partisans murdered Cilli. The king then treacherously seized Ladislas Hunyadi and put him to death; his younger brother Mátyás (Matthew) Hunyadi, then a boy of sixteen, he took to Prague, where he threw him into prison; only to die himself, still unmarried, a year later.

For the first time in Hungarian history there was now no candidate for the throne able to put forward a claim based even tenuously on heredity. There were, of course, pretenders enough, including the evergreen Emperor Frederick, but this time the nation was tired of foreign kings. The name of Hunyadi was magical among the small nobles, and it was easy for Szilágyi to organise them to favour of the surviving bearer of the name. On 24 January 1458, while the great men were still debating, a huge multitude of common nobles, assembled on the ice of the frozen Danube, proclaimed Mátyás king. Emissaries having with some difficulty extracted him from the keeping of George Podiebrad, in Prague (for the Czechs, too, had decided in favour of a national king), he was brought to Buda and enthroned amid scenes of national rejoicing.

Mátyás Corvinus, as he is commonly known from his crest, a raven, is, with the somewhat qualified exception of John Zápolyai, the only completely 'national' king to have worn the Holy Crown after the extinction of the old dynasty, and it is natural that Hungarian historians should have seen his reign, in retrospect, through something of a golden haze. The remarkable glamour of his personality is undeniable. He was, as his panegyrists never tire of repeating, a true Renaissance prince. He was exceedingly talented in every respect: a brilliant natural soldier, a first-class administrator, an outstanding linguist, speaking with equal fluency half a dozen languages, a learned astrologer, an enlightened patron of the arts and himself a refined connoisseur of their delights. His library of 'Corvina' was famous throughout Europe. Besides the illuminated MSS of which this mainly consisted (many of which he had specially wrought for him by Italian crafts-men), his collections, on which he spent vast sums, in-cluded pictures, statues, jewels, goldsmiths' work and other *objets d'art*. Under his patronage, architecture and the arts flourished in Hungary. Scholars of European repute lived and worked at his court and in the circle of the Archbishop-primate, János Vitéz. Some of them produced elaborate and scholarly works, still valuable in parts, on Hungarian history. The first book printed in Buda ante-dated Caxton. Sumptuous buildings sprang up in the capital and in other centres. Most of these were destroyed in the subsequent Turkish invasion, which also dispersed the remnants of his collections, but those which have survived, notably the magnificent Coronation church of Buda, show that Mátyás' Hungary could challenge comparison with most European states of the day. His reign saw the founda-tion of Hungary's second university – unfortunately, an-other short-lived creation.

The word 'Renaissance' is to be taken exactly, for especially after Mátyás had married, as his second wife, Beatrix of Aragon, daughter of the King of Naples, the influences of the early Italian Renaissance dominated his court. They brought with them the absurdities of the day. The cult of Attila and his Huns, at that time held to be the Magyars' ancestors, flourished. The historian Bonfinius traced the Hunyadi's own ancestry back to a Roman consul, himself the descendant of Zeus and the nymph Taygeta. But the classical trappings were used to enhance the national glory. When Mátyás' father-in-law sent him a Spanish horse-master, he replied:

'For centuries we have been famed for our skill in horsemanship, so that the Magyar has no need to have his horses dance with crossed legs, Spanish fashion.'

Seen unromantically, his reign, of course, appears as the usual mixture of good and bad. His first years were necessarily spent in consolidating his position, for he had many opponents, both abroad and at home. Even Podiebrad had demanded a heavy ransom for releasing him, and although the Emperor Frederick did not press his claim by arms, he, too, demanded a big price for suspending them, and for restoring the Holy Crown. The Czechs were still installed in north-western Hungary, the Turks still dangerous in the Balkans. Many of the magnates were very hostile to the young upstart, as they regarded him, and he soon became involved in a dispute with his own uncle and sponsor, Szilágyi, who had hoped to rule for him till he grew older.

Mátyás overcame all these difficulties with energy and skill. Podiebrad was paid off, Frederick bought off, through the mediation of the Pope; the Czechs were mopped up, an accommodation having been reached with Giskra. Szilágyi was sent on an expedition into the Balkans, which ended in his death, and the other magnates brought to heel. Two successful expeditions were carried out against the Turks, a chain of fortresses built along the southern frontier, and Hungarian suzerainty re-established, if in somewhat shadowy form – it was worth little unless enforced by garrisons, which could not be spared – over Bosnia, Serbia and Wallachia, and later, also over Moldavia.

It is by his acts after he had really become master of his country that Mátyás is to be judged. His electors had bound him stringently to observe constitutional forms, and this he always did, hearing the views of the Council and admitting the principle that the Diet should meet annually. He actually enlarged the autonomous powers of the counties. Nevertheless, the whole bent of his mind was towards the fashionable 'princely' absolutism of his age, and his respect for constitutional institutions was largely formal. In practice, he disregarded the Council; his real instruments were his secretaries, a body of men picked by himself, generally young and often of quite obscure origin. When the Diet proved recalcitrant, he bent it to his will, ruthlessly enough. His rule was in fact a near-absolutism, and the touchstone of it is, whether or no it was enlightened and beneficial.

In some respects, it was certainly both these things. He simplified the administration and made it more efficient, and carried through a grandiose reform of the entire judicial system, abolishing many anachronisms and abuses and introducing a simplified and accelerated procedure which was of particular benefit to the small man. He encouraged the towns, especially the smaller market towns, and while not alleviating the legal position of the serfs, in fact greatly improved their condition by the even-handed justice which he enforced, so that when he was dead they mourned: 'King Mátyás is dead, justice is departed.'

The central controversy of his day turned round his defence policy and the financial burdens which he imposed on the nation in support of it. He trebled the size of the *militia portalis*, following this up by the most famous of all his 'innovations', the creation of a standing army, some 30,000 strong, which ranked as part of the king's *banderium*' This force, which was drawn largely from the defeated Hussites, and was known, after its commander, 'Black. John Haugwitz, as the 'Black Army', was his most powerful weapon against all enemies, abroad or at home.

Since the upkeep of this force, supervening on the cost of his sumptuous court and his collections, involved an expenditure far beyond what could be met out of ordinary revenue, Mátyás reorganised the tax system in ways which cut at the root of the national tradition. He screwed up the profits from the regalia, introduced a *tributum fisci regalis* from which none of his subjects was exempt, and frequently – in the latter half of his reign, regularly – imposed a special *porta* tax of a florin per *porta*. Although he conceded the right of the Diet to vote this, yet in 1470, when that body objected, he dissolved it and had the tax collected by his servants. By these means he raised the royal revenue to the unprecedented figure of 6-800,000 forints; although in some years his expenditure far exceeded even this sum.

In the first years, the nation was prepared to accept extraordinary financial burdens to redeem the Holy Crown, rid north Hungary of the Czechs, and above all, to secure its defences against the Turks. But after his good beginning in the last-named field, Mátyás allowed his attention to be distracted to the west. He had then some excuse: the Austrians and Czechs were proving worse neighbours than the Turks, who remained passive for some ten years after their defeats. But Mátyás let himself be drawn into an ever-widening circle of campaigns in the Lands of the Bohemian Crown and Austria, in pursuit for himself of the Bohemian Crown, the dignity of Roman King and the succession to the Imperial Crown itself, after Frederick should die. In fact, he succeeded in 1469 in making himself master of Moravia, Silesia and Lusatia, with the title of King of Bohemia (although this was also borne simultaneously by Podiebrad) and, in 1478, in forcing Frederick to cede him Lower Austria and Styria. To his subjects, he justified these campaigns, and the taxes which he levied to finance them, by the argument that Hungary alone was no match for the Turks; that the sovereign princes of Austria and Bohemia would not help him and could not be trusted not to stab him in the back; and that he could therefore only organise the great crusade if he had at his disposal the resources of the Bohemian and Imperial Crowns. There was perhaps something in this argument, for the only source which sent Mátyás any help against the Turks was the Holy

See, which sent some rather jejune subsidies. But the Hungarians, although probably not oppressed by conscience-pricks over the blatant aggressiveness of Mátyás' wars, saw no profit in them, had no ambition to become the nucleus of a multi-national empire, and believed that Mátyás was simply gratifying personal ambition at the expense of the security of Hungary's southern frontier – which, in fact, the Turks raided again in 1474 and 1476, doing much damage. There was much grumbling, and in 1470 a party which included some of Mátyás' oldest supporters conspired to set Casimir of Poland on the throne, and next year Casimir actually crossed the Carpathians at the head of an army.

He found few supporters and the enterprise collapsed easily enough; but it cannot be said that in his lifetime Mátyás was ever beloved as Stephen I or Louis the Great had been.

Mátyás might nevertheless have established a new, native dynasty; but neither of his two wives bore him an heir. His only issue, a boy called John, was his illegitimate son by a bourgeoise of Breslau. One of Mátyás' main preoccupations as he grew older was to ensure this boy's succession, and he eventually reached agreement in principle with Maximilian of Austria whereby John was to marry Maximilian's daughter; Hungary was to hand back Austria and Styria to Maximilian; and Maximilian was to renounce his father's old claims on Hungary and recognise John as its sovereign. But on 6 May 1490, when actually on his way to the meeting which should have made the agreement definitive, Mátyás died suddenly, and the whole house of cards collapsed. The smaller nobles would have liked another ruler of the Hunyadi stock, but John's illegitimacy was a real objection, and he himself was of too peaceable and unambitious nature to press his claim hard. Maximilian was another candidate, but the magnates were afraid of him; what they wanted was, as one of them put it cynically, 'a

king whose plaits they could hold in their fists'. Such a man
was to hand in Wladislas Jagiello (Ulászló II in Hungarian
history), whom the Bohemians had chosen as their king in
1471 precisely for his negative qualities, a choice which he
had thereafter justified so amply as to earn from his subjects
the name of 'King Dobře' (King O.K.) from his habit of
assenting without cavil to any proposal laid before him.

In the event Maximilian contented himself with the
restoration of the Austrian provinces and with an agreement that if Ulászló died without heirs, Maximilian himself, or his heirs, should succeed. Thereafter he exercised
an increasingly close, although friendly, protectorate over
Hungary, which was not altered when Ulászló, after many
curious adventures, eventually married and, in 1506, became father of a boy. Another agreement was concluded in
1515 under which this boy, Louis, married Maximilian's
granddaughter, Mary, while his sister, Anne, was betrothed
to Maximilian's younger grandson, Ferdinand, who was to
succeed to Louis's thrones if Louis died without issue.

During these years Maximilian built up for himself a
considerable party in Hungary, especially in the west of
the country, but he also had many opponents. The
national party, strong among the smaller nobles, refused
to recognise the validity of the dynastic compacts, and a
Diet in 1505 actually passed a resolution never again to
receive a foreign king. This party's candidate, should
Ulászló's line die out, was one John Zápolyai, whose uncle
and father had risen from small beginnings to hold successively the office of Palatine under Mátyás, while John himself was Voivode of Transylvania and the biggest landowner
in Hungary.

Meanwhile, under King Dobře's rule, conditions in
Hungary plunged downhill with Gadarene rapidity. His
electors had forced him to repeal all Mátyás' 'innovations',
including his extraordinary taxation. This involved the
dissolution of the Black Army, the chief instrument of

Mátyás' personal power; for defence, the nation now reverted to the *banderial* system. The king had also to promise to convoke the Diet regularly, giving advance notice of the subjects which he proposed to lay before it, and to agree that no decree issued by him was legal without the Council's confirmation. He fell entirely into the hands of the clique round him, who plundered the royal revenues so ruthlessly that only a fraction of them reached the treasury. The annual revenue fell to under 200,000 florins. The king himself was reduced to selling off Mátyás' collections. Sometimes he had literally to beg for food and drink for his court. At one carnival the king's own estates could produce only eight turkeys.

The power of the magnates, which at the same period became almost total in Bohemia, was to some extent limited in Hungary by the resistance of the lesser nobles, who succeeded in asserting a right to a share in the membership of the Council, as also to attendance at the Diet. In 1514, too, they achieved a remarkable paper reaffirmation of their position in the shape of a codification of the Customary Law of Hungary, drawn up by the jurist Werböczy. This work, known as the 'Tripartitum', which, although never formally promulgated, was ever after universally treated as authoritative, laid down in explicit terms the complete legal equality of all nobles, as enjoying 'one and the same liberty'. In practice, this helped them little politically: even in the Diet the magnates could always get their way by prolonging the debates until the small men could stay away from their farms no longer.

It did, however, help to reaffirm the cardinal distinction between the free and the unfree population, and the most unhappy feature of the period was the swift deterioration of the position of the latter class. The phenomenon was not a specifically Hungarian one; it was occurring simultaneously in Germany, Bohemia and Poland, and even set in rather later in Hungary than in the neighbouring countries. But here, too, the peasants found their burdens progressively increased and their liberty, especially that of escaping from a tyrannous landlord, progressively restricted. The Diet of 1492, while confirming their right to change their masters, reduced their inducement to do so by making it illegal for any lord, including the king and the Free Districts (the prohibition was extended to the boroughs in 1498) to exact less than the minimum legalised dues and services. This Law was a serious blow to the market towns and the Districts, which under Mátyás had achieved a half-free condition, compounding their obligations for a relatively small annual sum. In 1504 peasants were forbidden hunting or fowling.

Then, in 1514, there came an extraordinary and terrible episode. The Cardinal Primate, Tamás Bakócz, aspired to the Papacy. He was not elected, but as consolation and diversion, entrusted with the organisation of a crusade. None of the big men volunteered, but a huge army of peasants and masterless men did so. Bakócz put them under the command of a Szekel professional soldier named Dózsa. Left without proper leadership or supplies, the wretched crusaders grew restive and presently Dózsa turned them not against the Turks but against the lords. The movement expanded into an almost nation-wide jacquerie. There was savage fighting in which fearful atrocities were committed on both sides. Then the revolt was put down. Dózsa was put to death by indescribable tortures. A Diet intoxicated by a spirit of almost inconceivable vindictiveness ordered the most savage reprisals against all leaders and all perpetrators of any atrocities, and their kinsfolk, and condemned the entire class of peasants, with certain exceptions, to 'real and perpetual servitude'. They became irrevocably bound to the soil, in which they were explicitly declared to have no ownership whatever – they were wage-earners pure and simple. Their corvée was raised to fifty-two days in the year, and their other dues and payments increased. This savage law, too, was enshrined in the Tripartitum.

Louis succeeded his father in 1516, but, a boy of nine, naturally could bring no remedy. Meanwhile the defences of the country went from bad to worse. The frontier garrisons were left without pay, the fortresses fell into ill-repair. The king disbanded his own *banderium* for lack of funds, and several of the magnates followed his example. Then, in 1520, the Turkish threat grew acute again. Suleiman the Magnificent succeeded to the Sultanate and at once sent Louis a demand for tribute; when this was rejected, he marched on Belgrade and took it. The country awoke to the danger and agreed to a general tax for establishing a permanent mercenary army, but this was to replace, not supplement, the existing system. The lords were relieved of the obligation of maintaining *banderia* and the lesser nobles from obeying the levée. The proceeds of the tax were embezzled and the army never raised.

Hungary was given a brief respite by the Sultan's decision to reduce Rhodes before turning north again, but in 1525 attack was again imminent. Messengers scoured Europe appealing for help, but hardly any came; the Empire was occupied with France, Poland with the Tatars, Bohemia was indifferent. When, in 1526, the Sultan commenced his advance in earnest, it was at first almost unopposed. The levée was, after all, proclaimed and the *banderia* re-activated, but when, in July, Louis set out from Buda he had at first only 3,300 men with which to meet the Sultan's 70–80,000 regulars and half as many irregulars. By the time the two armies made contact at Mohács, Louis' army had swollen to 25,000, but the detachments from Transylvania and Croatia had not yet arrived. Disregarding advice to wait for these, the Hungarians attacked on 29 August. The army was almost utterly destroyed and the king himself perished by some fatal mishap in the rout.

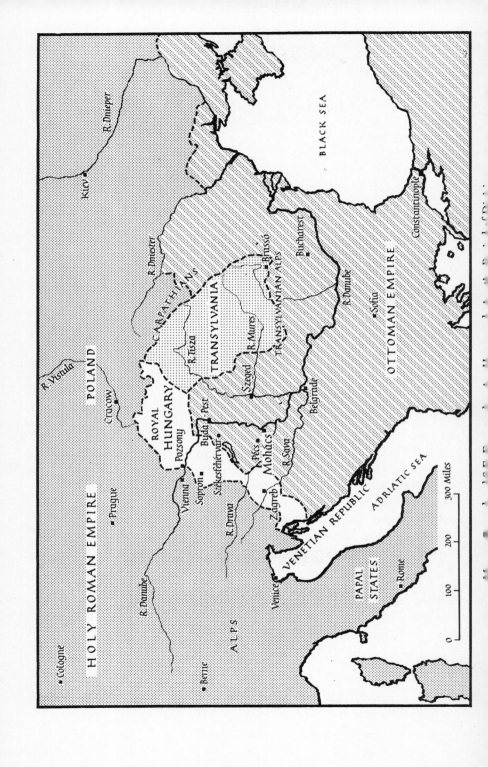

HOLY ROMAN EMPIRE

POLAND

ROYAL HUNGARY

TRANSYLVANIA

OTTOMAN EMPIRE

VENETIAN REPUBLIC

PAPAL STATES

ALPS

CARPATHIANS

TRANSYLVANIAN ALPS

BLACK SEA

ADRIATIC SEA

R.Dnieper

R.Vistula

R.Danube

R.Dniester

R.Tisza

R.Mures

R.Danube

R.Sava

R.Drava

• Cologne

• Berne

• Prague

• Cracow

Kiev •

Vienna ■

Sopron ■

Pozsony ■

Székesfehérvár ■

Buda ■ Pest

■ Pécs
Mohács ■

Zagreb ■

Venice ■

Rome ■

Szeged ■

Belgrade ■

Brassó ■

Bucharest ■

Sofia •

Constantinople ■

0   100   200   300 Miles

4

THE PERIOD OF DIVISION

THE battle of Mohács was the prelude to the most miserable period of Hungarian history: the well-nigh two centuries of partition, when the Turks lorded it over the heart of the country and reduced it to a near-desert; the Habsburgs held the western fringe of it in a grip which at times was not much less brutal than the Turks'; while the flickering lamp of the national independence survived only in remote Transylvania, and there precariously. To this day, Hungary bears on her body the scars of these dreadful decades. Yet the partition did not come about immediately, and but for the disastrousaccident of the youngking's death, it might never have come about at all. Suleiman had not come prepared to conquer Hungary, and after advancing as far as Buda withdrew his army again to the Balkans, only leaving garrisons in a couple of fortresses near the southern frontier, Pétervárad and Ujlak. But the king's death was the signal for another contest for the throne. Many of the magnates, and nearly all the lesser nobles, wanted a national king, in the sense of the 1505 resolution, and were prepared to accept Zápolyai; but Ferdinand of Habsburg had announced himself as Louis' lawful successor, and a certain party, while not conceding any legal validity to the Habsburg-Jagiello family compact, yet held that Ferdinand, with the resources of the Empire behind him, would afford Hungary the better protection against the Turk. It took time for them to persuade Ferdinand to submit to the forms of election, and meanwhile his supporters had crowned Zápolyai in all due form. Ferdinand's partisans nevertheless proclaimed him king, and then a complex military and diplomatic struggle broke out, which lasted for several years. Getting the worse of the earlier exchanges, Zápolyai appealed to the Sultan, who installed him in Buda, and with whose help Ferdinand's effective rule was confined to the western third of the country, but neither claimant was able to drive the other right out of the field, and the barren conflict went on until the whole country was heartily sick of it. At last, in 1538, Zápolyai's ablest adviser, a Croat Franciscan known as Friar George, or Martinuzzi, mediated the secret agreement of Várad, under which each claimant recognised the other's title and the territorial *status quo*, while Zápolyai, who was much the older man, and then unmarried, agreed that on his death Ferdinand (or his son) should succeed to the entire kingdom. If John Zápolyai had a son (he was then wooing the Polish princess, Isabella) this boy should be compensated with a duchy in north Hungary. On 22 July 1540, John died, but a fortnight later Isabella, whom he had married in the interval, gave birth to a son, John Sigismund, whom the anti-Habsburg party promptly recognised as king. Ferdinand sent an army against Buda, but now the Sultan decided to play for his own hand. In August 1541 he occupied Buda himself. He recognised John Sigismund as king, but as his own vassal, and, moreover, carved a great wedge out of the centre of the country and incorporated it in his own dominions. In 1547 Ferdinand was obliged to conclude a truce under which the Sultan recognised him as *de facto* ruler, subject to an annual tribute, of those parts of Hungary (the north and west, and the 'remnants of the remnants', as its own Estates called them, of Croatia) then actually held by him, while he continued to recognise John Sigismund's rule in the east. Ferdinand still hoped to recover Transylvania, and in 1551 Martinuzzi persuaded Isabella to renounce her son's claims in return for a duchy in Silesia for him, and monetary compensation for herself. Imperial troops then entered Transylvania, where they committed the grievous miscalculation of

assassinating Martinuzzi. The Sultan was, however, determined not to let Transylvania fall to his dangerous enemy,
the Habsburg, and in 1564, soon after Maximilian II had
succeeded Ferdinand, attacked again. More prolonged
fighting followed, in the course of which Suleiman died
while besieging the west Hungarian fortress of Szigetvár,
the defence of which, by the heroic Miklós Zrinyi, is one
of the famous episodes of Hungarian history. The Imperial
armies meanwhile stood idly by at Györ, and failed to
follow up the confusion in which the Sultan's death had
thrown the Turks. Isabella and her son were reinstated in
Transylvania, which in 1566 the Sultan formally declared
an autonomous principality under his own suzerainty; if
John Sigismund died without heirs the Transylvanians
were to elect his successor, subject to confirmation of
their choice by the Porte. In 1568 Maximilian recognised
this arrangement, and also accepted a new frontier far less
favourable than the old: starting from near Nagykanizsa
this now ran to the western tip of Lake Balaton, then
from the lake's eastern extremity to cross the Danube
between Komárom and Esztergom, skirted the foothills
above the Great Plain in the north, as far as Egér, and
thence ran south-south-east, approximately bisecting the
Tiszántúl. The trisection of Hungary was complete.

Of the three parts of Hungary, that which was directly
ruled by the Turks had the most to endure. Its sufferings
were substantially greater than those of the Balkan
countries through which the Turks had advanced earlier,
for there the mountains held secluded corners into which
the conquerors did not easily penetrate, and in which
survivors from the open lands could take refuge. Moreover, the Orthodox church came to terms with the
Crescent with a relatively good grace, and even the numbers of its former members who saved their lives, sometimes even their status and their properties, by adopting

Islam, was not inconsiderable. The open plains of central Hungary afforded a few secure hiding-places, and the faith of its catholic population proved admirably strong: the number of converts to Islam was minimal.

Further, their conquest had cost the Turks much fighting before it was completed, and the accepted fate of a prisoner taken in war by the Turks, if it was not death, was transportation into slavery. The process began with Suleiman's campaign of 1526; the advance of his army to Buda was marked by a swathe of burning villages, and its retreat was followed by a seemingly endless line of miserable captives, doomed to the slave-markets of Anatolia unless, as often happened, they were slaughtered on the way, as being too much trouble to transport. The scene was re-enacted after every campaign, and even the Sultan's recognised subjects, in time of peace, were not safe. There were, in fact, few years of real peace: at least on the frontiers, guerilla warfare was endemic, and during it, the Turkish irregulars, and still more, their Tatar auxiliary bands, were not particular on which side of the frontier they collected their victims. It was an especial misfortune for the country that Hungarian slaves were highly esteemed in Anatolia and fetched big prices. Sometimes victims were carried off from the heart of the country, or sold by resident masters, in times of what was nominally complete peace.

The fate of those who escaped slavery was a yoke which was often almost as heavy. In the territory ruled by the Turk, which was organised in four (later five) Pashaliks, the whole under the control of the Beglerbeg, Pasha of Buda, the government was entirely Turkish. All former title-deeds became null and void, and if a Hungarian noble remained behind (most of them fled), he lost his rank and all that went with it, and became a peasant among the peasants. The entire land passed into the absolute ownership of the state, which kept one-fifth of it 'for Allah', i.e., under its own direct management, while bestowing the rest in fiefs, usually small, among its own officials and soldiers. These thus formed a landlord class ruling over their peasants much as the native landlords had done. There was, however, this difference, that the fief was not hereditable, nor even granted for the beneficiary's lifetime. He could be transferred at any moment to another part of the Sultan's dominions, and the higher dignitaries were in fact seldom left long in one station. Even the legal dues and taxes, of which one part was paid to the state and the other to the landlord, were heavy, but the short-term fief-holder had also every interest in squeezing the last farthing out of his land and his peasants, and when illegal extortion was added to the legalised burden, it became crushing.

Conditions on the state lands, or *khases*, were, indeed, perceptibly better. There was little arbitrary exaction, and there are recorded cases of complaints going up to Constantinople and being remedied. The larger localities even enjoyed a measure of self-government, for the Turkish officials found it easier to deal with their inhabitants in bulk, through their own representatives, than man by man. They were thus able to pay their taxes collectively, which was much less burdensome, as preventing illegal exactions against individuals. Some of them, which lay well behind any frontier, came to enjoy a measure of prosperity, practised industry and especially trade (including a large trade in cattle with the west) on a substantial scale, and evolved a solid and self-respecting middle class.

The chief *khas* country was in the central plain, on the two banks of the Tisza, an area which lay some way behind the frontier, and was used by the Turks as a supply base for their frontier fortresses. The populations of this area forsook their villages and congregated in the relative shelter of the towns, and thus were born the curious 'village-towns' of the Alföld – Szeged, Nagykörös, Kecskemét, Cegled, Debrecen and the rest, each of which incorporated in its boundaries the territory of the deserted villages round it.

Thus the municipal area of Kecskemét at one time covered 475,000 acres, which had formerly housed thirty-two villages.

But even this security was very limited and the well-being modest indeed; the cattle-trade itself developed only because the population found arable farming too unrewarding or too dangerous, and the herds which reached the west consisted of wild, skinny beasts which had to be fattened for months in Germany or Austria before they were slaughtered. Such traders as prospered were usually Greeks, Armenians or Serbs, rather than Hungarians.

Generally speaking, the feature of Turkish rule at its best was barren unconstructiveness, and at its more frequent worse, savage destructiveness. Beyond a few baths, the Turks brought nothing whatever to Hungary, except fortresses, and what they found there, they destroyed, or allowed to fall into ruin. The most serious of all the effects, from the national point of view, was the depopulation brought about by the wars, the slave-raiding and the endemic pestilence, aggravated locally by the emigration of refugees. In this respect Hungarian historians have distinguished three zones. The first and worst covered the south of the country, up to the Maros in the east and a line extending westward from its junction with the Tisza to that of the Sárviz with the Danube, thence south-westward past Pécs to the frontier. This area, once among the most flourishing in Hungary, had borne the brunt of the first fighting, and its original population had been practically wiped out before the middle of the century. Later it was partially replaced by immigration from the Balkans, but the new population was far less numerous than the old and less rooted to the soil; they were semi-nomadic herdsmen, rather than farmers. North of this came the main *khas* country. Here more population had survived, and there had even been some immigration from the south. Yet even here, as late as 1720, a generation after the Turks had gone, the population of Debrecen, the largest of the local towns, was still only 8,000, and that of Szeged, under 5,000, and for perhaps 25 miles all round each of them, there was hardly a habitation to be seen.

The strip of land behind the semicircle of the frontier was rather more densely inhabited, for here were the garrisons, and the state saw to it that the Spahi lands should be occupied. When the population fled, or was massacred, new colonists were brought in. Buda, as the seat of the Beglerbeg, as well as a large garrison station, remained a considerable place. But even here a traveller found in Vác, in 1605, only a handful of peasants who knew only from hearsay that a rich town had once stretched round the sides of their poor huts. The frontiersmen were, incidentally, largely Serbs and Vlachs who followed the Turks when the latter evacuated the country.

With the men, the works of their hands vanished. The walls of the villages crumbled into the soil from which they had been fashioned. More durable buildings stood deserted and ruinous. Smiling fields reverted to swamp and jungle. The rude Balkan herdsmen lived in primitive cabins half sunk in the ground, which they left empty when danger threatened or even when pastures were exhausted.

The devastation wrought by the Turks was, of course, not confined to Turkish Hungary. When the Porte and the Empire were at war, which was frequently enough, the Sultan's armies spread ruin where they passed, but even the periods of 'peace' meant only that no large armies were set on foot; not that all hostilities were suspended. It was nearly thirty years before anything like a continuous defensive line for Royal Hungary was established, and then only along part of the frontier. The rest was protected only by a line of fortresses, often inadequately garrisoned. Turkish and Tatar marauders often slipped through the gaps, laying whole regions waste and massacring their inhabitants or carrying them off into slavery. Hardly any part of Royal Hungary was spared these visitations, and in the turbulent years preceding the liberation, no place could call itself safe. A considerable zone, in places forty miles deep, behind the whole length of the frontier actually paid a regular Danegeld to the commanders of the local Turkish fortresses to escape these vexations.[1]

The damage directly inflicted by armies or raiders was not the only burden which the neighbourhood of the Turks laid on Royal Hungary. The frontier fortresses and their hinterland covered a considerable part of the country and occupied the energies of much of its population. Young men took service under noted commanders and led adventurous lives of derring-do, paying the Turks back in their own coin. There was much that was romantic in this frontier life, in which the classes sank their differences before the common danger. Even duels between Christian and Turkish paladins were not infrequent. It also provided an excellent military training. But it was not a life in which wealth could accumulate, or the arts of peace flourish.

The loss of so much of Hungary to the Turks, and the difficulty and expense of defending the remainder, were the two main causes in the gradual deterioration of relations between Royal Hungary and its new dynasty which took

[1] There was a curious counterpart to this in that many of the villages on the Turkish side of the frontier, down to the line Pécs-Baja-Szeged, continued during most of the occupation to pay a proportion of their old taxes, tithes and rents to the representatives of the former recipients. These were usually collected by agents of the Hungarian frontier fortress commanders, who retained the money as part of their pay, setting it off against the sums due to them from the county authorities. The existence of these cross-payments was recognised by both states, and sometimes actually found mention in peace treaties. In allowing them, the Turks also recognised the existence of a sort of shadow county organisation on their territory, and permitted it a certain voice in their subjects' internal administration.

place in the sixteenth century, and of the progressive real, although not nominal, diminution of its political status.

In the first years after his accession, when he was still fighting to unite all Hungary under his rule (when it would have been by far his most important possession), Ferdinand gave the nation little reason to complain. Having once sworn to respect its constitution, he began by keeping his oath scrupulously enough. At first he left it to be governed for him by the existing Council, under the presidency of his sister, the queen-widow. In 1528 he deferred to the Hungarians' wishes by replacing Maria by a Palatine, Count István Báthory. Membership of the old Council now degenerated, indeed, into a titular honour, but the new Council which Ferdinand appointed to help the Palatine was composed of Hungarians, and Ferdinand did not interfere with their conduct of their business. He reserved two places for Hungarians in the *Hofrat* which he was organising as his central advisory Council for his dominions as a whole – it was they themselves who failed to take up the offer; and while he had begun by providing only secretariats for Hungarian affairs in his top-level central ministries, the *Hofkanzlei* and *Hofkammer*, when the Hungarians complained, he allowed them a court chancellery and a *camera* of their own, nominally subject to no orders except those issued by himself. He convoked the Diet regularly (as he did throughout his reign), levied no taxes without its consent, and deferred to its opinion when it resisted various innovations proposed by him.

But the hope of reuniting Hungary faded, and, especially after Ferdinand had succeeded his brother as Emperor in 1558, Royal Hungary had become no more than a small, outlying and exposed annexe to a mighty organism in which its special problems and interests inevitably counted for little. The Hungarians absence from the *Hofrat*, while emphasising their country's distinctive status, lost them their opportunity of pressing their case when issues of foreign policy were discussed. The orders to the Hungarian court chancellery, while still issued in the king's name, in fact came from central *Hofkanzlei*, while in 1537 the Hungarian *camera* was formally subordinated to the *Hofkammer*. Above all, Hungary lost her independence in the vital field of the national defence.

It had been obvious from the first that her own resources were insufficient even for the defence of her own frontiers, let alone the recovery of the rest of Hungary, and she herself had insisted that she must be helped to discharge the tasks. The first defensive arrangements were made by agreement between the Estates of Hungary and the neighbouring Lands. Austria proper and Bohemia undertook to help with the defence of the northern and eastern sectors, and, under the first arrangements, did no more than supply garrisons to reinforce those provided by the Hungarians themselves, on whom the brunt of the work fell. The supreme command over all these forces was then still in Hungarian hands, for the Palatine's rights included the command of all armed forces in the country, in the king's absence.

When, however, Báthory died, in 1534, Ferdinand did not appoint a new Palatine, but only a 'locum tenens'. This official, again, was a high Hungarian dignitary, and the change did not impair the nation's autonomy in those fields (which included the judiciary) which were still regarded as *interna*; but the national defence was no longer among those fields, for the locum tenens did not exercise the Palatine's vital prerogative. In 1556 the responsibility for the defence of all the Habsburgs' dominions was assigned to a central body, the *Hofkriegsrat*, and on this body the Hungarians, in spite of repeated protests, were never given representation.

The process was carried further still on the southern, or Croat, sector, where Inner Austria had agreed to help. Here it soon became clear that something more than reinforcement of the local Hungarian fortresses would be needed, and a whole new system was organised. The core of it was the chain of fortresses, the garrisons of which were generally German; while the population of the areas round and between the fortresses, this consisting largely of Serb and Croat refugees from the Balkans, was organised as a sort of militia, being given free land in return for a perpetual obligation of military service. In 1578 this strip of land, now divided into two Districts (the Croat and the Wend) was formally withdrawn from the jurisdiction of the Croat Estates and made into a 'Perpetual Generalcy', under the command of the Archduke Charles, then the ruler of Inner Austria. Later again, when the Habsburg dominions were again reunited under one monarch, this, too, came under the administration of the *Hofkriegsrat*. This was the genesis of the 'Military Frontier' which thereafter, until its dissolution under the 1867 Compromise, proved so effective a thorn in Hungary's flesh.

Thus Hungary received help indeed, but at the cost of submission to foreign control over an essential field of her national life, and she was allowed no say whatever in the great question of the recovery of her integrity. Complaints that she was being ruled by foreigners soon became loud: the unruly conduct of the foreign garrisons, who were often left unpaid and sought their own remedy by plundering the countryside round, became a standing grievance; and feeling became bitter indeed when Maximilian let Zrinyi and his men perish, and on top of that, recognised the Sultan's suzerainty over Transylvania at a moment when most Hungarians believed that it would have been possible to drive the Turks out of all Hungary.

Relations between the nation and its new rulers were already worse under Maximilian than under Ferdinand, for Maximilian, who had claimed to be succeeding his father *jure hereditario*, had signed no electoral diploma, had no personal memories of Hungary's former greatness and importance, and was accustomed to rule as absolute monarch in his other dominions. He was therefore less punctilious than his father had been about consulting the Diet, and refused to remedy any of the nation's constitutional grievances. He even promised the Imperial Diet that he would incorporate Hungary in the Empire. He was, however, personally an easy-going man, and did not interfere gratuitously in the nation's internal affairs. Matters took a sharper turn for the worse when in 1576 Maximilian was succeeded by the unbalanced Rudolph, and especially when Rudolph transferred his court to Prague. Hungarian affairs were now dealt with only at second hand; from the chancellery ta Vienna they were sent on to Prague, where – Rudolph shutting himself away with his circle of astrologers – all decisions were taken by a little clique of military advisers, who saw in the Hungarians only truculent rebels, to be weakened by all possible means. The commanders of the military garrisons claimed complete authority in their districts, and tried to usurp in them even the judicial power.

Now, too, a religious conflict supervened on the constitutional and military disputes. In the preceding half-century the Reformation had swept over Hungary, beginning with its German inhabitants, the burghers of the towns and the Transylvanian Saxons, who had, by great majority, adopted the doctrines of Luther. These, written as they were in German, had not penetrated widely among the Magyars, but after Mohács Calvin's latin writings had converted to themselves the greater part of the people, spreading with darticular rapidity because a very large number of the highest roman catholic dignitaries had perished on the field of Mohács. The Reformation was in itself an event of the first importance for Hungary. It breathed new vitality into a spiritual life which had become in many respects worldly, torpid and degenerate, lending it a fresh inspiration, and one which proved peculiarly well adapted to the national genius. Hungarian protestantism came to constitute a vigorous creative element in European life, and in particular, the especial embodiment of the spirit of national independence.

But the religious question was destined also to become a source of national weakness by dividing Magyar from Magyar, and as prelude to this, while the nation was still almost entirely protestant, a cause of conflict between the people and its rulers. Neither Ferdinand I nor Maximilian, who himself inclined strongly towards protestantism, had tried to impede the spread of it in Hungary, but by the time Rudolph succeeded his father, his uncles and cousins had almost completed the enforcement of the Counter-Reformation in Inner Austria and the Tirol, and Rudolph was soon at loggerheads with the protestants in his own dominions. Relations between him and his Hungarian subjects soon approximated to a condition of cold war, which was complicated and aggravated in 1591 by the outbreak of another official war, known as the 'Fifteen Years War', with the Turks. Both the course and the outcome of this were, however, altered, not only by a change in the nature of the Turkish power, but also by the emergence of Transylvania as a distinct political factor.

As we have seen, the separation of Transylvania from Royal Hungary had been the Sultan's work. After Mohács there had been little positive separatist feeling in either half of the country; Zápolyai had had his partisans in all parts of Hungary, and Ferdinand had had his (notably the Saxons) in Transylvania. Both anti-kings had claimed sovereignty over all Hungary, and the aim of all Martinuzzi's diplomatic manoeuvres had been to reach an accommodation between the rivals which should make possible the ultimate restoration of the national unity. Indeed, John Sigismund himself, even after the reaffirmation of his position in 1568, had secretly recognised Maximilian as his suzerain, and the national prince whom the Transylvanians had elected in 1570, after John Sigismund's childless death, a local magnate named Stephen Báthori, had also sworn secret fealty to the Habsburg.

But pending the achievement of unity, the east Hungarians had been obliged to conduct their own affairs. Martinuzzi, the political genius and authority of the time and place, had fallen back on the local institution which existed, the old 'Union of the Three Nations', created in 1437 and still functioning. In 1542 representatives of the Three Nations, meeting at Torda, solemnly renewed the Union and thereafter met regularly in Diet; after 1544 this was attended by representatives of the 'Partium', i.e., those counties lying west of Historic Transylvania whose geographical situation forced them into partnership with it (at the time these were Bihár, Zarand, Arad and the District of Lugos and Karánsebes). Again in 1542, a Council composed of representatives of the Three Nations and of the Chapter of Nagyvárad was established to advise the executive, then personified by Martinuzzi, who was acting as 'lieutenant' for Isabella and her son.

A little later, Transylvania introduced another innovation, a very important one, for which it afterwards became famous. Here, too, the Reformation had made much progress, but the two parties were so evenly balanced that neither dared challenge the other to a duel à outrance, and in 1550 the Diet proclaimed the free exercise of the catholic and protestant religions. The protestants then split into Lutherans and Calvinists, and in 1564 the Diet established 'tolerance' between these two. In 1572 it recognised the catholic, lutheran, calvinist and unitarian creeds as 'established religions', the followers of each to enjoy freedom to practise their faith and equal political rights. The Orthodox faith, that of the Roumanians, was 'tolerated', i.e., could be practised freely, but was not admitted to political equality.

Enjoying these local safeguards, the Transylvanian protestants were naturally apprehensive of the growing power of the Counter-Reformation in the west. Stephen Báthori was himself a catholic, but Maximilian's intrigues against him forced him into retaliation, and the differences between him and the Habsburgs were accentuated when the last Polish king of the Jagiello line died in 1572. Although Maximilian hoped to gain the throne, it was Báthori whom the Poles elected to it, in 1575, and thereafter he and his younger brother, Christopher, who governed Transylvania for him until his death in 1581, and thereafter ruled it as his successor, were the Habsburgs' enemies rather than their partners.

When the Fifteen Years War broke out, the picture seemed at first to be reverting to its old lines. Sigismund (Zsigmond) Báthori, who had succeeded his father in 1586, began by allying himself with Rudolph in return for the hand of Rudolph's cousin, Maria Christina, and recognition of himself and his descendants as hereditary princes. The allies at first won important successes over the Turks, but failed to follow them up, and a period of great confusion followed. Báthori, who was a man of unbalanced mind, subject to fits of insane cruelty, abdicated, returned, abdicated again, and the rule over Transylvania alternated between him, his nominees, Rudolph, a local leader named Moses Székely and the Voivode Michael of Wallachia. When Rudolph's troops were in Transylvania, their commander, Basta, inaugurated there a real reign of terror, executions going hand in hand with confiscations and simple spoliation. The same atrocities were committed in Upper Hungary, and throughout Royal Hungary the court took the opportunity to confiscate the estates of many Hungarians, among them the Palatine, Illesházy, on trumped-up charges of treason. The position grew so intolerable that at last one of Sigismund's generals, István Bocskay, himself previously one of the most loyal supporters of the Habsburg cause, revolted. He raised a new army, the backbone of which was constituted by the wild soldier-herdsmen of the plains, known as 'hayduks', and drove Basta, not only out of Transylvania, but also out of Upper Hungary, which rallied to him. A Diet offered him the crown, which he refused, but on 23 June 1606 he concluded with Rudolph the Peace of Vienna, which left him prince of a Transylvania enlarged, for his lifetime, by the counties of Szatmár, Ugocsa and Bereg, and also guaranteed the rights of the protestants of Royal Hungary. Then, through his mediation, the Peace of Zsitvatorok (11 November 1606) was concluded between the Emperor and the Porte. The territorial *status quo* was left unchanged, but the Emperor was relieved of his tribute to the Sultan.

These treaties ushered in a new period. For the next half century the Turks were unaggressive, and even their rule over their subjects lost something of its brutality. Some travellers brought reports of peasants faring better under Turkish masters than under Christian, and cases occurred of flight across the frontier eastward. Above all, the Turks were indifferent what form of error their *Rayah* chose to pursue; if anything, they were less hostile to protestantism than to catholicism, with its international connections. Harried protestants in Royal Hungary sometimes called the zealots of the Counter-Reformation 'worse than the Turks'.

The place of the Turks in the power-question was, however, now taken by Transylvania. Bocskay, indeed, died (poisoned, some said) a few weeks after the Peace of Zsitvatorok, and the usual scramble for power followed, then another bad reign by another bad Báthori. But then, in 1613, the Porte forced the Transylvanians to accept as prince the man who was destined to prove the most famous of all the line, Gabriel Bethlen, more commonly known by the Hungarian version of his name, Bethlen Gábor. Bethlen's rule, which lasted from 1613 to 1629, was in every sense re-

GABRIEL BETHLEN D. G. TRANSSYLVANIÆ PRINCEPS, PARTIVM VNGARIÆ REGNI DNS ET SICVLORVM COMES, Anno ætat.XXXIX, a Chõ Nato ƆIƆ ƆCXIX

17. István Báthory: ref. p. 73

18. *The fire tower at Sopron*

TWO TOWERS FROM EAST
AND WEST HUNGARY

19. *A Turkish minaret
at Eger*

markable. At home, while avoiding the cruelties and ex-
cesses of many of his predecessors, he established a singular
variant of patriarchal but sufficiently enlightened despotism. He developed mines and industry and nationalised
many branches of Transylvania's foreign trade, his agents
buying up the products at fixed prices and selling them
abroad at a profit, almost doubling his revenues by this and
other devices. He built himself a grand new palace in his
capital, Gyulafehérvár, kept a sumptuous court, and patronised the arts and learning, especially in connection with his
own, Calvinist, faith. He founded an academy to which he
invited any pastor and teacher from the rest of Hungary,
sent students abroad to the protestant universities of England, the Low Countries and protestant Germany, conferred hereditary nobility on all protestant pastors and forbade landlords to prevent their serfs from having their
children schooled.

Other parts of his revenue he devoted to keeping up an
efficient standing army of mercenaries, with whose help
he conducted an ambitious foreign policy, along new lines.
Keeping peace with the Porte, he struck out to the north
and west. Partly, no doubt, he was actuated by simple personal ambition, but he seems also to have been genuinely
anxious to protect protestant liberties, especially those of
his fellow-countrymen in Royal Hungary, against the rising
tide of the Counter-Reformation. This combination of motives led him to intervene when the Thirty Years War broke
out in 1618, and with the Imperial armies heavily engaged
in Bohemia, he overran most of Royal Hungary, where a
party offered him the crown in 1620. The Porte vetoed
his acceptance of this offer, but by the Treaty of Nikolsburg (31 December 1621) he gained the title of Prince of
Transylvania and of Hungary, a big frontier extension and a
duchy in Silesia, besides securing confirmation of the rights
of the Hungarian protestants. A series of further campaigns,
in the course of which Bethlen, with some difficulty, got

Transylvania recognised as a member of the 1626 West-minster Coalition, were ended by other treaties which did not alter substantially the position reached at Nikolsburg.

When Bethlen died suddenly in 1629, the Transyl-vanian Estates abolished most of his internal reforms with as much alacrity and decision as the Hungarian Estates had shown in abolishing those of Corvinus. György Rákóczi I (1630–44) was obliged to follow more conventional methods, and was himself a less original character, but he was a shrewd negotiator and – not less important – the owner of enormous private estates. The power which these gave him enabled him to consolidate his position at home, and he managed to maintain and even advance Transylvania's international status and prestige. He fought the Emperor again, when the protestants of Royal Hungary complained that their rights were being disregarded, beat him, and in the Treaty of Linz (16 December 1645) ex-tracted from him fresh guarantees even more far-reaching than those agreed at Vienna and Nikolsburg. Transylvania figured as a sovereign state in the Treaty of Westphalia.

Largely owing to this support from Transylvania, partly also to the division of the Habsburg patrimony prevailing at the time, Royal Hungary was able to preserve a good deal of political and religious liberty during the first half of the seventeenth century. Matthias, to whom Rudolph ceded the rule over Hungary, Moravia and Austria in 1608, had to submit himself to election and to sign a diploma promis-ing to respect the chartered privileges of the 'Status et Ordines'. In 1613 he wrote bitterly to his cousin Ferdinand that he was quite powerless in Hungary. The Palatine did what he pleased, without troubling himself about either orders or prohibitions. 'If I ask the Hungarians to support me against the Turks, no one budges, but if the Prince of Transylvania asks them for help, the tocsins ring in every county. They mean to depose our House.'

The Hungarians made no such move: Matthias was followed by Ferdinand II and he by Ferdinand III, but each had to sign a far-reaching diploma, and neither was strong enough to break his word on a large scale. Thus Hungary escaped almost entirely the inhuman enforcement of the Counter-Reformation under which Bohemia suffered so terribly, and was also spared the worst ravages of the Thirty Years War.

With the relative peace there came a revival, also relative and limited to certain circles, of attachment to the dynasty. This was chiefly the work of the great Hungarian Cardinal, Péter Pázmány, made Primate-Archbishop in 1616, who by his extraordinary persuasive genius succeeded in winning the great majority of the magnates (whose tenets, until the Peace of Linz, were automatically followed by their subjects) back to the catholic fold. The catholic magnates, including the prelates, came to form a party in Hungary which was at least loyal to the Habsburgs and on their side in the great national issue of east versus west, and their influence was the stronger because they now ranked officially as a separate Estate. Ferdinand I had introduced the institution, previously unknown in Hungary, of hereditary titles of rank, and the families so distinguished, with the great officers of the Crown (who were almost invariably drawn from among them) and the higher-ranking prelates now formed a separate Upper House ('Table') which deliberated separately from the representatives of the counties and boroughs who formed the 'Lower Table'.

Pázmány was active also in the cultural field. He did much to improve the standards of the clergy and to raise the level of education generally. He was the founder of the oldest Hungarian university to survive into modern times, an institution originally sited in Nagyszombat, although later transferred to Buda-Pest. The national culture of the day, in which Austrian, Italian and Polish influences blended curiously with those of the native soil, was highly interesting, and far from insignificant.

Pázmány's work was, however, not an unmixed blessing to Hungary. Against the cultural advance which it brought, and the relaxation of tension with the dynasty, had to be set the acute internal conflict which developed with this phase of its religious history, for the catholic Hungarians were no more tolerant towards their protestant fellow-countrymen than were the court's German and Spanish advisers, and the antipathy of many of them extended also to protestant Transylvania. It was returned in full measure by the protestants of Royal Hungary and by the Transylvanians, who in their campaigns in Hungary took especial delight in burning the castles and ravaging the lands of the catholic Hungarians. Thus Hungary came again to be deeply divided, by cleavages, both vertical – Royal Hungary versus Transylvania – and horizontal within Royal Hungary itself, where the catholic magnates were at odds with the lesser nobility, which in the main had remained protestant.

The position of the pro-Habsburg party – in so far as it can be so called – was in any case ambiguous and painful. Hated by their fellow-countrymen, they were also distrusted by the centralists in Vienna, who saw in the distinctive position which all Hungarians were determined to maintain, only an unnatural and undesirable anachronism. And they themselves were well aware that any concessions to them were unwillingly made and would be retracted if ever the opportunity presented itself.

The problem of reconciling Hungarian chartered privileges with Habsburg centralism was never really solved; and to aggravate it, there was the running sore of the Turkish occupation of central Hungary. If the Turks had abandoned organised aggression, this did not mean that the border forays, with their constant toll of Hungarian blood, had ceased. Moreover, the apparent weakness of the Turks should surely have made it possible to drive them out of

Hungary altogether, and it was the king of Hungary's sworn duty to do this. Sometimes individual Hungarians undertook private campaigns, some of which met with considerable success, but the Crown, occupied as it was with the west, refused to support them. It adhered, pedantically or honourably, to its truce with the Porte and let the dismemberment of Hungary continue.

The uneasy balance between the three factors which had been established in 1606 was destroyed when György Rákóczi II of Transylvania, who had succeeded his father in 1648, overreached himself, allowing himself to be drawn into Charles X of Sweden's Polish schemes. In January 1657, seduced by the prospect, held out to him by Charles, of acquiring the crown of Poland, he led an army across the passes, having consulted neither the Transylvanian Estates, nor the Porte. The enterprise was a complete disaster: the army was encircled by the Tatars and most of its members killed or carried off into slavery. By ill fortune, Mohammed Köprülü, the architect of the Ottoman Empire's last renaissance, had just become Grand Vizier. He led a great force against Transylvania and captured, one by one, the great fortresses guarding it. The end of a confused struggle was that Transylvania lost the bulk of the outlying western territories which had furnished most of its real strength. A new prince – Mihály Abafi – was installed, who was a simple puppet of the Porte's.

It was the end of Transylvania both as a European Power and protector of Hungarian liberties, and it also brought about a crisis between the Estates of Royal Hungary and the dynasty. During the fighting, both the Transylvanians and the west Hungarians had appealed passionately to Vienna for help, insisting that now was the chance to end Turkish rule in Hungary. Here, again, the moment was singularly unfortunate. Leopold I, who had just ascended the throne, was among the most convinced catholics of his line, and his advisers, Lobkowitz, Portia, Auersperg and the rest, were among the most extreme devotees of 'Great Austrian' absolutism. Further, Leopold was preoccupied with his struggle against France for the hegemony over Germany, and reluctant to offend the sultan. He did send a small force under his famous general, Montecuccoli, into Transylvania, but when the Turks took this, and hostilities which had been opened independently in south Hungary by Miklós Zrinyi, great-grandson of the hero of Szigetvár, as a *casus belli*, and attacked Hungary, the old story was repeated. Montecuccoli left Zrinyi to his fate. He defeated the Turks signally at Szent Gotthard, on the Austrian frontier, on 1 August 1664, but instead of following this up, Leopold on 27 September concluded the Peace of Vasvár, which would have been more appropriate had Austria been the defeated party: under it, he recognised the Sultan's gains in Transylvania, ceded him a fortress in west Hungary, and even submitted to paying an indemnity.

The vicious circle was now complete. The Hungarians' embitterment was so great that for the first time, an important party in West Hungary, including leading catholics, turned against the Habsburgs. A group of the highest magnates in the land, including the Palatine himself, Ferenc Wesselényi, opened negotiations with the Porte, France, and other powers. The conspiracy was betrayed and several of the leaders executed. Now Ferdinand's minister, Lobkowitz, organised reprisals on the grand scale. Three hundred noblemen lost their estates. The Cardinal-Primate, Szelepcsényi, and his right-hand man and later successor, Kollonics, seized their chance to press home the Counter-Reformation. Protestant pastors and teachers were ordered to renounce their faith, or leave their homes; those who refused were sent to the galleys. In 1673 the Constitution was suspended and Hungary placed under a Directorate, headed by the Grand Master of the Teutonic Order, with a Council composed half of Germans, half of Hungarians.

The official languages were declared to be Latin and German, and officials were required to know 'Slavonic' but not Hungarian. These measures could not long be maintained in their full severity, for the discontent threw up a leader in the person of a young north Hungarian nobleman named Imre Thököly, who, gathering behind him a force (known after Dózsa's followers, as 'kuruc', or crusaders) of refugees, disbanded soldiers and hayduks, and catching Leopold at a disadvantage – war had broken out again between the Empire and France – forced him, in 1681, to restore the Constitution, re-convoke the Diet and promise to remedy most of Hungary's grievances, besides acknowledging Thököly himself as quasi-sovreign of north Hungary.

But this meant no real reconciliation; three Hungarians out of four had now reached the stage of regarding the Habsburgs and 'Austria' as their mortal enemy. And it was just at this moment that the great war opened which ended by bringing all Hungary under Habsburg rule. In 1683 the Sultan, encouraged by Thököly's successes, sent another vast army northward. It swept across Hungary and reached the walls of Vienna itself. Now, however, the tide turned. On 12 September the beleaguering army was caught unawares, defeated disastrously, and driven back in rout. This time the victory was not squandered. By the end of the year, all Royal Hungary was free. In 1686 Buda was taken after a month's siege, its fall bringing with it the liberation of the rest of the Dunántúl and the Alföld as far south as Szabadka. In 1687 it was the turn of Transylvania and the rest of Central Hungary, except for the corner contained by the Maros and the Tisza, and the Imperial forces even penetrated deep into the Balkans. Louis XIV's invasion of west Germany enabled the Turks to retake Belgrade and re-enter south Hungary, but on 26 June 1699, after some years of less severe and mainly local fighting, the Sultan signed the Peace of Karlowitz, under which he relinquished all Hungary except the Maros-Tisza corner and the long-lost Croat territories across the Save.

So Hungary was liberated and almost completely re-united at last, but at a dreadful cost. The Hungarians' own losses in the operations had been not inconsiderable, for while it is true that the main regular forces were German, Hungarian auxiliaries played important parts in many of the actions. The material devastation was enormous. The vast Turkish army left a train of ruin behind it in its advance, and still more, in its disorderly retreat. Where fortresses held out (and some did for two or even three years) the besiegers scorched the earth round them to cut off the defenders' supplies. What the country suffered at the hands of its liberators was little less. The West Hungarian counties were required to pay the lion's share of the provisioning of the army, and above this, the soldiers billeted in the villages looted, ravaged and raped at will, so that the villagers fled before them. 'What profit will Your Majesty have', the Palatine asked Leopold, 'if He rules only over forests and deserted hills?' In a hundred years, he wrote, Hungary had not paid so much to the Turks as now it was required to pay in two to the armies of occupation. The peasants were perishing of starvation, selling their wives and daughters to the soldiery. According to another writer, many peasants sold their children to the Turks for money with which to satisfy the demands of the soldiers.

The general devastation was, indeed, probably worse than it had ever been. The figure traditionally given for the total population at the end of the wars is 1,500,000 for Inner Hungary and 800,000 for Transylvania, plus perhaps another 250,000 for Croatia and the Military Frontier. Modern investigators believe this to be an underestimate, and put the grand total at least three, conceivably four millions. But this was little enough for a country the size of Hungary; moreover, such population as there was was mainly concentrated in the northern counties and in Transylvania. In 1692 the total population of the three counties

20. *A Turkish djami in Pécs*

21. *The capture of Buda from the Turks, 1686: ref. p. 87*

23. *Ferencz Rákóczi II: ref. p. 92*

22. *Maria Theresa*

of Baranya, Somogy and Tolna was officially put at 3,221 souls, 1,652 of them in the city of Pécs alone. Between the Danube and the Tisza the inhabited places were usually a day's journey apart.

Political persecution, too, recommenced as soon as a district was in Imperial hands. Some of the Imperial generals instituted real reigns of terror. In 1683 Carafa, the most notorious of them, after extorting huge sums from the citizens of Debrecen, reported that he was on the track of a dangerous conspiracy against Leopold's life, and after putting numerous nobles and burghers to the torture, had twenty-two of them, all completely innocent, executed.

And now Leopold's anti-Hungarian advisers held that the time had come to proceed to the complete subjugation of the country which Thököly's rebellion had interrupted. After the capture of Buda, the Privy Council met to discuss the modalities of the coronation of Leopold's elder son, Joseph, and some of the participants argued that Leopold was entitled to introduce a completely new system, *jure belli*. On this, as on several other occasions, Leopold showed himself more moderate than his advisers, and at a Diet convoked in 1687 he agreed to confirm the existing Constitution, subject to three modifications: the succession was made hereditary in the male line of the Habsburgs, the *jus resistendi* (which Wesselényi and his fellow-conspirators had invoked as justifying their action) was abolished; and to Joseph's promise to observe the country's laws and privileges was added the saving clause: 'as the King and the assembled Estates shall agree on the interpretation and application thereof.'

After this, however, Leopold did not again convoke the Diet, and his rule was, in fact, a malevolent dictatorship exercised by the *Hofkriegsrat*, the *camera* (which was staffed largely with Germans) and Kollonics. It is true that a very drastic plan proposed by Kollonics for reorganising the country (in ways some of which would have benefited it) was not adopted, but this was because the Archbishop of Kalocsa succeeded in persuading Leopold that it could not be carried through without the consent of the Diet, which Leopold preferred not to ask. Enough was done without this to put the saying into circulation that Kollonics' object was first to pauperise Hungary, then catholicise it, then Germanise it. 44,000 of the 60,000 soldiers which constituted the Imperial army were quartered in Hungary, which the military commissioners in charge of them bled white for their maintenance.

The protestants were harried unmercifully. In 1690 a Commission, called the *Neoacquistica Commissio*, was set up to check title-deeds in the reconquered territories. Even where the heirs at law of the former owners were able to establish their titles, they were required to pay a heavy indemnity for reinstatement. Where they could not pay this, or in the more frequent cases where a claim was disallowed, or no claimant came forward, the Crown disposed of the land as it would. A few estates were purchased by Hungarians, notably the Esterházys, but more were sold to foreign buyers, or given to Imperial generals in arrear of pay. The Cumanian-Jazygian Free Districts were sold to the Teutonic Order and their populations reduced to villein status. The Crown at first treated the whole of south Hungary simply as territory conquered from the Turks. The Military Frontier was extended to run the whole length of the Turkish frontier, as far as Transylvania, the new areas, like the old, being organised in military Districts under the *Hofkriegsrat*. The hinterland was afterwards restored to the counties for administrative purposes, but the Crown kept almost all the land in them for itself.

It was especially on these *neoacquistica* lands that the process, to which we shall return later, of colonising the soil of Hungary with non-Magyars, was initiated even before the Turks were fairly out of the country. This began, indeed, almost fortuitously with the arrival of sundry

small bands of refugees from the Balkans, who were established more or less provisionally in Hungary, and by far
the most important immigration of the time was not originally meant to be permanent: in 1690, when the Austrian
armies evacuated Serbia, they were accompanied by a big
body of Serbs, usually estimated at 40,000 fighting men,
or 200,000 souls in all, under the Patriarch of Ipek, Arsen
Crnojević. They were settled provisionally near the
southern frontier, and were to have returned to Serbia
when it was reconquered, but after the Peace of Karlowitz
were of necessity allowed to remain in the country. They
were promised free exercise of their religion and the right
to elect their own archbishop and Voivode. Most of them
were now settled in the Military Frontier, but considerable numbers outside, although usually adjacent, to it,
notably in the angle between the Drave and the Save.

Transylvania was treated only a little less ruthlessly. In
1687 Leopold agreed with Apafi, the ruling prince, to
recognise his title, subject to recognition of himself as
suzerain. Apafi's son was to succeed him, and when he in
his turn died, the Transylvanians were to recover their
right of electing their own prince. Leopold promised to
respect the Transylvanian Constitution. When Apafi died
in 1690, Tököly, with Turkish support, defeated the local
Austrian garrisons and in an effort to save the situation,
Leopold issued a diploma guaranteeing the autonomy and
rights of the Principality, but he refused to sanction the
succession of the young Apafi and ruled Transylvania
through his own governors.

It is arguable that the Kollonics era was more dangerous
to Hungary's national existence than any she had previously
experienced, but the excess of the evil ended by bringing
its own remedy. It evoked from the first much resistance,
especially in the north-east, which lay a little outside the
effective reach of the Imperial arm, and became the refuge

of every kind of political revolutionary: persecuted Protestants, nobles ruined by the *neoacquistica*, disbanded soldiers, masterless hayduks. Here spontaneous rebellion, the
un-organised protest of poor men against their oppressors,
broke out in 1697 and was renewed year after year. Then,
looking for a leader, the rebels fixed their eyes on Ferenc
Rákóczi II, grandson of György Rákóczi II and of Péter
Zrinyi, and stepson of Thököly.

Leopold had not confiscated the young man's estates,
which were the biggest in that part of Hungary, but after
having him educated by Jesuits in Bohemia, and then attached to his own court, had allowed him to go home. A
gentle and unassuming soul, Rákóczi was one of the most
reluctant rebels in history. He drifted into the role mainly
out of pity for his wretched fellow-countrymen and did not
finally yield to persuasion until Leopold had had him imprisoned and friends had contrived his escape and smuggled
him into Poland. Now he could no longer resist the ap-
peals, and in June 1703 he entered Hungary, calling on all
who would to follow him.

The moment was favourable, for war had just broken
out again between the Empire and France, and Hungary
had been almost devoided of its garrisons. There was,
moreover, hope of help from France and Poland. Soon the
greater part of Hungary had joined the new leader and the
last great rebellion which the country was to know for
150 years was in full swing.

The Rákóczi rebellion is that on which later Hungarian
historians have looked back with more romantic pride
than on any other in their history. Its national and popular
character (in it the nation was united, and class distinction
sunk, as never before or since) and the noble and unselfish
character of its young leader have lent its memory a peculiar charm. In fact, any hope that it would end in giving
Hungary back its full independence vanished on the day
when Marlborough's victory at Blenheim destroyed the

vision of 'French and Hungarian soldiers meeting in the streets of Vienna'. For the rest of its seven-year course it was simply an increasingly forlorn struggle against growing odds. It brought with it more destruction, more depopulation (aggravated by a terrible outbreak of plague) and, towards its end, more disunion among the Hungarians themselves. And when at last peace was signed at Szatmár on 30 April 1711, the terms, which had been negotiated between the commander of the Hungarian troops on the Imperial side, Count János Pálffy, and Rákóczi's lieutenant, Count Sándor Károlyi, were less favourable than the court had offered five years earlier. On paper, brought no immediate improvement at all, simply confirming the constitutional and religious position as defined in 1687–8, with the addition that the king promised to convoke a Diet at which any complaints could be voiced, and offered an amnesty to anyone, including Rákóczi himself, who took an oath of loyalty to the Crown within three weeks.

Nevertheless, the bloodshed had not been in vain. Since the revolt had started, Leopold had died, and with Joseph I, still more with his brother Charles, in whose name the peace was actually concluded (Joseph having died on the eve of it), new men and new ideas had come to reign in Vienna. Charles had none of his father's antagonism towards the Hungarians: he was convinced that 'it was very important that quiet should prevail in Hungary' and that 'the Hungarians must be relieved of the belief that they are under German domination'. He was honestly prepared to treat the nation generously, and the Hungarians, on their side, were sick of the vain struggle and more than ready to accept the terms – which, indeed, were generous enough in the situation. Practically all of them except Rákóczi himself and a few members of his immediate entourage accepted the amnesty, and the Diet which met next year at Pozsony did so in a spirit of general good will. The most difficult parties to the negotiations were, indeed, the

Hungarian *labanc*[1] nobles, whom the amnesty deprived of the hope of further enriching themselves at the expense of their fellow-countrymen. Charles again swore to respect the national rights and liberties and promised solemnly to rule Hungary only in accordance with her own laws, existing or as legally enacted in the future, and not 'according to the pattern of other provinces'.

The remaining details took several years to work out, partly because the whole problem of Charles' relationship with his subjects now became inextricably involved with his endeavours to secure for his daughter, Maria Theresa, the undivided succession to his dominions, and Hungary's law did not yet bind the nation to accept the succession in the female line. Ultimately, however, the 1723 Diet agreed to this (with the reservation that the wearer of the Holy Crown must be legitimate, roman catholic, and an arch-duke or archduchess), and made the fundamental concession that so long as this link with the Habsburgs' other dominions existed, Hungary would regard herself as thereby united with them 'indivisibly and inseparably', this union being valid 'for all events and also against external enemies'. Only if the line became entirely extinct did the nation recover its right to elect its monarch, and the automatic connection with 'Austria' come to an end.

Charles swore again, in his own name and that of his successors, not to rule Hungary 'after the pattern of other provinces' but only in accordance with its own laws, existing or to be agreed between king and nation at future Diets, which were to meet every three years. He would defend the integrity of the country, and not incorporate any part of it in his other dominions.

Of the accompanying agreements, the most important was that which regulated anew the long-standing problem

---

[1] A word meaning literally 'foot-soldier', which had come to be used for the pro-Habsburg party, as contrasted with the 'easterner' kuruc party.

of defence by providing for the creation, as supplement to the noble levée, of a standing army, to be composed as to one-third by Hungarians, recruited by 'voluntary enlistment', and two-thirds by foreigners. It was to be stationed in Hungary, and Hungary agreed to pay for its upkeep by a tax the amount of which had to be agreed with each Diet. The army was to be under the control of the *Hofkriegsrat*, but Hungary was promised that she would now be given representation on that body.

The *Consilium Locumtenentiale* was now reorganised and recognised as the top-level administrative organisation. It was to sit in Pozsony, under the presidency of the Palatine, who was to be assisted by twenty-two councillors appointed by the king from among the prelates and the higher and lower nobility. The independence of this body, and of that of the Hungarian court chancellery and *camera*, of any non-Hungarian office, were confirmed.

5

THE EIGHTEENTH CENTURY

THE next period of Hungarian history, that covered by the
remainder of Charles' reign and by the reign of his daughter,
Maria Theresa, is one on which Hungarian commentators
of later days have passed singularly various judgments. For
some of them have seen it as an age of sorely-needed rest
and successful recuperation; others, as one of stagnation
and even of national decadence. In fact, it contained features which would support either view, and these call for
description in some detail; for short and uneventful, on
the surface, as the period was, it yet produced the formation and alignment of the forces of whose conflict, after it
had closed, the modern Hungary was born.

The supreme blessing enjoyed by Hungary during this
half-century was that of peace; first and foremost, peace
between the nation and its rulers. When, a few years after
the Peace of Szatmár, war broke out again between Austria
and the Porte, Rákóczi, from his Turkish exile, tried to
raise again the old standard, but no one listened to him.
For a time, it is true, the peace was still uncordial and
suspicious. When, in the last years of his reign, Charles
embarked on another Turkish war, and this proved both
expensive and inglorious in its ending, discontent was rife
again; so much so that when Maria Theresa had to meet the
Diet after her father's death, there was a very real possibility that pent-up discontents might find explosive outlet.
At the best the malcontents might take advantage of her
difficulties to demand inordinate concessions; at the worst
they might ally themselves with the King of Prussia. As is
well known, the scene, one of the most famous in Hun-

24. *Maria Theresa and her Hungarian bodyguard. From an old print*

garian history, passed differently; when the lovely young queen appeared before the Diet, her babe on her arm, it voted by acclamation 'vitam et sanguinem pro rege nostro, Maria Theresa', i.e., a substantial force of enlisted men beside the noble levée itself. But it had been a narrow squeak. The famous shout had not been nearly so spontaneous as was represented: hard bargaining behind the scenes had preceded it, and rumour whispered that the Diet had added under its collective breath: 'sed non avenam.'

But the crisis had been weathered, however narrowly, and it was followed by a period during which the relationship was, up to a point, really cordial. Maria Theresa was genuinely grateful to the Hungarians for their response, which, if it did not materialise on quite the scale promised, yet undoubtedly saved the existence of the Habsburg monarchy as a Great Power. She regarded them as 'fundamentally a good people, with whom one can do anything if one takes them the right way', and set herself, not merely to keep them from rebelling, as her father had done, but to awaken in them a positive loyalty towards her throne. She admitted the magnates to posts at her court and in the central services, diplomatic and military, of the monarchy, encouraged them to send their sons to the Theresianum, the famous academy founded by her in Vienna for the sons of the aristocracy, and not infrequently paid their all too prevalent debts, or at least advanced them money to tide them over their crises. For the lesser nobles she founded the Royal Hungarian Bodyguard, to which each county sent two youths of noble birth. She succeeded in fact in generating, at least in the circles reached by her benevolence, a real attachment to the dynasty, and in the country at large, a sincere acceptance of the indissoluble nature of its link with the monarchy.

Charles' first Turkish war brought the recovery of the remaining corner of Hungary, evacuated by the Turks in 1718. His second was fought in the Balkans, and Maria

25. *Sopron: Baroque architecture, 18th century*

Theresa's wars in the west. Thus Hungary saw no hostile armies during the period. She contributed towards Maria Theresa's wars not inconsiderable forces, some of which earned much distinction, but her sacrifices in blood were small, and in money, moderate. The *contributio* (war-tax) was fixed in 1724 at just over 2,100,000 florins. This was raised to 2,500,000 in 1728, to 3,200,000 in 1751 and to 3,900,000 in 1765, plus certain further sums from newly reincorporated areas.

This prolonged peace of course made possible a very real recovery in many directions. The population increased very rapidly, large-scale immigration reinforcing the effects of a high rate of natural increase. By Joseph II's reign it had risen to a total of about 9¼ millions (just under 6½ millions in Inner Hungary, nearly 1,500,000 in Transylvania, 650,000 in civilian Croatia and 700,000 in the Frontier). The growth was, of course, especially fast in the areas which had been the chief sufferers under the previous devastation: in the county of Bács-Bodrog, the population rose from 31,000 to 227,000; in the Bánát, from 45,000 to 774,000. The increase was almost pure gain for the country, which could absorb it easily; it was only in a few areas of the north, and in Transylvania, that rural congestion began to show itself, and migration down to the plains drained off most of these local surpluses. In spite of the growth of allodial farming, the taxable area of the country, i.e., that contained in 'urbarial' peasant holdings, multiplied fivefold. In many of the former devastated areas, especially where German colonists were settled, the whole face of the countryside was changed. Swamps were drained, forests cleared, land brought under the plough. Where no sign of human habitation had broken the solitude, unless the hovel of a gypsy or a Vlach herdsman, neat villages now stood amid fields of smiling corn. In the north and west, where foundations had survived on which to build, there was evidence of prosperity and even of luxury. Some of the great landlords here disposed of enormous rent-rolls and other resources. The annual income of Prince Esterházy, the richest of them, was estimated at over 700,000 florins; that of Count Batthyány at 450,000. Two other magnates had incomes of over 300,000 florins, four more at over 150,000, and there were many fortunes of 50–60,000 florins. The wealth of the roman catholic church could vie with that of the lay magnates: the net income of the Primate-Archbishop was put at 360,000 florins, that of the Bishop of Egér at 80,000 and of Nagyvárad at 70,000.

The chief outward and visible sign of this was constituted by the great mansions which began to dot the countryside almost in profusion. That built by Prince Esterházy at Esterháza (one of several owned by him) contained 200 rooms and stabling for 200 horses, and cost 12 million gulden to erect. If this was the most magnificent of them all, those of the Grassalkoviches, Batthyánys, Festetiches and not a few others could bear comparison with those of the leading aristocracy of most European countries. Well over 200 great palaces were built in Maria Theresa's reign alone, with a large number of smaller manor-houses, while the town residences of the magnates, comfortable homes of burgesses, and many new churches and other public buildings, adorned Pozsony and Buda.

In the palaces of the magnates and the new churches, the baroque culture of the central Europe of the day was at home, sometimes magnificently expressed. Prince Esterházy supported a private theatre in which nightly performances were held, opera, German comedy and Italian *opéra bouffe* alternating under the direction of Haydn. The ceilings of the great palaces and churches were adorned with frescoes by fashionable painters. In 1723 the Crown had claimed the control of education, and Mariá Theresa showed real interest in this subject. She had the University of Nagyszombat transferred to Buda-Pest, and patronised the foundation of many other schools, both secondary and elementary. Under the *Ratio Educationis*, issued in 1777, the whole country was divided into nine districts, each of which was to be covered by a network of educational establishments of all grades. The Hungarian clergy, too, spent much of their revenues on educational purposes.

The shadows in the picture were, however, not inconsiderable. The malignant political persecution had ceased, but its cessation had not given the country back its real independence. Through her concurrence in the Pragmatic Sanction Hungary was now by her own admission, and indeed more firmly than ever, relegated to the status of a component of a larger complex with multiple extra-Hungarian interests. She had still no means of influencing the international relations of that polity, for she was not represented on the court chancellery, through which they were conducted, and when the new *Hofrat* was established as the supreme advisory organ to the monarch on matters of general policy, it, again, at first contained no Hungarian member; later, a Hungarian *Referent* was appointed to it, but rather as an expert on Hungarian affairs than a representative of Hungarian interests. The whole field of the nation's defence had slipped definitely out of its hands with the institution of the standing army, which made the effective national defence force (for the noble levée had now become a recognised last resort) a mere component of a larger body, mainly non-Hungarian in composition and entirely so in respect of control over it, for the promise that Hungary should be represented on the *Hofkriegsrat* was never fulfilled. Indeed, the standing army developed into a permanent and powerful instrument for the enforcement of the monarch's will in any case in which it conflicted with that of the nation.

The Crown was almost equally free in the exercise of

its financial prerogatives, which extended not only to the management and enjoyment of the revenues from the Crown estates, but to the minting of money, and the levying of customs, excise and indirect taxation in general. Even while recognising the 'independence' of the Hungarian *camera*, Charles had announced that he would give it its orders 'through the *Hofkammer*'. In practice, and after a time, officially, the *camera* again became a mere department of the *Hofkammer*, and Hungary had no control either over its operations or over the disposal of the money passing through its hands. Half its net revenues went to the upkeep of the court in Vienna.

Still, foreign affairs, defence and cameral finance had always been royal prerogatives, and the first two of these, at least, were bound to rank as central services of the *Gesammtmonarchie*. All other fields of public life were *interna*, to which Charles' promise applied that Hungary should be governed only through her own laws. But as the business of government grew more complex, the Crown regularly claimed as falling within its own competence every subject on which no earlier law specifically entitled the Diet to be consulted; thus in succession it claimed education, 'colonisation', religious questions, industrial legislation, and, finally, the regulation of the peasants' obligations, to constitute *politica*, i.e. questions which the Crown had power to regulate by rescript, without consultation with the Diets. It is true that it passed its orders in these fields through the Hungarian court chancellery, and that that body remained nominally independent of any authority except the monarch, but they were none the less orders, and the *Consilium*, by which they were executed, was, again, responsible to the chancellery, not the Diet. And Charles, again, left the office of Palatine vacant when its holder, Miklós Pálffy, died in 1734, appointing instead another Viceroy.

The powers of the Diet were, in fact, practically confined to voting (or refusing) extraordinary or increased supplies of money or recruits, and after he had got his way over the succession, Charles convoked it only once more, in 1734, when he asked the nobles to renounce their exemption from taxation. When they refused to do this, he did not again consult them. Maria Theresa was no less autocratic. When Charles died in 1740 she had to convoke the Diet for her coronation, and in her extremity she had to supplicate it for help against her enemies. In return for this help, besides confirming 'for ever' the nobles' liberties, she appointed a new Palatine and dismissed some of the previous Viceroy's foreign advisers. But after this, she, too, convoked only two more Diets (in 1751 and 1765) and when the second body rejected her proposals to improve the peasants' conditions, she dismissed it and enacted her reforms by rescript. She too, left the office of Palatine unfilled after 1764.

All this means that except in a few respects, Hungary was being governed exactly like any Austrian or Bohemian Land, and most of the differences were created only through the non-extension to Hungary of the reforms introduced in Austria in 1748–9 and thereafter. Then, indeed, the differences became important. The Hungarian court chancellery was not merged in the new Austro-Bohemian *Directorium*. The new system of bureaucratic control was not extended downward, as it was in Austria through the *Kreisämter*: the counties retained their old autonomy and organisation. Finally, when the nobles of Austria and Bohemia renounced their exemption from taxation, those of Hungary retained theirs, and with it a bargaining power much greater than possessed by their western colleagues after they had consented to the institution of decennial 'recesses'. The Diet could not, indeed, in practice refuse the *contributio* once fixed, nor get it reduced, but the Crown could not get it raised, nor call out the noble levée, without the Diet's consent.

A particular grievance under which Hungary suffered was the continued dismemberment of the country. When Michael Apafi II died in 1713, Charles simply took the title of Prince of Transylvania. The only change introduced by Maria Theresa (except that she formally admitted her title to derive from the Holy Crown) was to promote Transylvania to the rank of a 'Grand Principality'. It had its separate court chancellery, *Gubernium* and *Thesauriat*. When the last corner of Hungary was recovered from the Turks in 1718, the area, baptised the 'Bánát of Temesvár', was kept as a separate crownland, administered, like the Military Frontier, from Vienna; it was only in 1779 that it was liquidated, its southern fringe being attached to the frontier, while the remainder was organised in counties. The civilian counties between the lower Save and Drave, now known as 'Slavonia', were placed for administrative purposes under the Ban of Croatia, although still ranking as parts of Hungary proper for purposes of taxation and sending representatives to both Diets.

The system of government in these areas was as autocratic as in Inner Hungary. The Transylvanian Diet was, indeed, convoked regularly, but it was so packed with *ex officio* members as to forfeit any claim to represent the people. The military administration in the Bánát and the Military Frontier was purely authoritarian.

The economic progress which the country was making looked, as we have said, remarkable, and was so in certain fields, but it was uneven, and in other fields even laggard. In the latter part of the period it was not of Hungary's advance that men were speaking, but of its backwardness. The whole economic picture was dominated by the appalling state of the communications, especially in the Plains. Here the roads were mere tracks, impassable for heavy traffic during much of the year; the rivers were often blocked by shoals or fallen tree-trunks. It was only on estates belonging to enlightened landlords, and where the geographical situations were exceptionally favourable, that arable farming for profit was possible, and only on these, and in some of the newly-established German colonies, that agricultural methods reached even the central European standards of the day. Even these had not usually got beyond the threefold rotation of crops. In the Magyar parts of the ex-Turkish areas, the twofold rotation of crop and fallow was still usual, while the Serbs and Roumanians merely scratched each year a different patch of the expanses on which they pastured their herds. Only vineyards were manured; otherwise, dung was used for fuel, to make walls, or to fill in potholes in the roads. The fabulous harvests which had dazzled early travellers had been the response to cultivation of soil which had lain virgin for two centuries; they were already dwindling as these primitive methods exhausted the stored-up fertility. Threshing was done by teams of horses or of oxen 'treading out the corn', and crops were commonly stored in underground pits (a device originally adopted to conceal them from marauders), where often they rotted. It was no uncommon thing for a year of super-abundance, in which much of the harvest had not even been gathered, to be followed by one of dearth, sometimes of actual famine.

Nearly all the farming was in fact for subsistence, for the modest needs of the local market. Cattle, driven on the hoof into Austria, and wine were more important as agricultural exports. But most of the Hungarian cattle were still kept in the open all the year round, an existence which proved too hard for a high proportion of the calves. The survivors were lean, stringy beasts, which the importers bought cheap before fattening them for slaughter. Wine was still exported in large quantities up to the middle of the century, but the best market for it, Silesia, was lost after Frederick the Great seized that province, and the Austrian Government started a tariff war with Prussia.

Thus the rewards even of agriculture were meagre, at any rate from the point of view of the national finances. And yet agriculture was the source from which fully 90 per cent of the population still derived its living even at the end of the period. The census of 1787, the first to enter into much detail, gave 18,487 priests (many of them monks) and only 5,001 professional civil servants and members of the free professions combined. To this figure may be added some 10,000 lower grade civil servants, who were not listed separately, and 5,000 or so teachers. Most of these were at least half farmers. There were 48 Royal free and 16 other boroughs in Inner Hungary, 9 in Transylvania and 8 in Croatia. The largest of these, Debrecen, had a population of just under 30,000; of the rest, only Pozsony, Buda, Pest and Szabadka topped the 20,000 mark; several had under 2,000. It is true that there existed also some considerable agglomerations which did not possess urban charters; these included Kecskemét, which in population ranked next below Pest. But these memorials to *khas* life under the Turkish rule were really just enormous villages, or collections of villages, counted administratively as one, and the same was true of some of the titular towns, Szabadka, Szeged and Debrecen itself. Their inhabitants were simply farmers, and the cottages which lined their streets were inhabited in the months when field-work was possible only by the economically inactive members of each family; its able-bodied members were camping out on their fields, perhaps many miles away.

The chief occupation of many other towns, Tokaj, Gyöngyös, Ruszt, even Buda, was viticulture. In 1777 the towns contained only 30,921 persons listed as employed in industry, nearly all of it on the smallest scale: there were 13,394 independent master-craftsmen, 12,316 journeymen and 4,671 apprentices. Most of the peasants' simple needs hardly required the services even of a craftsman: they were supplied by their own women folk.

The gold and silver mines were nearing exhaustion and the first coal-mines only just opening.

Most internal trade was equally primitive.

And this backwardness was, in part, thrust upon Hungary from Vienna, of deliberate policy. In part only, for the first cause lay in the devastation which the country had suffered under the Turks and in the wars of liberation, and the slow pace of its recovery up to the middle of the century had been due to its own inability to overcome this *damnosa hereditas*. Among the handicaps there must indeed be counted that of the national psychology. Centuries of history had rendered the Hungarian noble, great or small, quite incapable of counting industry or trade as a career fit to rank with landowning or soldiering. And the peasants were no more enterprising than their masters. They were not easily persuaded to supplement their incomes by housework, even when the opportunity offered. Travellers noted that 'the abundant blessings of nature made them dull and lazy. If they had bread and bacon to last them the year, and a warm coat, their needs and their monetary ambitions were satisfied.'

As a consequence, most of such trade and industry as existed was in non-Magyar hands. The members of the guilds – who, however, had become as narrowly restrictive as imagination could conceive – were still mostly Germans. The trading class and pioneers of capitalist development in Hungary were Serbs, or the class collectively known as 'Greeks', a term which included not only true Greeks, but Kutzovlachs and other Balkan elements. These were not only the shopkeepers but the industrial entrepreneurs, who travelled round the country and bought up the products of the peasant craftsmen.

The Austrian repressive policy developed out of what were quite reasonable initial considerations. The planned economic development of the Monarchy was originally undertaken on a serious scale to make good the loss of

Silesia, and it was natural enough to site the new factories in Bohemia and round Vienna, in proximity to the main markets and where the populations had an old tradition of skill, assigning to Hungary, which in any case was suffering from a shortage of labour even for agriculture, the role of producer of raw materials. This division of functions was in any case only meant to last until conditions in Hungary changed. Maria Theresa specifically forbade any discrimination against Hungary, where she personally founded several factories (including the famous Herend porcelain works, still in production today). But she herself agreed that the state should not found or subsidise factories in Hungary which competed with Austrian enterprises, and the Austrian and Bohemian magnates whose interests were bound up with the new developments (and who dominated the economic council which was in charge of the new planning) found ways of getting this ruling to apply to almost any state enterprise in Hungary. A suggestion that private individuals should be prohibited from founding factories was not adopted, but the economic council, through whose hands applications for privileges, subsidies and other facilities passed, saw to it that these were never, or hardly ever, granted to Hungarians. Where, nevertheless, such establishments came into being, their products, and those of the guilds (which did not come under the authority of the council) were handicapped by an internal tariff which allowed Austrian manufactures to enter Hungary free, except for payment of a small fiscal duty, while Hungarian exports to Austria were made prohibitively expensive by over-valuation of them on the frontier. The internal market for Hungarian manufactures was further restricted by the facts that no court (the chief consumer of luxury goods) resided there, and that all the requirements of the army were produced in Austria except the food, which was supplied locally, often at under the cost of production.

Hungary's industrial subjection to Austria was made almost complete by the institution (first in 1754) of a high tariff wall, applying both to exports and imports, round the whole Monarchy. Articles which Austria could not produce, and which were therefore allowed to enter the Monarchy, had to be bought from Austrian middle-men.

Worst of all, the discrimination came to be extended to agriculture. In the early stages, some government money was spent on agricultural improvements in Hungary, some of them useful: the cultivation of the silkworm in the Bánát is an example. But if the Austrian cereal harvest was poor, Hungary was sometimes forbidden to export hers elsewhere than to Austria, while if the Austrian harvest was good, the Hungarian was excluded. Even Hungarian wine could not be sent abroad unless accompanied by an equal quantity of Austrian wine. The only export which was almost entirely unrestricted was that of cattle.

The discrimination was regularly justified by the argument that as the Hungarian nobles had retained their freedom from taxation after the Austrian had renounced theirs, they would, given equal treatment, undercut Austria; and further, that Hungary's contribution to the common exchequer in direct taxation was unduly light. It is true that the 'war tax' was not raised *pari passu* with the growth of the population, and thus came to be much lighter than that paid per capita in Bohemia or the Netherlands; yet an Austrian expert, Count Zinzendorf, calculated that if a complete balance-sheet had been drawn up, including the Crown's revenues from the *camera*, the cost of maintaining the army, etc., Hungary would have been found to be paying more than her quota. The weight of the taxation was, moreover, greatly increased by the extreme shortage of currency among the peasants, on whose shoulders the payment fell.

There was much that was unsatisfactory also in the cultural field. The fine flower of the baroque culture was savoured chiefly by a small privileged circle. During most of the period, catholic education was chiefly in the hands of the Jesuits, and was directed primarily to the propagation of the faith, and as means to this end, to the training of missionary priests. The weight of it was laid on theology and the humanities, and it was essentially aristocratic in spirit. It produced elegant courtiers and learned and subtle bishops, who were themselves often the scions of the highest families in the land, but it did not penetrate to the masses. The intellectual level of the parish priests was low, as their stipends, too, were meagre. The Piarists, who were the Jesuits' main rivals and succeeded to their position when the Jesuit Order was dissolved in 1773, were much more democratic and their curriculum less restricted, but they had much leeway to make up. In the 1770s only 4,145 of Inner Hungary's 8,742 communes had schools at all (an average of 7·5 schools to every 10,000 of the population) and in 3,883 of these only one teacher was registered; the exceptions were in areas of mixed population.

And all the facilities and favours in this field were for the catholics. The question of the protestants' status, left in 1722 for agreement between the parties, was settled by Charles in 1731, after the parties had reached deadlock, by the *Carolina Resolutio*. This upheld the restrictions imposed by Leopold. Protestant services could be held only in a few specially designated places, outside which only private worship was allowed. Conversion to protestantism was forbidden. Protestants had to observe catholic festivals and their clergy were subject to the visitations of catholic prelates. A catholic oath was required from all persons entering the public services, which were thus practically closed to protestants. For a while, protestant students were forbidden to attend foreign universities.

In this respect Maria Theresa, being herself a devout catholic, was less tolerant than her father, who took his personal religion more lightly. Moreover, her name inspired catholic zealots to press the theory that Hungary was the 'regnum Marianum', a country peculiarly dedicated to the service of the Mother of God. For the protestants, on the other hand, her reign was 'the Babylonian captivity'. They were subjected to many further grievous restrictions. Their colleges actually declined in number and wealth. That they survived at all, and even maintained a high level of learning, was a tribute to the courage and solidarity of the population; it was achieved in the face of strong governmental opposition, and at the cost of painful sacrifice.

An important improvement was brought about in the cultural standards of the Ruthenes and some of the Roumanians by the introduction among them (against strong resistance which limited its extension) of the Uniate church; but the level of the populations which remained true to the Orthodox creed (the Serbs and over half the Roumanians) remained deplorably low.

The chief charge brought by the Hungary of the nineteenth century against that of the eighteenth was of having allowed the national spirit to decay. It was certainly the case that by the end of the century the magnate class was only half Hungarian. It was not, indeed, an ethnically foreign class like that of Bohemia; for whereas the Germans, Spaniards and Irishmen among whom the estates of the Czech rebels had been distributed after the Battle of the White Mountain had found these habitable and profitable, and had struck their roots in them, the foreign beneficiaries of the *Neoacquistica* had often found the geographical and human conditions in their new homes too intractable, and had sold them back to Hungarians or to Greek speculators, who in turn had sold them on. Those who had survived, or had come in later – for even after the liquidation of the *Neoacquistica* it had not been difficult for a foreigner to buy an estate and acquire Hungarian 'indigenate' – had Magyarised, and become indistinguishable from the old stock.

But on the class as a whole, Maria Theresa's policy of the sugar-loaf had worked with great effect. They spent much of their time and their rent-rolls in Vienna, intermarried with the 'Imperial' German-Austrian and Bohemian aristocracy, looked for their culture, not to Hungary (where, indeed, its products were thin enough on the ground) but to Vienna or Paris, and forgot, or failed to learn, the Magyar language itself. If few of them were 100 per cent centralists – national pride and an appreciation of the material advantages which went with a patent of Hungarian nobility forbade this – they were yet unquestioning supporters of the Gesammtmonarchie and essentially alien from the rest of the nation.

This was enormously important politically, for few as they were – the families bearing hereditary titles at the end of the eighteenth century numbered only 108 (two princely, 82 of counts and 24 baronial) – they owned between them about one third of the soil of Hungary. They also, as we have seen, formed a separate 'Table' of the Diet and no Resolution by the Lower Table was valid unless endorsed by the Upper. Their monopoly of the high offices of state was almost complete.

In default of the magnates it was chiefly on the *bene possessionati* middle nobles in their county strongholds that the leadership of the national cause devolved. Many of them took their responsibilities seriously and conscientiously, and in so far as Hungary emerged at the end of the period with its political institutions as nearly intact as they were, its national life as vigorous, the merit must go to these men. Most of them were national also in the narrower sense of the term. They felt themselves to be Magyars, spoke the Magyar language, affected Magyar usages. It is true that this was the period at which the Magyar language, regarded as a means of expression, was at its lowest ebb. The nation had never renounced the tradition that its official documents were couched in Latin, and since the sixteenth century the debates of the Diet and even the county congregations, and the proceedings of the Courts, had come to be conducted in that language. Partly for that reason – to fit budding administrators and jurists for their careers – education above the primary level was given mainly in that language, and after Latin, the *Ratio Educationis* gave the largest place (above the primary level) to German.[1] Thus Magyar in the eighteenth century was hardly a literary language, but it was none the less a living one, spoken currently by an educated class. Thus when the time came for the full political national revival, the Magyar people, like the Polish, had to hand a class which was already fully national; it did not, like the Slovenes or Ruthenes, have to create one.

The achievement of the Hungarian nobles had, however, its weaknesses, although these were not all of their own making. Those critics who castigate them so severely for the exclusive stubbornness with which they defended their own class privileges should in fairness remember that this was the only major political question on which the Crown commonly allowed them any voice at all: it usurped almost all constructive work as its own prerogative. Nor is it by any means certain that the instinct was absurd which warned the Hungarian nobles always to mistrust any proposal emanating from Vienna. If their outlook was narrow, what else could be expected from these local squires whom the deplorable communications cut off during much of the year from contact with all but their nearest neighbours?

Yet the narrowness was there, and it was true that they were too easily satisfied, looking no further so long as they

---

[1] It is interesting that in the urban boys' schools there were three 'foreign' pupils (presumably the sons of army officers) to every four Hungarian'.

26. Part of Veszprém

27. Hungarian
gentleman, 18th century

28. *Tihány abbey* (18th century)

possessed the wherewithall for abundant living and for the limitless hospitality which was their pride; also true that they too easily attributed these blessings to the successful defence by their ancestors of their privileges, not asking whether time had not changed the value of those privileges. It was especially unfortunate that the most treasured among them, the exemption of their land from taxation, entailed them in a direct conflict of interests with the peasants, so that their defence of it did breed among them a great class egotism.

This was particularly apparent in their attitude towards the peasants, where, incidentally, they made no national distinction: a true noble should be Magyar, but the converse, that a true Magyar should be noble, was not admitted. The Hungarian nobles of the eighteenth century went right back to Werböczy and to Werböczy's own authorities in their identification of Hungary with themselves. The gulf had never been wider in the national history, or at least not since the old days of slavery, between the *populus* and the *misera contribuens plebs*, whose function in the state was still simply to work for his betters. 'God himself has differentiated between us', wrote one contemporary, 'assigning to the peasant labour and need, to the lord, abundance and a merry life.'

For the first decades of the period the material condition of the peasants, too, degenerated. The savage enactments of the Tripartitum had proved short-lived in practice; as early as 1547 a Diet had repealed the *adscriptionem glebae*, seeing in the misfortunes of the previous years Divine punishment for the oppression of the poor, 'whose cry goes up incessantly before the Face of God'. In the sixteenth and seventeenth centuries the peasants suffered greatly from war and from the exactions of the foreign garrisons and the Austrian treasury, but their legal position did not greatly deteriorate. A very considerable proportion of them achieved free or partially free status, holding their lands on 'contracts' which were often not unfavourable.

But the return of law and order, and the growth of commercial farming in an era of labour shortage, coupled with the economic conditions which left land still almost the only source of wealth, brought a renewal of the pressure. Old customary freedoms were overridden, common lands enclosed, dues and services multiplied. To the landlords' exactions were added those of the state, for besides the war-tax, which rested exclusively on their shoulders, the peasants had now to supply food and transport for the local units of the standing army, and might themselves be pressed into service in it (for the 'recruiting' normally took the form of shanghai-ing). Finally, the 'house-tax', levelled by each county (again exclusively from the non-nobles) to meet the costs of local administration, rose sharply. In Transylvania conditions were worse still: here the *robot* was four days a week, and there was also much rural over-population, so that misery was acute in the whole province, including the Szekel districts.

Charles did not willingly interfere in the relations between landlord and peasant, but after serious disturbances had broken out in Slavonia, he worked out an *urbarium* for that area, laying down the minimum legal size for a peasant *sessio* and the maximum services which the landlord might exact. This, however, never became law. Maria Theresa did not raise the question seriously at her Coronation Diet, at which she needed the nobles' support, but asked the Diet of 1751 to raise the war-tax without increasing the burden on the peasants. The Diet retorted that the way to alleviate the peasants' position was to reduce the tax and to abolish the discriminatory tariff. In 1756 the queen simply promulgated Charles' *urbarium* in Slavonia, and hoped to persuade the Diet which she convoked in 1764 to adopt a similar system, and to accept the taxation of its own land. Although the unrest was now widespread the Diet refused flatly. Maria Theresa did not try to enforce the extension of the land-tax, which would have been contrary to her own sworn word, but now had the rest of Hungary (Transylvania excluded) surveyed, and in 1767 simply enacted an *urbarium* for it by rescript.[1]

The *urbarium* registered all land then worked as peasant-holdings, and thus liable to tax. Further alienation of such land, except under permit, was forbidden. The size of a *sessio* was fixed at an area ranging according to locality and the quality of the land from 16 *hold*[2] arable plus 6 *hold* ley for the best land in Sopron and Pozsony to 38 plus 22 for poor-quality land on the Tisza, plus, in every case, one *hold* for house, garden and farm-buildings. The peasant's obligations to his landlord were fixed at one day's *robot* (labour) weekly per full *sessio* if performed with draught animals and cart, or twice as much hand-labour, plus the old 'ninth' paymentintroduced by Louis the Great, and certain other dues and payments which varied according to locality. The obligations of a peasant holding less than a full *sessio* were proportionately less. A peasant was declared legally free to leave his holding if he had paid up all his dues. Royal Commissions were appointed to supervise the work of the patrimonial Courts of Justice.

This enactment must have improved the peasants' conditions, which some observers now described in very favourable terms. The *robot* was, at any rate, far lighter than in Bohemia or Galicia, where it was 156 days a year per full *sessio*, while even in Styria it was 104. On the other hand, the Hungarian peasant was worse off than the Austrian in that he lacked the protection which the latter enjoyed through the *Kreis* officials; the 'noble county,' with all its administrative and judicial apparatus, was and remained a class institution.

And the way in which the reform had been brought about deepened still further the cleft between noble and

[1] It was not introduced in Croatia until 1780.
[2] 1 *hold* = 0·576 hectares = 1·43 English acres.

peasant. Although humanitarian considerations had entered into it, the primary motive behind it had been simply to secure for the Crown a larger fraction of the peasants' production by limiting that of the landlord. Nevertheless, the Crown was now able to figure as the protector of the peasants against the tyranny of the nobles, and was widely so regarded by the peasants themselves.

The period also saw the consummation of what, in its long-term effects on the national destinies, was the most serious of all its developments: the great transformation of the ethnic character of the population.

The beginnings of the change reach back, of course, to far earlier periods. The Turkish advance through the Balkans had already driven many Serbs, Vlachs and Bosnian Croats to take refuge in Hungary. Then had come the Turkish invasion and occupation of Hungary itself, the brunt of which had fallen on its most purely Magyar areas, while the national homes of the Slovaks, Ruthenes and Roumanians in north Hungary and Transylvania had escaped relatively lightly. It is true that many Magyars had escaped into these parts, but those saving themselves by flight were outnumbered many times by those slaughtered or carried off into slavery, and while the non-Magyars, too, had their losses, these were much less heavy and were partially offset, in the case of some of them, by further immigration: substantial numbers of Serbs and Vlachs followed the Turks into the Alföld, other Roumanians slipped unobtrusively into Transylvania; and there was a big immigration of Croats, not only into the old Slavonia, (now officially known as 'Croatia'), but northward into the Muraköz, and more sporadically, all up the Austro-Hungarian frontier.

It has been calculated that when the wars of liberation began, some 50 per cent of the total population was still Magyar; but the ravages of these wars, again, were heaviest in the Magyar areas, and the end of them was accompanied by more waves of immigration. The biggest of these, the organised immigration of the Serbs under their Patriarch, has already been mentioned, and besides this great body, many smaller groups entered Hungary both from the Balkans and from Wallachia. Serb and other South Slav elements occupied the old Lower Slavonian counties, now known simply as 'Slavonia', and much of the south of Hungary proper; the Vlach element multiplied in Transylvania and, driven by the pressure of population and harsh social conditions, spilled out into the Partium.

This led on to the systematic operation known as the *Impopulatio*, viz., the settlement by the Crown (and on a smaller scale, by some of the big landed proprietors) of the vacant lands at their disposal. In some instances great landowners who owned estates both in the north and the centre populated the latter by bringing down peasants from their other properties: it was in this way, for example that the Slovak colony round Békescsaba, still in existence, came into being. Even a few Magyar peasants were moved in this way. But the purpose of the operation was to increase the total population, which could not be done by moving men from one part of the under-populated country to another; and in fairness it must be recalled that the economic doctrines of the day held the multiplication of population to be a desirable objective in itself. To this, however, were undoubtedly added, in the Crown's mind, the political and economic considerations that the Magyars were a politically unreliable element, which it was desirable to weaken, and a backward one in its agricultural methods.

So another stream of non-Magyars was directed into the country: a few freak groups brought from as far afield as France, Italy, Catalonia and South Russia, a few political, religious or moral deportees from Austria, but the great majority recruits, enlisted by agents, from the smaller states of south Germany, a fact which led to the application to them all by the Hungarians of the generic name of 'Swabians'. The process began under Charles, was at its fullest flood in the middle years of Maria Theresa's reign and was not officially wound up until 1786.

The chief receiving areas were the Bánát (from which Magyars were excluded by deliberate policy) and the other empty lands of South Hungary, Bács-Bodrog, Baranya and Tolna, in which the Germans were settled in such numbers as to earn for the district the popular name of 'Swabian Turkey'; but Germans were settled in considerable numbers also in other parts of Hungary, including the western environs of Buda itself.

Meanwhile, the inconspicuous immigration of Roumanians had been going on, and there had been other smaller but not inconsiderable movements: several thousand Armenians settled in Transylvania; a steady trickle of artisans and other specialists, these chiefly from Austria and the German districts of Bohemia-Moravia, entered the towns. The Jewish population, too, although still small, was on the increase.

The Magyar element re-asserted itself not ineffectually in certain parts of the country. When the central and northern parts of the Alföld were cleared of the Turks, not only did the old landowning class, in so far as it had survived, flock back to re-occupy its ancestral acres, but the same road was taken also by a large number of Magyar peasants, lured by the larger holdings and easier social conditions. The surviving non-Magyars of these areas Magyarised (it was in Maria Theresa's reign that the Cuman language finally died out). These areas became almost solidly Magyar, and the same became true of much of the Dunántúl, except its western fringe, its south-eastern corner, a few smaller areas, and the towns. But this centripetal movement depleted the Magyar stock in the peripheral areas, and as they moved down, the non-Magyars moved in after them.

It is calculated that by the end of the *impopulatio*, the Magyars numbered only about 3,350,000, or some 35 per cent of the total population. The Roumanians now numbered about a million and a half, the Slovaks a million and a quarter, the Germans a million, the Serbs and Croats about three quarters of a million each. The remainder was made up of Ruthenes, gypsies, Jews and smaller nationalities.

An ethnic map of the country drawn at the end of Maria Theresa's reign which did not take density of population into account and ignored small ethnic islets, would have looked very much like one drawn in 1900. It would have shown the Magyars in a large, or clear, majority only in the central parts of Hungary. In the west, the fringe was German. In the north, the main ethnic line between the Magyars on the one hand and the Slovaks and Ruthenes on the other followed approximately the line where the foothills of the Carpathians melt into the plain. In Transylvania and the Partium, the Roumanians were probably now in a small absolute majority. Croatia proper was almost solidly Croat, the Slavonian counties chiefly Serb, and the rest of the south a hotch-potch of Southern Slav, of various brands, German and Roumanian, with a relatively small admixture of Magyars.

The Serbs were always a thorn in the Hungarians' flesh. From the first, they regarded themselves as the Emperor's men, whose function it was to fight any of his enemies, including, or for preference, Hungarians. They certainly did not propose, if they could help it, to exchange their accustomed life of herdsmen-soldiers for the arduous state of peasant cultivators on some Hungarian nobleman's estate. They battled hard for continued recognition of their 'national' status, if possible on a territory of their own, where they would form a separate polity under the Emperor.

The Hungarians succeeded in getting this latter demand

rejected, and the Serbs' 'national' privileges reduced to ecclesiastical autonomy. Through their church, however, the Serbs kept alive their feeling of national cohesion, and, most of them, their implacable hostility towards Hungary, and this was the easier because a high proportion of them were settled in the Military Frontier, where the authorities welcomed and fostered the attitude.

There were national stirrings during the period also among the Roumanians. Between the Orthodox Roumanians and the Hungarians, again, the religious difference helped to accentuate the contempt in which the latter held the former, as an unstable and altogether inferior race, little superior to gypsies. The Roumanians in their turn endured with sullen hatred their position of inferiority and the increasing social pressure which was put on them as the Transylvanian nobles drove them into settled work under conditions which were peculiarly burdensome. The conscious Roumanian national revival was, however, initiated by the leaders of the Uniate church, who came forward with the theory that the Roumanians of Transylvania were its true autochthonous population, the descendants of the Roman colonists of Dacia. They used this theory as an argument to demand recognition of the Roumanian nobles as a fourth 'nation' of Transylvania, and of the Orthodox faith as a fifth 'recognised' religion.

The remaining non-Magyars had not yet become troublesome. The Croat nobles lived in harmony with their Hungarian colleagues; the non-nobles here had nothing to say. There was some friction between the Hungarians and the German peasant colonists, who also regarded themselves as the subjects rather of the Empire than of Hungary, and the German burghers – this last as much on social and economic as on strictly national grounds. This was not, however, very serious, and in the case of the peasants, rather tended to diminish as they settled in. Slovak and Ruthene nationalism was still dormant. The Hungarians, for their part, did not see in the non-Magyar quality of the peasants (as distinct from the Serbs) any particular danger. Yet the danger, although still latent, was there, and only a little later it was destined first to threaten and then to destroy the Hungarian state itself.

6

RENAISSANCE AND REFORM

THE truce between dynasty and nation was broken when, on 29 November 1780, Maria Theresa died. Her elder son, Joseph, who now succeeded to the sole rule (he had been co-regent for some years, but his mother had kept him in fairly tight leading-strings) was a man of the younger generation. Steeped in the new French political philosophy of his day, and, moreover, profoundly impressed by the example of Frederick of Prussia, impatient of obstacles and blind to difficulties, he aimed at welding his dominions into a centralised polity, ruled by himself on the principles of enlightened absolutism through a single bureaucratic machine, working on uniform administrative principles and even with a uniform philosophy of life. So obvious was the incompatibility of his programme with the vested liberties of such of his dominions as had retained them, that he refused to commit himself to any oath to preserve them. As regards Hungary, in particular, he refused to submit himself to coronation, having, instead, the Holy Crown transported to Vienna, to be kept there as a museum piece, and thus earning the nickname of the 'hatted king'. He then set about enacting his reform programme by rescript.

Some of his earlier measures actually satisfied wishes which had long been expressed in Hungary. The Patent of Toleration, issued in 1781, remedied the chief grievances of the non-catholic Christians (protestants and Greek Orthodox alike) by allowing them full freedom of public worship and complete equality with catholics of civil and political rights, including admission to public office; the Jews, although not receiving full civic rights, were granted freedom of worship and made subject to the ordinary laws. Other of his edicts, if they could not expect to be generally popular, were certainly beneficial to much of the population: chief of these were the Livings Patent, which dissolved a number of religious Orders and applied their property to founding new parochial livings, each with an elementary school attached; and his Peasant Patent, which definitively assured the peasants liberty to leave their holdings, on payment of their dues, marry, and put their children to any trade.

But much even of these measures was unpopular, and not only among the classes obviously suffering under them: the catholics and the landlords were enraged, but the protestants and the peasants were not satisfied. There were two chapters of enactments which snapped the national patience. One related to the old question of noble taxation. When the nobles refused to renounce their exemption, Joseph applied extreme economic pressure. The high tariff duties round the Monarchy were replaced, in the case of many commodities, by complete prohibitions, and the importation into Hungary of manufactured articles from the Austrian provinces and Galicia became completely free, whereas Hungarian exports to Austria had to pay the full duty applicable to foreign goods. Joseph then announced his intention of imposing a general land tax, under all circumstances, and began a survey of the nobles' lands.

Even more spectacular were the administrative and educational changes. The distinctions between Inner Hungary, Croatia and Transylvania were expunged, and the whole country, except the Military Frontier, which was retained,[1] brought under one gigantic *Gubernium*. This was divided into ten Districts (in delimiting which the old Croat-Hungarian frontier was ignored), each under a Commissioner. The counties lost their autonomy; the Föispáns disappeared, and the Alispáns and minor officials became

---

[1] As said above, the Bánát had already been abolished in 1779.

Government employees. German replaced Latin as the language of administration, the changes entering into force immediately in the central offices, after one year in the counties and three in the lowest instances. Any official not mastering the language before expiration of the grace was to be dismissed. Knowledge of German was also made the condition of admission to the Diet, and education completely Germanised: by 1786 Joseph had got so far as to order that German was to be the sole language of instruction for all subjects in all schools. Only religion might be taught in the pupils' mother tongue in the primary schools, and intending priests might study Latin in the high schools.

Then, in 1787, Joseph embarked on an ill-advised Turkish war. A large army was quartered in south Hungary, and the country flooded with demands for recruits and with requisitioning orders. The whole nation, including the peasants, seethed with discontent. The proscribed counties, re-assuming their old powers, put themselves at the head of the resistance. A party made contact with Joseph's rival, the King of Prussia. Then Belgium revolted; the war went very badly, and Joseph himself fell mortally sick. On 28 January 1790 he yielded, and revoked all his rescripts relating to Hungary except the Toleration Patent, the Peasant Patent and the Livings Patent, then promised to convoke a Diet and ordered the Holy Crown to be brought back to Hungary. Three weeks later (20th February) he died.

The reign of Joseph II was perhaps the most dynamic in Hungarian history. No single aspect of the national life, political, social, economic, cultural or national in the modern sense of the term, was the same after it as before it. But many of its most important positive after-effects showed themselves only a generation later, when they appeared as manifestations of the *Zeitgeist* which Joseph's intemperate wizardry had helped conjure up. The immediate mood of the Diet which met soon after his death was one of unqualified reaction. Some of its speakers, indeed, voiced political doctrines on the social contract and the sovereignty of the people which could have come straight from the contemporary Paris, but without exception, they were talking strictly in terms of the historic Hungarian nation and its rights *vis-à-vis* its monarch; its right, that is, to preserve intact its ancient institutions.

Joseph's brother and successor, the shrewd and circumspect Leopold II, handled this dangerous situation with great skill. He gave the Diet a new and solemn pledge, which in substance simply repeated Charles' declarations of 1715 and 1723, but was now embodied in a Law,[1] that Hungary was a wholly independent kingdom, not subject to any other land or people and to be ruled only by its own lawfully crowned kings and in accordance with its own laws and customs. He also consented to having the loopholes stopped which his predecessors had utilised to evade this obligation. The king had to submit himself to coronation within six months of his predecessor's decease. He must convoke the Diet triennially. He would rule by law only, and not by rescript or patent.

With Joseph's recantation, the administration had already reverted to the *status quo ante* his innovations, the old organs, central and local, simply taking over again with their former constitutions and competences. Leopold confirmed this, with only two modifications, both on the highest level. Transylvania and Croatia recovered their separate status, and Leopold also set up a separate 'Illyrian Chancellery' for the Hungarian Serbs. He rejected, however, a 'Supplex Libellus Valachorum' in which the Roumanians of Transylvania had asked for recognition as a 'nation', although, or perhaps because, some of them had perpetrated a terrible jacquerie seven years earlier.

[1] This Law (Law X of 1790) was thereafter counted by the Hungarians as the fundamental guarantee of the national status.

For the rest, Leopold prevailed on the Diet to enact legislation in the sense of the three Patents which Joseph had not revoked, and in return, agreed to a law proscribing the use of 'a foreign language' (under which German was meant) as an official medium, but rejected a request (from which the Croats had dissented, and which was not pressed), that Latin should be replaced by Magyar as the official language of all public services, including the Army. All that he would concede here was that provision should be made for the teaching of the Magyar language at the university and in the gymnasia, with a view to the training up of a future supply of Magyar-speaking officials. 'For the time being', government was to be carried on in Latin. Several other *postulata* for immediate change fared no better. It was, however, agreed that the Diet should set up a number of committees which were to present to its successor proposals for reform in a great number of fields, including many in which Maria Theresa had not allowed the nation a voice.

Things might have developed either way from this beginning. On the one hand, documents recently discovered show that Leopold was secretly entertaining plans for imposing drastic changes in Hungary, not in the direction of Germanisation, but in that of a far-reaching democratisation of the entire political system. On the other hand, the committees took their work very seriously, and some of them worked out some extremely interesting and constructive proposals, especially in the economic field. But now there followed a series of events the combined effect of which was singularly detrimental to all ideas of social or political progress. The French Revolution degenerated into terrorism. Leopold died suddenly, on 1 March 1792, and was succeeded by his son Francis, a man of extreme mental timidity, in whose eyes the only hope of saving his own throne and humanity lay in freezing any situation which promised to avert revolution. The settlement which Leopold had reached in Hungary seemed to him to answer this description, and at his coronation Diet he confirmed it with few changes, the most important of which was the cancellation of the Illyrian Chancellery. The Hungarian Estates, for their part, found any settlement welcome which safeguarded them against the twin dangers of Josephinian revolution from above and Jacobin revolution from below.

In 1795 feeling on both sides was hardened by a queer event. The police came on the tracks of a fantastic Jacobin plot, the leading figure in which was a dubious and enigmatic character, the Abbé Martinovics, who had been an agent of Leopold's, and employed by him on preparations for an attack on the conservative opposition to a 'revolution from above'. But after Leopold's death the plans had lost shape, retaining their revolutionary character while losing their link with the Crown, which was no longer privy to them. They had, moreover, acquired new sympathisers, some quite hare-brained, but others serious and sensible, and, for that very reason, really dangerous. The revelations, true or invented, made by Martinovics under interrogation, increased Francis' determination to refuse any change which might conceivably lead to revolution, while the arrests (which were numerous) made in connection with the conspiracy, and the glimpses afforded by the trials of obscure forces stirring below the surface, finally cured the Estates of any taste for adventure.

The period which followed was much rather one of cold war, than of genuine and cordial peace. The respect which Francis paid to the Hungarian constitution was perfunctory enough. In the first years of his reign he duly convoked the Diet every three years, but only to ask it for subsidies and recruits for his wars. By constitutional tradition, the proceedings of a Diet opened with consideration of the royal *postulata*; when agreement on these had been reached, the turn came of the Estates' *gravamina*. It was Francis' habit simply to dissolve each Diet as soon as he had extracted from it what satisfaction he could extract of his own demands. The nation's wishes were never formally discussed at all; the reports of the committees of the Leopoldinian Diet were simply laid *ad acta*, and if the later Diets got any concessions at all, they were extracted in the course of the bargaining over the *postulata*.

This meant that they were meagre to a degree. The two main wishes expressed by the Diets of these years were for wider use of the Magyar language in education and public life, and for revision of the inequitable economic relationship with the Austrian provinces. In the former field, Francis, under pressure, made one or two further concessions: in 1792 Magyar had been made a compulsory subject in higher and secondary schools in Inner Hungary,[1] and after 1805 it became permissible to correspond with the chancellery and the *Consilium* in Magyar. The economic system was not altered in any material respect.

For twenty years, nevertheless, each party got enough out of the truce to make it worth keeping. Francis obtained considerable votes of men and money, while Hungary could reflect that her contribution was still light compared with that which Francis' other dominions had to pay, and except in 1809, when the *insurrectio* was called out (for the last time), did not fall on the nobles. If the Diets were almost always barren, yet the shadow of the censorship and the political police fell but lightly on Hungary, whose nobles could with justice regard themselves by their own standards the freest class on the Continent. The wars touched Hungarian territory only twice, and each time only for a few weeks, and in other respects brought the country actual gain, for the land-owners were able to make big profits out of the wheat for which there was an almost unlimited demand, at high prices.

Even so, tempers became frayed on both sides, and an

[1] i.e., excluding Croatia as well as Transylvania and the Frontier.

open clash was again and again averted only by the tact and skill of the Palatine, the Archduke Joseph, who combined, in a quite remarkable degree, loyalty to his brother with sympathy for the Hungarians. But even he was worsted in the end, on the issue of the common finances. The one thing which Francis had been powerless to keep stable had been the value of his money. Since the beginning of the wars, the expenditure of the Monarchy had regularly, and largely, exceeded its revenue, and the government had met the deficit by issuing paper money, the value of which, in terms of prices, had sunk rapidly, and while the paper had in law to be taken at its face value, it was quoted in Augsburg at a discount of some 800 per cent. In 1811 the Austrian Finance Minister carried through a drastic operation, reducing the nominal value of the currency by 80 per cent, and the Diet was asked to take over the funding of 100 million of the 212 million gulden to which the national debt had thus been reduced, besides paying an extraordinary subsidy towards the amortisation of the remainder. It refused, and in 1812 Francis dissolved it and enacted the desired measures by rescript. For thirteen years Hungary was now again ruled without a Diet.

The discontent now became acute; so much so that when in 1825 a renewed threat of war compelled Francis to convoke the Diet again (after attempts to get what he needed direct from the counties, by unconstitutional means, had broken down on their ingenious resistance), its proceedings were so dangerously turbulent that he found it expedient to make a sort of apology and to promise not to repeat his offence.

Some Hungarians count this Diet as marking the end of the long period of torpor and the beginning of the exciting 'Reform Era' which followed it. This is only half true. A spirit of defiance was, indeed, apparent in the pertinacity and acerbity with which speakers voiced their grievances, but except on one point, the Diet's attitude was still the old one, unchanged in any particular; it was simply that the encroachments, financial and other, of the Crown's servants on Hungary's ancient liberties must cease, and those liberties be restored intact.

The only demand which could not have come straight out of the Middle Ages was still the request, which had become regular since 1790, for wider use of the Magyar language in the administration, the Courts and education, and this did indeed reflect a modern spirit, which had begun to stir even before Joseph's day (the first signs of it go back to the last years of Maria Theresa's reign), but had been greatly stimulated by the violence offered to it by Joseph II, and since his death had grown more vigorous with every year: a spirit of pride in the national language as the embodiment and vital necessity of the national spirit.

The last decade of the eighteenth century and the first quarter of the nineteenth had been a time of inspiring activity. Lexicographers had set themselves to the heavy task of re-fashioning and enriching the Magyar tongue, developing it into an instrument in which modern thought could be expressed and modern literature written. As the lexicographers cleared the way, the poets, romantic novelists and playwrights followed on their heels. Many of their achievements were crude and tentative, but in some, real genius — in a few cases, some of the greatest that Hungary has ever known — shone through what were still imperfect forms, and good and bad alike were hailed with enormous enthusiasm. The cult of the language was accompanied by a similar fashion for the national costume, dances, and whatever else was specifically Magyar.

Yet even this was still modern only in a peculiar and restricted sense. As the Hungarian noble class embraced most educated Magyars, it followed that nearly all their writers and intelligentsia were nobles born, and they instinctively saw the picture of the nation through the spectacles of their class. Where any writer was of non-noble origin, the chances were that he was a quasi-noble by adoption, for the attainment of certain academic qualifications conferred the status of *honoratior*, which brought with it some of the privileges of nobility, and with them, almost invariably, the 'noble' outlook on the world. Thus practically every figure of this first phase of the literary renaissance, whatever his own economic circumstances, identified Hungary with its noble class, drew his inspiration from the wells of the national tradition, and heartened the present with the memories of a past which had grown glorious by defending its immemorial freedom. The new spirit in no way diminished the social and political exclusiveness of Hungarian nationalism.

The new Magyar nationalism agreed with, and in its turn helped to reinforce the assumption that the Hungarian polity must be the preserve, as it had been the creation, of the Magyar element in the country. It was on this assumption that the repeated requests were made to the Crown to substitute Magyar for Latin as the language of state, and the non-Magyars of Inner Hungary would not have been very much affected had the change been made, so long as representation in the Diet and the county Congregations, and employment in the public services, was confined to nobles, and so long as the *de facto* situation prevailed that the politically active noble class, except for the denationalised magnates at the top, already spoke and felt Magyar. As for education, although extreme proposals were bruited at two of the Diets, the Crown's refusal to make any substantial concessions in this field was enough to prevent complications from arising.

The only conflict (except that with Vienna) which the new movement had so far evoked had been with the Croats. Here the position was really different, since the language of the ordinary Croat nobles was Croat, and when, at the Leopoldinian Diet, the Hungarians first proposed the abolition of Latin, they tried to allow for this by offering that the Croat language should enjoy in Croatia any position gained by Magyar in Inner Hungary. The substitution of Magyar for Latin in the central Diet and services would still have left the Croat deputies or employees in the *Consilium* at a disadvantage compared with the Magyars, but the latter did not feel it reasonable that they should continue to renounce what they regarded as their natural right to transact their national affairs in their own language (besides imposing on themselves the continued burden of acquiring a second language) for the benefit of so small a minority. There were less than 20,000 noble persons in Croatia, compared with over 300,000 in Inner Hungary[1], and the 20,000 included not only the magnates, lay and ecclesiastical, most of whom either spoke both languages equally well, or neither of them, but also the 'sandalled nobles' of Turopolje (Turmezö), near Zagreb, a separate community living under their own count, who aspired to no office and were, incidentally, solid for the Hungarian connection. Croatia had only two virilist members of the Upper Table, the Ban and the Bishop of Zagreb, and only three delegates to the Lower Table — two representing the Zagreb Diet, and the Count of Turopolje.

The Croat delegates had nevertheless objected to the proposal on principle, maintaining that the Diet had been acting *ultra vires* in trying to pass it into law; for the use of the neutral Latin was founded on immemorial *pacta conventa* between the two associated kingdoms of Hungary and Croatia, and no change could be made without the assent of both parties. This attitude of theirs had shown a rift between Hungary and Croatia which was destined afterwards to widen into a great gulf, the more impossible

[1] The census of 1787 showed 9,782 male nobles (of all ages) in Croatia, and 155,519 in Inner Hungary. This census counted the Slavonian counties as part of Inner Hungary, but these contained only 160 noble families all told.

to bridge because of the fundamental nature of the central question, whether Croatia was indeed an 'associated kingdom' or only an 'adjunct of Hungary' – a question on which neither party was ever able to convince the other, just as they could not on the second great disputed point, the appurtenance of the Slavonian counties. During the period of torpor, however, the cloud remained on the horizon, and did not even bulk very large on it, for Francis' summary Diets afforded no opportunity for the raising of constitutional issues, or even for detailed discussion of the language question, while from 1811 to 1825, the years of neo-absolutism, no discussion was possible at all. It was also important that during the latter period the Croats who could have argued their case were fewer than ever, for between 1809 and 1815 a substantial part of Croatia was out of the Monarchy altogether, as part of Napoleon's Kingdom of Illyria, and when this was liquidated, Vienna kept the civilian portions of the areas so detached under its own administration until 1824.

Furthermore, Croatia during this period was even more untouched by any true spirit of modernity than Hungary itself. Political Croatia, like political Hungary, consisted of its nobles; and the Croat nobles were not only fewer on the ground than their Hungarian colleagues (2·9 per cent of the total population, against 4·8 per cent) but even more divorced from their people. Towns were rarer, the peasants even more oppressed, the exclusive predominance of the catholics more absolute, for the Croat delegates had invoked the same argument of *pacta conventa* to prevent the extension to Croatia of the alleviations which Hungary introduced for its Protestants in 1790. The Croat nobles had hitherto shown no interest whatever in the Croat language, steadily insisting on Latin, not only in the central services, but locally; when, in 1805, Francis had made the concession mentioned above, the Congregation of Várasd had solemnly resolved that the suppression of Latin would mean 'the end of culture and of the nation, which would no longer understand its own laws'. This arch-conservatism did not, indeed, render the Croats' opposition to Hungary any less determined, and perhaps made it in some respects even more dangerous, since it struck an answering note in Vienna.

The spirit of the Diet which was convoked in 1830, to strengthen the government's arm in view of the July revolution in Paris and the unrest in the Netherlands, Italy and Poland, was hardly different from that of 1825. Its members were as anxious as Metternich himself that the revolution should not spread. They used the government's embarrassment, indeed, to extract another linguistic concession, the most important which they had yet gained: it was enacted that thereafter no person not conversant with the Magyar language should be admitted to the public services in Inner Hungary, and the same requirement was to be made, after four years' grace, for admission to the Bar. The chancellery and *Curia* were instructed to answer in Magyar communications addressed to them in that language by the counties, and Magyar might also be used in the Courts. But for this price, they cheerfully voted 48,000 soldiers for the safeguarding of the existing order. But Francis had taken the opportunity to have his son and prospective successor, Ferdinand, crowned proleptically, and for reward had consented to listen, at a new meeting, to the nation's long-postponed *gravamina*. A terrible outbreak of cholera in 1831 was made the excuse for leaving the Diet unconvoked that year, but in 1832 it met; and the atmosphere in which it did so was magically transformed.

It is easy, and up to a point true, to say that this change was simply the natural reflection of altered world conditions. The great deflationary crisis which had followed the boom of the war years was passing in its turn. England was in the full swing of its industrial expansion, and even in the

Habsburg Monarchy the winds of modern capitalism were setting the withered leaves rustling and wafting messages of a new world in which fortunes were to be made by those who understood its language. The bourgeoisie was stirring, even the peasants were not the unquestioning, unresisting clods that their grandfathers had been.

Pertinaciously as Francis and Metternich had tried to seal off the Monarchy from the new world, the victories of Liberalism in western Europe had shown that despotism was not invincible. The stirrings which had begun in Austria in 1830 need no more explanation than this, but in Hungary, with its special tradition that saw the very existence of the nation as dependent on the preservation of the old institutions, more was necessary.

But this special impetus had been given, by two events. One was an outbreak of peasant unrest in the areas devasted by cholera in 1831 so serious as to convince the nation that the situation of the peasants could no longer be left where the legislation of 1791 had settled it. Some, indeed, saw the remedy in more repression, but a considerable number believed that only real reform could avert further outbreaks. The other event was the publication of István Széchenyi's book *Hitel* ('Credit').

Count István Széchenyi was the scion of one of Hungary's great historic families, and heir to a tradition of national service; his father, Ferenc Széchenyi, had been the founder of the great national library which still bears his name. The young Széchenyi's own outlook was itself conditioned by his origins and his early experiences, which had included service in a hussar regiment; he saw the world through the eyes of an aristocrat, and one to whom loyalty to the dynasty was axiomatic. But his was a brooding and mystic spirit which became wholly possessed by a burning and compassionate love of his country and of the Magyar people. His whole outlook and inspiration were essentially religious. It was with the soul of Hungary that he was con-

cerned, and subscribing to the view that 'the soul of a
people resided in its language', he had electrified the Diet
of 1825 by offering to contribute a year's income from his
estates towards the foundation of a National Academy of
Sciences for the improvement of the Magyar language.
But his vision went beyond this. He had travelled in western Europe, especially England, and looking at his country,
he was shocked by its backwardness, by the morally in-
defensible degradation in which the masses of its people
lived, and by the selfishness of their exploiters. His origin-
ality, and his unique effectiveness, lay in the fact that although what he cared for most was the moral regeneration
of Hungary, his approach to the problem was severely practical, even materialistic. His diagnosis, which was couched
in unsparing terms, was that Hungary was not at all an
Eden of successfully guarded freedom, but rather a 'great
fallow-land', a place and a people deserving of infinite well-
being, spiritual and material, and capable of achieving it,
but at present, poor and neglected, a prey to political
sterility, social oppression, economic backwardness. And
with extraordinary hardihood he told his fellow-nobles
that the blame for this lay, spiritually, with their own
short-sightedness and egotism, and institutionally, with
the sacrosanct Hungarian constitution itself, which was not,
he declared, a bastion at all, but a prison in which they
themselves were the most unfortunate inmates and their
own pockets the worst sufferers. Their cherished exemption from taxation prevented the accumulation of funds
to finance indispensable communications, and without
these the produce of their estates was unsaleable; the *aviticitas*, by declaring their lands inalienable, prevented them
from borrowing on the security of them for improvements;
the landlord-peasant nexus made the peasants surly malcontents whose forced labour, unwillingly rendered, was,
Széchenyi calculated, only one third as productive as a
free man's hired labour.

The effect of *Hitel* and of the works with which Széchenyi followed it up – *Világ* ('Light') in 1831 and *Stadium* in 1833 – was like that of an explosive charge which breaks a river block and sends pent-up waters pouring suddenly and turbulently down. The orthodox were scandalised beyond measure. Copies of the books were publicly burnt in several county congregations, and·their author savagely denounced for a traitor to his country and his class. But to the very considerable number of Hungarians who had felt obscurely that their country was ailing, without being able either to diagnose the disease or to prescribe the remedy, they came as a revelation, and it may fairly be said that with, and in large part thanks to, their appearance the period of Hungarian history known as 'the Reform Era', began.

The years which followed were extraordinarily stimulating ones, an intoxicating contrast to the sterile decades before, a time when it was indeed bliss to be alive, and very heaven to be young. Once Széchenyi had sounded the trumpet which sent the walls crumbling, reformers pullulated. Before the Diet, which did not rise till 1836, was over, the magnate and paternalist social reformer Széchenyi was himself a back number in the eyes of the angry young men hatching out in the aula of the University, and thronging the purlieus of the Diet itself – for it was the custom of deputies to bring with them, as secretaries and to give them experience, bands of young *jurati*, who formed an audience to the proceedings and often, in the absence of any fixed rules of procedure, a tumultuous chorus. Their learned apparatus, such as it was, came chiefly from the French and German liberal philosophers, whose works easily slipped past the slipshod censorship into Hungary; their catchword and panacea was liberty, especially national liberty, and the rising sun of their allegiance was the man who soon became Széchenyi's great rival, Lajos (Louis) Kossuth.

Kossuth was a member of that dangerous class which possesses birth and brains, but no means. He was, moreover, a protestant. His family was noble, so that public service or politics were open to him, but his genius being his only fortune, he had entered active politics only comparatively late in life, and that through a curious side door. After qualifying as a lawyer, he had spent his early manhood managing the estates of a wealthy widow in his native north-eastern Hungary. The widows of magnates were, by tradition, entitled to send proxies to the Lower House, and in 1832 this lady sent Kossuth, then already thirty years of age, to Pozsony in this capacity, and here he became intoxicated with the new spirit, but proxies were not allowed to speak. He fell, however, on a brilliant idea: no official record was kept of the debates, and Kossuth had the thought of issuing an unofficial journal of them. This was less a transcript than a highly-coloured commentary, calculated to win sympathy for the causes which Kossuth had at heart. Most brilliantly written, for Kossuth proved himself a journalist of quite extraordinary capacity, they served their purpose admirably, and at the same time made their author, at one bound, the idol of the younger and more impatient reformers.

Like Széchenyi, Kossuth loved his country and his own people with a profound passion, saw in their existing condition many evils, and burned to remove them. But both his diagnosis and his remedy differed from Széchenyi's. Széchenyi was both, as we have said, instinctively loyal, as an ex-officer and a magnate, to the dynasty, and also intellectually convinced that Hungary's own interests demanded a considerable measure of integration into the Monarchy. Not only was she far too weak to challenge Vienna to a conflict, but the connection was necessary both for her security and also, given her paucity of capital, for her economic development.

Kossuth, a true child of his age, regarded liberty as the

universal talisman – liberty of all kinds, and above all, national liberty, as the pre-requisite without which no social, economic or cultural advance was possible at all. Blind to the advantages which Széchenyi recognised in the connection with Vienna, he saw only the oppressive side of the *de facto* control which the central authorities had come to exercise over Hungary. The very first objective of the reform movement must be to emancipate her from this control; after this political battle had been won, all the rest would follow. His programme was, in fact, a repudiation of Széchenyi's advocacy of collaboration and a reversion to Hungary's traditional *gravaminal* policy, only now in the interests of national development, not of stabilisation.

Kossuth's social and political tenets constituted a curious and not altogether logical mixture. He was as axiomatic as any man in his instinctive identification of political Hungary with its noble class (of his own membership of which he was deeply proud), and in all his political thinking he assumed that the leadership in Hungary should and would remain in the hands of that class. Nevertheless, his burning national feeling itself came to generate in him, as he grew older, an increasingly pronounced social radicalism. Partly out of genuine love and compassion towards his fellow-men, partly with the political purpose of strengthening the Hungarian nation against Vienna, he came to wish, as he once put it, 'not to abolish our noble liberties, but to extend them to the whole people'. He came thus to accept the abolition of all ancestral restrictions which confined liberty to the noble class alone, and to advocate, not only the extention of taxation and the abolition of *robot*, but the complete emancipation of the peasants. An extended franchise, freedom of the Press and association, penal reform and an inexhaustible list of further innovations, from which little was missing that Hungary needed to modernise herself, found their places on his list.

Kossuth would probably in any case soon have overshadowed Széchenyi, for his was obviously far the more popular appeal: how much more romantic (and more in the the national tradition) to declaim against a foreign oppressor, than to follow an austere path of self-criticsm, self-discipline, self-sacrifice! And while his position had automatically placed Széchenyi in front at the outset – no one but a magnate could even have published *Hitel*, still less have found readers for it – once the first step had been taken, he was at a heavy personal disadvantage. He spoke the Magyar language itself haltingly; not only was the argumentation of his books dry, but their language was difficult and contorted. Kossuth had a resonant and beautiful organ; he was equally magical as speaker and writer, inexhaustibly fluent, irresistibly convincing, never at a loss for a phrase or an argument.

Széchenyi and Kossuth are the two most picturesque and most publicised figures of the Reform Era, and it is fashionable to describe its course in the terms of a duel between the two men and their respective principles: evolution or revolution, with Austria or against it – the more tempting because a bitter personal antagonism developed between them. But this is to over-simplify the picture. Even among those who found themselves forced to accept the necessity of the political struggle, there were almost as many ideas on what Hungary needed as there were reformers. The parliamentary leadership, in so far as the phrase is applicable at all, for no parties existed before 1847, of the reform movement during the decade, lay not with Kossuth (who was not a deputy until 1847) but with Ferenc Deák, a quiet, unassuming medium land-owner from Zala, distinguished equally for his complete rectitude, his unfailing good sense, his encyclopaedic legal knowlege and his unequalled legal acumen. A very important intellectual leaven was provided by a little group headed by Baron József Eötvös and known in derision as the 'centralists', or 'doctrinaires'. Unlike Kossuth, who regarded the counties with mystical devotion, and still saw them as bulwarks against centralist oppression, the centralists held them to be strongholds of reaction and obscurantism, and argued for a central government, responsible to the electorate and thus not under the control of Vienna, but itself administering Hungary with modern efficiency. In spite of this, they did not share Kossuth's nebulous allergy to all things Austrian, and were genuinely concerned to preserve the unity of the Monarchy. Socially, they were more radical than Széchenyi, and even, in reality, than Kossuth himself. In the Reform period, and even after it, so far as their persons were concerned, they were heavily overshadowed by the far more spectacular and popular Kossuth; yet, as will be seen, it was the essentials of their programme, hurriedly adopted by Kossuth when he saw its relevance, which laid the foundations of the reform of 1848.

Outside the strictly political circles, too, new forces were stirring. The literary movement entered on a new phase: it no longer looked back, but forward. Petőfi and others of its great figures were revolutionaries, like the young Shelley and Wordsworth.

But new ideas and new enthusiasms were now no longer the monopoly of the Magyars. Up to 1830 the Croat representatives in the central Diet had steadily followed their old path, opposing any suggestion to replace Latin as an official language anywhere, and for that matter, any proposal for social reform. But the re-incorporation of the ex-French districts had brought into Croatia a whole army of young men who, under the French regime and in the schools instituted by it, had imbibed a romantic nationalism of the most heady sort, flavoured (rather sporadically) with advanced social doctrines and, above all, belligerently impatient of any shadow of subordination of Croatia (which they conceived in the most extensive geographical terms) to Hungary. The new nationalism swept over Croatia like a heath fire in time of drought, setting students and young 'intellectuals' aflame, throwing out fiery streams of grammarians, lexicographers, poets and political journalists, and penetrating even the aristocracy. In 1832 a Croat magnate, Baron Rukovina, addressed the Sabor in Croat, a language which it had not heard for centuries. The next year Count Jankó Drasković, an elderly man, a member of one of Croatia's leading families, a Court Chamberlain, a member of the House of Magnates and a colonel, had the Slovak Kollar's protest against linguistic Magyarisation, *Sollen wir Magyaren werden?*, published in Croatia, then producing a work of his own in which he set forth a political programme for the constitution of Croatia, not only with Slavonia and Fiume, but also with the two 'Illyrian' governments of Austria (Dalmatia and the Slovene areas) and perhaps Bosnia, as a separate political constituent of the Habsburg Monarchy, with Croat as the language of administration and education.

At this point the Croat linguistic, and for a time also the political, movement were given a curious twist by a young man named Ljudevit Gaj, who for a time figured as their *spiritus rector*. Educated under Pan-Slav masters, Gaj held all Slavs to be brothers in the wider sense, but accepted the division of them into four main groups, one of which was the Southern Slav, or 'Illyrian', comprising the Croats, Slovenes, Serbs and Bulgars. He hoped to see all of these merge in a single nation, and the pre-requisite for this was to get them all to speak and write a single language.

The results of his linguistic endeavours were rather peculiar. He persuaded the Croats, and up to a point, the Slovenes, to adopt a new orthography, modelled on that of the West Slavs, but the Serbs and Bulgars rejected this, and continued to use the Cyrillic alphabet. Orthographically, therefore, the Southern Slavs continued to divide on religious lines, the catholics using Gaj's Latin script, and the Orthodox, the Cyrillic. Linguistically, on the other hand, Gaj and the Serbian linguistic maestro of the day, Vuk Karadžić, agreed on a common language, the 'što' dialect, generally spoken in the Serb lands, although not the Croat. Gaj persuaded the Croats to adopt this, but the Slovenes refused. Gaj had thus assassinated his own language, replacing it by one which was Serbian in content and Czech in orthography.

Politically, few disciples, and they almost all Croats, fully adopted Gaj's Illyrian doctrine. The Serbs, in particular, rejected it as a devilish machination of Rome's, and most of the Croats also disliked and distrusted the Serbs.

There were, of course, even some who were genuinely attached to Hungary and wanted no change in the Hungaro-Croat relationship, but this group, although politically important by virtue of the official positions held by some of its members, notably the Count of Turopolje, was numerically small. The great majority, to whom the name of 'Illyrian party' was applied, although inaccurately, really subscribed to the particularist Croat programme set out in Drasković' pamphlet. Meanwhile the larger Illyrianism, or at least the idea of Serbo-Croat brotherhood, was there to be trotted out as an additional stimulus to anti-Hungarian feeling.

Vienna, indeed, after first encouraging Gaj's Illyrianism, ended by taking fright at its Pan-Slav and pro-Russian implications; the Pasha of Bosnia, too, complained that the movement was spreading sedition among his peasants. The movement was forbidden, but not so the Croat particularist movement, which appeared to Vienna a useful counterweight against Hungary. It was given its head; and it may be said that the unbridled licence of the Croat national Press, and the venom of its attacks on the Hungarian state and the Magyar people, exceeded even what the Magyars allowed themselves in their counter-utterances, although these were vicious enough.

The new nationalism was now spreading also to the non-Magyars of Hungary, and analogous antagonisms were developing. Each side blamed the other lavishly for this, but the truth was that here, too, two views were confronting one another which were at least equally intelligible, but mutually incompatible, while the development of the conflict was a hen and egg story if ever there was one. The Magyars' profound conviction that the Hungarian polity was essentially theirs was certainly understandable, in view of its history; and in wanting its official language to correspond with what they regarded as its national character they asking no more than what every independent European nation regarded as its axiomatic right. When they now began to press actively their demand for the increased use and diffusion of their language to a point which involved imposing it, in greater or less degree, on the non-Magyars, this was in the first instance largely the reflection of the widening and democratisation of their own conception of the nation, the recognition of the existence as a political factor of other elements in the population, besides the nobility. If their view of the nature of the polity was accepted as justified even under modern conditions, it was even a liberal move to provide non-Magyars with sufficient schooling in Magyar to enable them to enter the national political community. It is fair to point out that there have been cases enough in history where national minorities have asked for no more than this, and that even now, some of the non-Magyars asked for no more. But others felt — no less in accordance with the spirit of the age — that they had the same natural right as the Magyars themselves to use their own language, cultivate their own national attributes, take pride in their own national pasts, and that to force another language on them was an unnatural tyranny. Their view was that the multinational country which Hungary was, when its total population was taken into account, ought to be organised as a multinational polity, and that

29. *Count István Széchenyi: 'a brooding and mystic spirit, wholly possessed by a burning and compassionate love of his country': ref. p. 135*

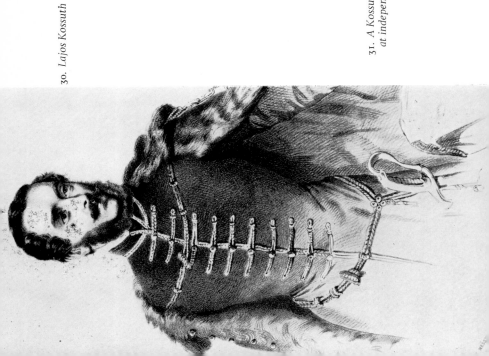

30. *Lajos Kossuth*

31. *A Kossuth banner used at independence meeting in the U.S.A.*

the languages of administration and education should adapt themselves accordingly.

What prevented either side from yielding, or even seeking a compromise, exacerbated the conflict and made collision ultimately inevitable, was the presence of outside factors: above all, Vienna, with its age-long hostility to Hungarian nationalism and its historic policy of allying itself with the non-Magyars; but to this was added in the 1830s the spectre, which then loomed very large, of Pan-Slav agitation, subverting the loyalty of Hungary's Slavs. In the eyes of many Magyars, the only complete safeguard against these dangers would have lain in Magyarising the entire population, and while only a few extremists (although there were such) ever dreamed of carrying so enormous an operation to completion, there were many who felt that a large measure of Magyarisation, something far beyond the provision of schools for a few aspiring civil servants, was a simple and legitimate matter of self-defence. Conversely, the more Magyars there were, the larger would be the number of champions of Hungarian nationality against the tyranny of Vienna. Ardent spirits added: the larger the army championing and enjoying the blessings of freedom and progress (which they proposed to bestow on Hungary) instead of reaction and obscurantism.

These considerations led the Magyars to be impatient and intolerant and to pay less consideration than they would probably otherwise have given to the natural susceptibilities of the nationalities, which they interpreted as sympathy with the enemies of the nation – thereby, of course, breeding such sympathy; although here again the shadow of the hen should not obscure the egg, for the designs both of Vienna and of Pan-Slavism were real, and both really possessed sympathisers in Hungary.

At the beginning of the 1830s all this lay rather in the future than the present. The Swabians and Ruthenes seemed so far untouched by any national feeling whatever. The

Serbs were passing through a quiescent period, although the literary movement which was developing under the auspices of Vuk Karadžić was instinct with Pan-Serb nationalism, which was also growing in Serbia. The Roumanian movement was still almost confined to Transylvania. Only a handful of Slovak intellectuals had so far adopted the theory of Czecho-Slovak identity, while rather more (like many of the Czechs themselves) were nebulously Pan-Slav. Others were particularist Slovaks, and quite prepared to make common cause with the Hungarians. The situation was, however, full of latent dangers, and Magyar chauvinism, by making the most of these, was already increasing them.

In the event, the course taken by the developments of these years, and, in particular, both the contents and the course of the Hungarian reform movement, were largely determined by the attitude taken up towards it by Vienna. It was hopeless to expect anything during the lifetime of Francis, whose aversion from change of any sort had become almost pathological with advancing years, and for this reason the first three years of the Diet which met in 1832 were practically barren. After Francis' death on 2 March 1835 the government of the Monarchy was taken over for the simpleton Ferdinand by the *Staats- und Konferenzrat*, which was not a body from which the Hungarian reformers could expect much sympathy. Of its three effective members, the Archduke Ludwig held it to be an injunction of piety to keep his brother's 'system' intact. Metternich was not anti-Hungarian, if only out of snobism, and the shallow corpus of inductive conclusions which he called his political philosophy included the beliefs that allowance must be made for Hungary's national individuality and respect accorded to the Hungarian constitution; but what he valued in that constitution was precisely its antique elements, which seemed to him a guarantee against revolution.

Kolowrat, the 'overlord' of the interior and finance, was a Josephinian at heart, not against authoritarian reform; but he regarded Hungarian nationalism as a dangerous disruptive force, his intellectual convictions in this respect being reinforced by strong pro-Slav, and in particular pro-Czech, prejudices.

The policy followed by the *Konferenzrat* towards Hungary was in fact wavering and inconsistent, and probably depended largely on which of its members happened at a given moment to be interesting himself most in the country. Its first moves, when in 1836 the 'Long Diet' rose at last, were severely repressive. The key government posts were filled with men who were both extreme centralists and unbending reactionaries. Kossuth was arrested, as were several of the young *jurati* and Baron Miklós Wesselényi, a fiery and extremely popular Transylvanian magnate and friend of Széchenyi's. At the same time, Kolowrat was lavishing encouragement on the Croats.

But the resulting outcry was very formidable. Even the moderate Hungarians rallied against this new oppression. Moreover, the international situation grew threatening again. Metternich wanted money and recruits from Hungary, and dared not provoke the nation too much. In 1840, accordingly, there was a change of policy in the direction of conciliation. The most unpopular officials were replaced, the Diet convoked and placated by considerable concessions in several fields, and Kossuth and Wesselényi amnestied.

The result, however, was only to whet appetites, and to play into the hands of the extremists. For one point on which the Opposition had protested particularly strongly, and on which the government had promised to mend its ways, had been its violations of the principle of free speech. When, then, the proprietor of one of Hungary's few papers, the *Pesti Hirlap*, made Kossuth its editor, he was allowed to write pretty well what he would. The brilliance of his writing sent the circulation of the *Pesti Hirlap* soaring until it was being read over all Hungary; the aura of martyrdom with which his imprisonment had invested him helped to lend his words an almost oracular authority, and soon he was far the most popular man in Hungary, and exercised far the greatest influence on its opinion.

This had a big effect in strengthening the reform movement on social issues, for thanks to Kossuth's real enthusiasm, and to his peculiar genius for presenting political and social reforms as national desiderata, political opinion in the country was during these years largely won over to the emancipation of the peasants and to many other good causes. But his influence also helped to keep alive the eternal spirit of opposition to Vienna, and further to exacerbate the nationalities question. A wave of extreme chauvinism swept during these years over Hungary and Croatia alike, and here again Kossuth was the inspiration and leader of the extremists, while Széchenyi sacrificed almost the last remnants of his popularity by protesting against Magyarisation as both unchristian and politically unwise. He and Kossuth were now openly at loggerheads, and attacking one another in barbed pamphlets.

For the Diet of 1843 the government mobilised all its resources, and again kept the Opposition down to a small number, largely thanks to the tempestuous support which it organised for itself among the sandalled nobles, to whom the taxation of their land would have been a serious blow. It was, however, now still hoping to conciliate the Hungarians, and sanctioned a considerable number of reforms in the social field. On the question of Austro-Hungarian economic relations there was an interesting regrouping of forces. The development of the German *Zollverein* under Prussia's patronage had led Metternich and certain other members of the inner ring in Vienna themselves to favour abolishing the internal tariff between Austria and Hungary and the constitution of the Monarchy as a homogeneous economic unit, all parts of which should be treated on a footing of strict economic and financial equality. Precisely in 1843, however, Kossuth had been converted by reading List's *Nationale System der politischen Oekonomie* to the idea of protection for Hungarian industry. His influence secured the rejection of the government's offer, as a counter to which Kossuth then launched a 'Buy Hungarian' campaign which at first enjoyed considerable popularity. It is true that this soon died away, and when the opportunity next occurred the country preferred to adopt the customs union.

Finally, the government, which already in 1840 had made further concessions on the language question, now gave way on it almost completely. A Law was enacted which made Magyar the official language of all institutions of Greater Hungary, i.e., of the Diet, the chancellery, the *Consilium*, etc., and of all internal administration in Inner Hungary. The king also promised to Magyarise all schools in Inner Hungary. The Croat deputies to the Diet, if unable to speak Magyar, were allowed a six years' grace in which they might continue to speak Latin, and the law did not affect the language of internal administration in Croatia. Communications from Hungarian to Croat authorities were to be in Magyar and no longer in Latin. The Slavonian counties and Fiume were counted as part of Hungary, and, after six years, had to use Magyar for internal purposes; up to that date, they were allowed to use their own languages.

This final victory in the long linguistic battle was hailed with enormous rejoicings in Hungary. But the effect of the laws on the relationship between Magyars and non-Magyars was disastrous. The Slovaks, on whom a great weight of entirely unjustified pressure was also being put, especially by the leaders of the Lutheran church in north Hungary, were at last stung into protest. They petitioned Vienna for redress, and now for the first time a Slovak national opposition became a considerable factor within Hungarian political life. Similar, although less widespread, protests came from Roumanians in the Partium and from some of the Hungarian Germans. The Croats besieged Vienna with petitions for complete or virtual separation from Hungary, and sent back, unread, communications addressed to them in Magyar. The situation in respect of the Serbs grew increasingly dangerous, less as an effect of the laws, which were only very partially applied among them, than because of developments in the Principality of Serbia, where the Minister President, Garašinin, was revolving a plan of his own for uniting all Serbs and Croats under the rule of Belgrade, and sending his agents into Hungary to make propaganda for the plan.

A very similar situation was, meanwhile, developing in Transylvania. Here, too, the excitement of the Josephinian period and the Leopoldinian Diet had been followed by a long stagnation. Francis did not convoke the Diet between 1808 and 1834, and the authorities quietly filled the elective posts in the *Gubernium* with their own nominees. In the early 1830s, however, agitation for reform and for union with Hungary set in. At first this was conducted almost single-handed by Széchenyi's friend, Wesselényi, whose fellow-nobles were slow to join him, partly out of particularist feeling, partly on social grounds: social conditions in Transylvania were much more backward even than in unreformed Hungary (the *robot* commonly ran at four days weekly), and the extension to the Principality of the reforms for which the Liberals were pressing in Hungary would have shaken their whole position. From 1840 or so onward, however, national feeling began to outweigh calculation among many of them. They adopted the programme of union with Hungary, and pending its achievement, demanded a more dominating position for the Magyar element in Transylvania. The Diet had been convoked again regularly since 1837, and in 1841–2 its

Magyar members put forward a motion to make Magyar the exclusive language of the Diet, the *Gubernium* and the other central offices, and of higher education; the Saxons were to be allowed a period of grace before the Law was fully applied to them. The Crown refused to sanction this proposal, but a Law on these lines was enacted in 1846, when the Diet, incidentally, passed another Law making social conditions harder than ever.

The reactions of the non-Magyars were, of course, strongly unfavourable. The Saxons, who were experiencing a national renaissance of their own, protested vigorously against the identification of what they maintained to be by right and tradition a multinational state, with the Magyar element in it alone. They declared themselves opposed to union, and spun what threads they could to Vienna. The Roumanians could afford to be fairly indifferent about the language of an administration in which they did not participate and an education which they did not receive, but there was among them, naturally, much discontent with their miserable social conditions, and national feeling, after a period of quiescence, was growing stronger again with the increase in numbers and quality of their own educated class, and with the parallel movement (itself largely fostered by émigrés from Transylvania) in the Danubian Principalities. There was already considerable latent and embryonic irredentism among them, but when they revived an official programme, it was still that of 1791, for recognition of their 'nation' and their religion within the framework of the Transylvanian constitution. They, too were bitterly opposed to the union with Hungary, as making this impossible and as·calculated to bring them under even heavier Magyar pressure.

After the 1843 Diet, Metternich tried new tactics. A group of the younger Hungarian magnates, calling themselves the 'Progressive Conservatives', had come to the conclusion that some reform was necessary, and a certain measure of it even desirable, but it should be carried through by the government, with due safeguards against extremism, both social and national. In 1843 this group, then under the leadership of Count György Apponyi (its founder, Aurél Dessewffy, had died prematurely) reached agreement with Metternich on a programme of political authority and economic reform. The Föispáns were to undertake the direct administration of the counties, in which they were to enforce the government's will; where unable or unwilling to do so, they were to be replaced by 'administrators'. The Opposition was to be excluded, as far as possible, from the Diet, and the procedure of that body was to be thoroughly recast and made orderly. The customs union with Austria (which promised advantage to the magnates, for by this time the growth of population in Austria had gone so far that Hungary could place practically all her agricultural surplus there) was accepted, together with its consequences, the most disagreeable of which would be the introduction into Hungary of the tobacco monopoly. There was to be a big programme of public works carried through with the help of Austrian financial houses, and such internal reforms as seemed beneficial; the group was not entirely opposed to seeing noble land taxed.

Apponyi was now appointed Vice-Chancellor (in 1846 he became Chancellor), and his associate, Baron Samuel Jósika, Vice-Chancellor of Transylvania. Some items of the programme were put in hand immediately. Administrators were appointed in no less than eighteen counties, and some important public works initiated, including the regulation of the Tizsa, of which Széchenyi took charge. Legislation, however would have to wait for the next Diet, which was announced for the autumn of 1847, when its first business would be to elect a successor to the old Palatine, who had just died.

In preparation for this, the supporters of the regime, including many conservatives who were far from progressive, constituted themselves into a 'government party'. The Opposition, in reply, drew together, and in June 1847 produced an 'Oppositional Declaration'. Thanks to Deák, who drafted it, this document was meticulously loyal, but it condemned the existing regime, in the roundest of terms, as 'foreign and non-national' and unconstitutional, being contrary to the provisions of the Law of 1790. For the rest, since all fractions of the signatories had insisted on having their own wishes included, the Declaration emerged as a somewhat amorphous but very comprehensive document, representing the lowest common multiple, rather than the highest common factor, of Hungarian liberal and national aspirations. It demanded a genuinely national ministry, responsible to a parliament, exercising effective control over the collection and expenditure of revenue; extension of representation to non-nobles in the counties and municipalities; general equality before the law and equality of status for all 'received' religions; complete and compulsory redemption of all peasant servitudes, against compensation for the landlords[1]; taxation of noble lands, abolition of the *aviticitas* and the institution of an adequate credit system; freedom of the press and abolition of the censorship on books; the re-incorporation of the Partium and union with Transylvania, if voted by the Transylvanian Diet. On the tariff question it trod warily, but protested against the inequalities to which Hungary had previously been subjected in industrial and commercial respects. Hungary was prepared to negotiate amicably with the Austrian Lands, but not to have conditions imposed on her.

It was with these two programmes that the Diet met in the autumn of 1847. In spite of strong pressure by the government, the two parties were approximentely equal in

[1] Opinion on the peasant question throughout the Monarchy had been enormously influenced by the bloody Galician jacquerie of 1846.

strength, but the Liberals, who were led by Kossuth, (elected for Pest county, and now for the first time sitting in his own right) had, on the whole, the advantage in the Lower House. It could be assumed that a considerable fraction of the social reforms, the resistance to which was crumbling even among the magnates, would go through, but the question of the central political control was different. On this the government was determined not to give way, and in fact, after the Diet had duly elected the old Palatine's son, Stephen, to his father's office, it almost at once reached deadlock on this central question. This was still unresolved, and seemed, indeed, past resolving, when events in the outer world violently snapped it and within a few weeks brought the reformers what, if they could consolidate it, would amount to total victory.

7

REVOLUTION AND REACTION

On the night of 29 February – 1 March the news of the fall of Louis Philippe reached Vienna. The immediate reaction of the honest Viennese bourgeoisie was unromantic, but effectual; fearing that Metternich would organise a European crusade against the revolution, and would finance it by a new issue of uncovered paper money, it stampeded to the National Bank to change its notes into silver, and the Bank, whose reserves of silver were quite inadequate to meet a general run, had to close its doors. Kossuth's political genius rose to the occasion. Sensing in a flash the relevance to the situation of the centralists' demand (which he had previously not taken very seriously) for a responsible government for Hungary, he on 3 March submitted to the Lower House a draft Address to the Crown, which contained most of the Opposition's programme, but especially insisted on the need for a responsible government, as the only way to safeguard the nation against arbitrary misuse of its resources. The corollary, he added, was that Austria should receive similar institutions.

The Lower House accepted the Address with acclamation, but it could not even be submitted to the Magnates, for the government had called the Palatine and officers of the House to Vienna to consult on the possibility of dissolving the Diet and installing a dictatorial regime. But on the 13th revolution broke out in Vienna itself. Metternich resigned, as did Apponyi. The intimidated magnates in Pozsony now accepted the Address, which a deputation of both Houses, led by the Palatine, carried to Vienna. They were sped on their way by a mass demonstration of the youth of

Pest. Threatened on all sides by revolution and fearing that refusal would result in Hungary's declaring itself independent, the *Staatskonferenz* yielded. Ferdinand declared himself 'prepared to fulfil the wishes of the nation'. Count Lajos Batthyány, a Liberal magnate, was appointed provisional Minister President, and in his turn formed a provisional ministry – a team of all the talents, which included Széchenyi, Kossuth, Deák and Eötvös. It remained to give legal satisfaction to the nation's wishes, which the Diet now proceeded to formulate.

So far as the internal political and social structure of the country was concerned, this amounted to little more than translating into the form of draft laws the programme of the United Opposition. The form of state which emerged was that of a limited monarchy. The king, or in his absence, the Palatine, exercised his executive powers through a responsible ministry, resident in Budapest; no enactment by him was valid without the counter-signature of the competent minister. The 'responsibility' of the ministers was to a bi-cameral parliament, an Upper House, the composition of which was provisionally left unaltered, and a Lower House of deputies elected on a wide suffrage. The franchise for the counties and municipalities was extended similarly.

Taxation became universal. The tithe was abolished, as were all payments and services due from the holders of urbarial land of 'peasant' rank,[1] who thus became the freehold proprietors of their holdings; the compensation for the landlords was left 'to the honour of the nation'. The Patrimonial Courts disappeared; the law was to be equal for all. The *aviticitas* was abolished. All 'received' religions were placed on a footing of complete equality. Freedom of the press and of assembly were guaranteed. A National Guard was established.

[1] Only persons holding a quarter *sessio* or upwards qualified for this title. Holders of less than a quarter *sessio* ranked with landless men as 'cottars' (*zsellérek*).

The 'national' postulates of the Opposition also received full satisfaction. The Partium were reincorporated
unconditionally; the union with Transylvania was enacted,
subject to the consent of the next Transylvanian Diet.
The re-incorporation of the Military Frontier was tacitly
assumed in the provisions of the franchise Law which provided for its representation in parliament. The laws did
not touch overtly on the status of Croatia, but the validity
of the Hungarian case on the points in dispute between
Hungary and Croatia was similarly assumed by the provisions in the franchise Law which laid down the number
of representatives to be sent to parliament by the Frontier,
the Slavonian counties, the towns of Fiume and Eszék and
'the counties of Körös, Zagreb and Varasd', whose representatives, alone, were to attend the 'Provincial Diet' of
Croatia. The laws did not touch on the language question,
which remained as defined by previous legislation; only
the language of parliament was declared to be Magyar.

The *Staatskonferenz* accepted most of this without argument, declaring itself disinterested in any questions which
were of internal Hungarian concern. It was, on the other
hand, actively interested in the maintenance of the central
services, which it regarded as essential to the preservation
of the unity of the *Gesammtmonarchie*. It began by objecting
to the creation of a ministry of defence, or even one of
finance, and yielded only when its attitude evoked such a
storm as to reawaken the spectre of a declaration of independence. The resultant solution was in many respects
ambiguous. The draft laid down the principle that the
executive must 'respect the unity of the Crown and the
intangibility of the link with the Monarchy', but did not
define the nature of that link. The cabinet included a minister *a latere*, or liaison minister, resident in Vienna, whose
duty it was to represent Hungary in all matters of common
interest with the rest of the Monarchy, and whose counter-
signature was required for all enactments issued by the king

when acting in his wider capacity, but the fields of common interest were, again, not defined. They were tacitly assumed to include foreign affairs. In both defence and finance the Hungarians had their way: they got an independent minister of defence, under whose control (and thus that of parliament) the Hungarian Army now stood; the king reserved his rights only in respect of 'the employment of the Hungarian army outside the national frontiers, and appointments to military office'. The ministry of finance was entirely independent, and all revenues from the *camera* came under its jurisdiction. The Hungarians agreed that their country would have to contribute towards the expenses of the court, but the amount of the quota and the means of determining it were left unsettled, and no agreement was reached on the very crucial question whether Hungary was to take over a share of the accumulated national debt; so far, she had not consented to do so, but the Austrians had not accepted the position as definitive. The question of an independent Hungarian national bank had not been raised.

When this agreement, such as it was, had been reached, Ferdinand came to Pozsony and on 11 April gave his sanction to the corpus of legislation summarised above, and known to history as the 'April Laws'. The new government thereupon legally assumed office.

That April day was truly one of glory for Hungary; but how certain would its glory prove? Socially, the outlook seemed assured. The magnates were hostile, but unless supported from outside, they were too few to be dangerous. The young radicals' and students' demonstration in Pest on 15 March had helped frighten the magnates into quicker submission, but the students' 'twelve points' had contained little more than what the laws now gave. Further middle-class unrest showed itself only in the form of some anti-Jewish rioting; the burghers as a class were behind the new government. The ex-villein peasants were not interested in national politics, but in extending and consolidating their own gains. The cottars and agricultural labourers had, indeed, come out practically empty-handed, and remained so, for the question of partitioning the allodial land was hardly raised, and then only to be rejected (only the small vintners were ranked on the same footing as the villein peasants); but the mentality of most of this class was still pre-revolutionary. Thus the countryside, on the whole, remained quiet, although there were a few disturbances in the chronic storm-centre of the Tisza. The industrial workers could be disregarded, or repressed.

There were, however, two quarters from which danger threatened. One was 'Vienna', which had surrendered only reluctantly on the question of the central services, and would certainly endeavour to recover the lost ground if it was ever in a position to do so. The other was the camp of the discontented non-Magyars. Between these an alliance was quickly struck which in little over a year brought the whole work of the Hungarian reformers down in ruin.

By a piece of singular ill-fortune for Hungary, the office of Ban of Croatia happened to be vacant, and on 22 March, the day before his own resignation and just before the appointment of Batthyány was confirmed, Kolowrat secured the appointment to that post of one, Colonel Josip Jellačić, an enthusiastic 'Illyrian' and fanatical anti-Magyar. Three days later, Jellačić was installed by acclamation at a mass meeting in Zagreb, amid shouts for the realisation of the Triune Kingdom. Jellačić announced that he would not submit to 'the present Hungarian government', and when he went to Vienna to complete the formalities, refused to take the oath as Ban on the ground that this would prevent him 'from remaining a firm supporter of the Crown at the head of the Southern Slav Movement'. After many provocative gestures, he formally 'broke off relations' with the Hungarian government on 19 April.

On 10 May a gathering of Slovaks at Liptószentmiklós

asked for national rights within Hungary. On 15 May a mass meeting of Roumanians at Balászfalva (Blaj) protested against the Transylvanian Diet's voting the union with Hungary before the Roumanians were properly represented on it. The Saxons demonstrated in a similar sense. It is true that when, on 30 May, the Diet pronounced for the union, the Saxons voted with the majority, but this was a matter of tactics. They remained only partially reconciled, while the Roumanians were openly hostile.

At this time the court was in a painful quandary. Its most urgent needs were to prevent revolution from breaking out where it had not yet done so, and to find reinforcements for its armies in Italy. Eternal hotbed of potential revolution as Hungary was, it had up to that stage behaved completely loyally; it was also the biggest potential source of reinforcements, especially since the court had conceded the claim of the Hungarian ministry of defence to authority over the Military Frontier regiments. Batthyány, who visited the court in Innsbruck early in June, promised to get the new Diet to vote 40,000 recruits for Italy if the court would disavow Jellačić, and accordingly, Jellačić, who in his turn set out for Innsbruck on 12 June, was icily received, and hardly had he left Innsbruck when a royal rescript rebuked him publicly for disobedience to orders and divested him of his honours and dignities.

He was, however, being secretly encouraged and used as mouthpiece by the Austrian centralists, led by the minister of war, Count Latour. Batthyány met him in Vienna, and offered him very wide concessions for Croatia, but his reply was that he could accept nothing less than the central control by Vienna of defence and finance, as well as Hungary's promise to take over part of the national debt. The negotiations, of course, broke down.

Meanwhile, the Serbs, encouraged from Vienna and also from Belgrade (which had sent some 10,000 armed irregulars to help), had held a congress which had demanded national and territorial autonomy, in alliance with Croatia, and had opened hostilities in south Hungary. Kossuth replied on 11 July by asking parliament to authorise the raising of 200,000 men 'to defend the endangered fatherland', and a credit of 42 million florins. Ten days later the request for reinforcements for the armies in Italy came before the House, and now the radicals, led by Kossuth, persuaded the House to refuse the men except on political conditions which were probably *ultra vires* and certainly absurd.

But the Austrian 'reaction' was now settling in the saddle. In mid-June Windischgrätz had put down the rising in Prague and converted the Czechs to loyalty. At the end of July Charles Albert capitulated to Radetzky in Italy. On 4 September Jellačić was formally reinstated in all his dignities; on 11 September he led an army across the Drave. Batthyány resigned; pending the appointment of a new government, the authority, under the Palatine, passed to a Committee of National Defence under Kossuth, who, the royal sanction for the Army vote not having been received, authorised the conscription of the new force and the issue of paper money to cover the expenses. The last ho peofcompromise disappeared when Count Lamberg, whom the Palatine had appointed Royal plenipotentiary, with instructions to negotiate with Jellačić, was lynched by a mob in Pest.

The successor to Batthyány's government was never installed, and in its default Kossuth was now the *de facto* dictator of Hungary. It was open war between Hungary and the court, and, at first, the Hungarians had the better of it. The Imperial authorities, their hands full with a renewed outbreak of revolution in Vienna, were unable to help Jellačić, who proved a very incompetent leader in the field. Heavily defeated by the young Hungarian armies, who had thrown up a leader of genius in Arthur Görgey, a youthful ex-officer of the Imperial forces, he was driven back across the frontier. But Vienna capitulated on 28 October and on 2 December Ferdinand abdicated in favour

of his nephew, Francis Joseph. Kossuth, rightly seeing that
the measure was directed against Hungary – its whole purpose was to release the regime from Ferdinand's pledge to
respect the April Laws – refused to recognise the abdica-
tion as legal for Hungary. A few days later, Windischgrätz and Jellačić led two new armies into Hungary, with
the avowed purpose of crushing the 'rebels'. Their first
advance carried them into Pest in a fortnight. Windischgrätz proudly announced final victory, and on 4 March an
Imperial manifesto announced the dissolution of the
Austrian Constituent Assembly and the constitution of the
entire Monarchy as 'an indivisible and indissoluble constitutional Austrian Empire'. This was to consist of a
number of 'crownlands', and Hungary was to be par-
titioned into no less than five such units: Hungary proper,
Transylvania (to include the Partium), Croatia-Slavonia
(with the Muraköz, and including Fiume), the Military
Frontier and a new 'Serbian Voivody'. The Hungarian
constitution, said the manifesto, remained in being so far
as its provisions did not conflict with those of the new
constitution, and subject to the introduction of institutions
guaranteeing equal rights for all nationalities and 'locally
current' languages.

To this the Hungarian parliament, meeting in the Calvinist church at Debrecen, replied on 14 April by proclaiming Hungary, within its historic frontiers, a fully independent sovereign state. The House of Habsburg was
declared forfeit of the throne; Kossuth became provisional
Head of the State with the title of Governor (Kormányzó).

For a little longer the issue still hung in the balance.
Windichgrätz' assumption that Hungarian resistance was
broken proved premature. Kossuth's eloquence and genius
rallied his supporters to extraordinary efforts. Görgey, in
a series of brilliantly conducted operations, drove the Imperial armies far back, and even recaptured Buda. A Polish
volunteer, General Bem, carried through another most

skilful campaign in Transylvania. But the odds were too
heavy, especially since many of the Hungarian officers, including Görgey himself, were caught in a conflict of con-
science over the dethronement of the Habsburgs. Mutual
suspicion between Görgey and Kossuth hampered the conduct of the operations. The foreign Powers to which Kossuth appealed for help refused to move; on the other hand,
the Czar Nicholas I, who was concerned lest the revolution
spread to Poland, had already intimated his readiness to
support Francis Joseph in the interest of monarchic solidarity. Now Francis Joseph asked his help. In June two
Russian armies entered Hungary, bringing the forces of
Austria and her allies up to some 370,000 men, with 1,200
guns, against the Hungarians' 152,000 men and 450 guns.
The defenders were driven inexorably back into south-
eastern Hungary. On 11 August Kossuth handed over his
powers to Görgey and fled to Turkey, with a few of his
most obstinate supporters. On the 13th Görgey surrendered at Világos to the senior Russian commander, Marshal
Paskievicz, who reported to the Czar:

'Hungary lies at the feet of Your Majesty.'

The capitulation of Világos was followed by another of
the reigns of terror of which Hungarian history is so full.
At first the country was placed under a military administration headed by Haynau, the notorious 'hyaena of
Brescia', who boasted that 'he would see to it that there
should be no more revolutions in Hungary for a hundred
years'. Thirteen Imperial officers who had served as
generals in the Hungarian army were hanged at Arad on
6 October and on the same day Batthyány, who had tried
to cut his own throat, was shot. There were many more
sentences of death, and about 100 executions; then an
amnesty saved the lives of the remaining destined victims,
but for a while, the fortress-prisons were full. The rank
and file of the *Honvéd* were as a rule conscripted into the
Imperial forces and sent to foreign stations.

In July 1850 the military regime was replaced by a civilian one, which was at first called 'provisional' but made 'definitive' in 1853. The treatment to which Hungary was now submitted was no longer brutal, but carefully calculated to eliminate all traces of the nation's independence. The division of the country into the five crownlands was confirmed, Inner Hungary being further subdivided, for administrative purposes, into five Districts, each under a commissioner, and Transylvania into five more. The autonomy of the counties and municipalities was abolished. The administration was purely absolutist and bureaucratic; it was conducted by a civil service drawn chiefly from the Czech and German districts of Bohemia, and reinforced by a newly instituted gendarmerie. The language of administration and of most secondary and all higher education was German; primary education was, in principle, in the pupil's mother-tongue. The tariff wall between Hungary and Austria was abolished and the tobacco monopoly introduced into Hungary.

The regime was not in every respect unbeneficial, especially to the poorer classes and the nationalities. The peasants benefiting by the 1848 reform, about 625,000 heads of families, were left in possession of their freeholds, the average size of which was estimated at about 12 *hold*. No compensation whatever was required of them. The more enterprising among them developed into solid yeoman farmers. The nationalities enjoyed more cultural freedom, on the lowest level, than before. 2,000 kilometres of railways were built, and a big network of roads. There was also some industrial development, and some credit institutions came into being.

But for the backbone of the nation, the middle and smaller nobles, the times were ruinous. The compensation paid to the former landlords (certain aulic favourites excepted) was not only niggardly, but paid only after long delays. Money cost 30-40 per cent. Some 20,000 foreclosures were made in under twenty years. A large part of this class fell into destitution. Such wealth as the country now produced flowed largely into the coffers of the Viennese holding banks. General taxation was crushingly heavy; the yield of direct taxation before 1848 had been 4,280,000 florins, and of indirect, 5,300,000; the corresponding figures in 1857 were 41,500,000 and 65,600,000. These burdens weighed as heavily on the nominal beneficiaries of the regime as on its avowed victims, and so, for that matter, did the Germanisation and the centralised bureaucracy. 'What you are getting as punishment,' a Croat once remarked to a Magyar, 'we are getting as reward.'

Thus almost every class and every nationality in Hungary was soon chafing against the absolutist regime, but until its grip relaxed, they did no more than chafe. The exiled Kossuth sought tirelessly for an international situation which should give Hungary back the full independence which she had bestowed on herself in 1849, but although some foreign Powers were willing to use Hungary as a tool, none was prepared to risk a new policy of adventure, and, no less important, it had been by no means all the nation that had wanted full separation in 1849, or wanted it now. At least as numerous were those who desired an accommodation with the Crown, provided that it did justice to Hungary's historic rights and her needs.

As time went on, the adherents of the latter view gradually fell into line behind Deák, who now emerged from the retirement into which he had withdrawn early in 1849. Deák had disapproved of the dethronement of the Habsburgs, in which he had had no hand, and believed in the necessity of agreement with Austria. He maintained with complete firmness that the April Laws were legally valid, and that any subsequent modification of the situation created by them, unless made by agreement with Hungary's lawful parliament, was legally null and void, and unacceptable. But he recognised that the laws regulating

Hungary's relationship with the rest of the Monarchy were in truth imperfect, and agreed that a modification of them by consent would be acceptable.

An important point in Deák's thesis was that while recognising no negotiating partner save Hungary's own crowned king, he was prepared that the agreement when negotiated should contain provision for consultation with the constitutional representatives of Austria; he even thought such provision essential, for, like Kossuth, he was convinced that constitutionalism in Hungary would not be safe if the monarch was absolute elsewhere. An unacknowledged corollary was that Hungary, while legally uninterested, was in reality vitally concerned with what form the Austrian constitutional settlement took: it was very important for her that it should be one which rested on factors whose interests coincided with her own.

In return for an acceptable settlement, Deák offered Hungary's loyalty; so long as it was refused, he advised the nation to practise passive resistance to all illegal demands made by the regime and its agents.

The possibility of an accommodation became real after Austria's defeat at Solferino in 1859 had convinced Francis Joseph that the centralist forces in the Monarchy were not strong enough to hold down simultaneously all the elements of national and social opposition. It was, however, only slowly that he came to recognise the inevitability of making concessions precisely towards Hungary, the *bête noire* of Austrian absolutism and centralism. He began by inviting notables from his various dominions to form a 'Reinforced Imperial Council', but the Hungarians who accepted the invitation, although all belonging to the extreme aulic aristocracy, yet combined with their Bohemian colleagues to insist on the restoration of the 'historic constitutions'. The 'October Diploma' of 1861 in fact reinstated these on paper, but half-heartedly, for while restoring the chancellery and the *Consilium*, it still provided for a strong central executive and a *Reichsrat* with competence extending to all questions affecting the Monarchy as a whole. Hungary's separate status was recognised only in a provision that questions relating only to the western half of the Monarchy were to come before a 'Restricted Reichsrat', to which the Hungarian Diet might be regarded as a partner. Then, four months later, came the 'February Patent' of 1861, nominally an elucidation of the Diploma, and this in fact carried the centralisation a long step further. The competences of the local legislatures were severely reduced, while the *Reichsrat* blossomed into a genuine central bi-cameral legislature, to which Hungary was required to send its representatives, to meet on an equal footing those of the other Lands. Hungary would thus have been degraded to the position of one Land among the others, and, to add to the grievance of principle, placed in a permanent minority, being allotted only 85 seats out of the 343 in the *Reichsrat*. Further, although the Voivody, which had satisfied no one, had been dissolved under the Diploma, Transylvania and Croatia continued to figure as separate Lands, and the Military Frontier was maintained.

Elections (on the 1848 franchise) were held, but the Diet which then met flatly refused, under Deák's guidance, to recognise the legality of the Diploma or the Patent; the only difference between its members related to the form in which the refusal should be expressed. Francis Joseph replied by dissolving, first the Diet, then the county congregations, and reinstating a new *Provisorium*, chiefly military in character. Deák, however, stuck to his point with quiet persistence, and by this time Hungary was not alone. Every political factor in the Monarchy was in arms against absolutism, and while the aims of most of these were mutually incompatible, Hungary found a valuable ally in the German 'Constitutional Party' in Austria (very powerful because of its connections with Viennese finance), which saw in the realisation of the Hungarian wishes the best guarantee against the Slavs gaining the overweight in Austria.

In 1865 Francis Joseph abolished the *Provisorium* and suspended the February Patent. In December the Diet was re-convoked, and in January 1866 the reunion of Transylvania with Hungary was in effect sanctioned by an order permitting the Transylvanian Diet to attend that of Pest. Negotiations for a settlement now opened seriously. They were interrupted by the outbreak of the Austro-Prussian war, whose disastrous course for Austria put the Crown in a position in which it could not easily have refused much more extravagant demands – for which, indeed, the more extreme Hungarian nationalists pressed. Deák, however, as he had not abated his terms when Hungary was weak, refused to raise them in her hour of advantage. Agreement was reached at the beginning of 1867. Hungary recovered her integrity and her complete independence in internal affairs. Foreign affairs and defence were designated as questions common to Austria and Hungary, each being placed under a 'common' minister; the unitary nature of the defence services was further safeguarded by a stipulation that 'all questions relating to the unitary command, control and internal organisation of the whole army, and consequently also of the Hungarian army, as a constituent part of the whole army, are recognised as falling within the competence of His Majesty'. A third 'common' minister was in charge of the finance for these two portfolios. The problems relating to these portfolios were discussed by delegations from the two parliaments. The proportion of the common expenditure to be born by the two halves of the Monarchy was initially fixed at 70-30, but was to be re-discussed, by the Delegations, every ten years, as were questions relating to commercial and tariff agreements; for a start, the whole Monarchy formed a single customs unit.

On 17 February, after this had been agreed, a responsible Hungarian ministry was formed under Count Gyula Andrássy, who had been Deák's principal assistant in the negotiations. On 29 March parliament accepted the 'Compromise', and on 8 June Francis Joseph was crowned and gave royal assent to the laws. The Crown had throughout made its consent to its concessions to the Hungarians conditional on their reaching agreement with Croatia and enacting legislation to safeguard in Hungary the principle of national equality which had been cardinal in Austria since 1848. Negotiations on both points had been proceeding, and on the former a committee appointed by the 1861 Diet had produced a remarkable interim report. Now the discussions were resumed, and laws on both subjects were sanctioned in 1868. Under the Hungaro-Croat Compromise (*Nagodba*), the Croats were forced to renounce the hope of making theirs a wholly distinct polity within the Monarchy: it remained linked with Hungary, and although the wording carefully described it as the theoretical equal of Hungary proper, the Ban of Croatia was nominated by the Hungarian Minister President. Its territorial claims were, on the whole, generously treated: it received the Slavonian Counties and, in theory, also Dalmatia, although not Fiume or the Muraköz. It was represented on the Delegations when Austro-Hungarian 'common' affairs were discussed. Questions left to Hungary as *interna* under the main Compromise were divided again into Hungaro-Croat 'common' affairs and Croat *interna*; the chief of the former were coinage and currency, commercial policy, and communications, while all cultural affairs and local administration and justice were Croat *interna*. Croatia sent representatives to the Hungarian Diet for the discussion on 'common' affairs; they were allowed to speak in Croat. Other affairs were dealt with in the Croat Sabor. The official language for Croat *interna* was Croat. Croatia's contribution to the common expenditure was fixed at a figure which made full allowance for its low taxable capacity.

The Nationalities Law began with a remarkable preamble which stated that all citizens of Hungary formed, politically, a single nation, the indivisible, unitary Hungarian nation, and that their equality of rights could be qualified only in respect of the official usage of the various languages and that only so far as necessitated by the unity of the country, the demands of administration and the prompt execution of justice. To meet these requirements, the language of parliament, administration, and the courts, and of the university, was Magyar, but non-Magyar languages were offered ample scope in the administration and justice, from the county level down. The lowest level officials were bound to use the language of the members of the public with whom they were dealing. In principle, every schoolchild was to receive instruction in his own mother-tongue up to the point where higher academic instruction began. The churches had the right to prescribe the language of instruction in the schools controlled by them. The free use of any language in private life was guaranteed.

8

THE ERA OF DUALISM

THE Compromise placed Hungary in a position which in many ways was more favourable than she had enjoyed since Mohács; in some respects, the nation had never before in its history been so truly master of its own destinies. From Pozsony to the Iron Gates, from the Tatras to Nagykanizsa, a single law reigned, administered by one government, which was able to express its will, and that of the parliament to which it was answerable, in a far wider field and with far fewer limitations than ever before. In all internal affairs – and that term included the Hungaro-Croat relationship and the nationalities question – the Crown retained only those limited powers of intervention which the central European political philosophy of the day commonly allowed to a constitutional monarch. These included the right to appoint the Minister President and to dissolve or prorogue parliament, but not to rule indefinitely without a parliament, nor to veto legislation enacted by it; although this last omission was largely rendered superfluous by his power to choose the Minister President of his will and by a right conceded to him by convention to give or refuse 'preliminary sanction' to a Bill before it was introduced.

It was true that Hungary was not autonomous in the conduct of her foreign relations, or her defence. For these purposes, she still formed only a part of the indissolubly and inseparably interlinked complex of the Habsburg Monarchy, and her interests in these fields had to be co-ordinated with those of its other components, through 'common institutions'. Yet even here the improvement in

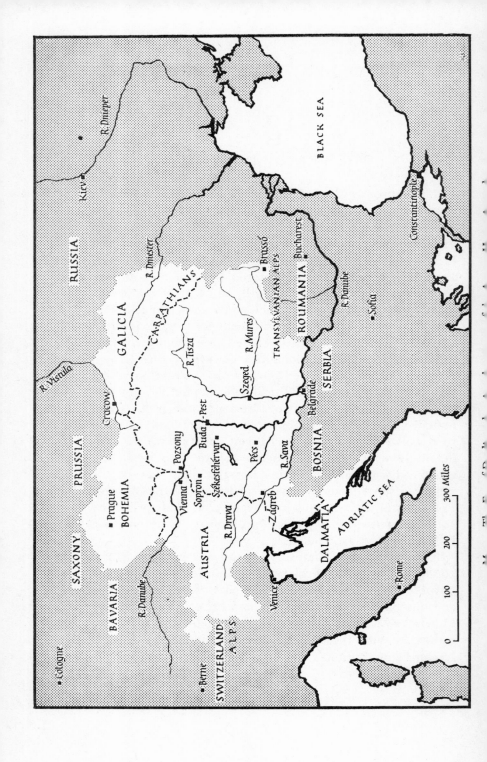

her position was enormous. While the conduct of foreign
affairs was still the monarch's prerogative, he now had to
exercise it through a responsible minister, who, by convention, was chosen alternately from the 'Austrian' and
Hungarian halves of the Monarchy. Moreover, any likeli-
hood that Hungary's interests would in the future be
sacrificed, as they had been so often in the past, in causes
which did not interest her, was much diminished by the
pragmatic fact that after the loss of Lombardo-Venetia
Hungary was larger in area than the rest of the Habsburg
dominions put together and by far the largest single unit
in them. It was easily arguable that the protection afforded
her by the Austrian connection now far outweighed its
dangers.

She had an equal voice, in law, in the tariff policy of the
Monarchy and in other questions affecting its economic
and financial interests as a whole. The customs union with
Austria could be denounced; for the present, it met the
interests of the leading Hungarian circles. The quota of
30 per cent which she had agreed to pay towards the
common expenditure was, again, subject to revision;
meanwhile, it could not be regarded as inequitable.

The real and large benefits which the Compromise conferred on Hungary were, however, half-hidden from the
eye of the nation by the mists of suspicion engendered by
the centuries in which the Austrian connection had brought
it so much disadvantage; whereas there were certain
points on which it was difficult for it to feel itself truly
independent, even now. Easily the most conspicuous of
these were those connected with the common army, over
which, as has been said, Francis Joseph had retained a large
measure of control. It was psychologically impossible for
him to regard this force otherwise than as the instrument
of his personal rule, which must place loyalty to himself
above any other consideration, including that of national
sentiment. This was also the spirit of his senior officers,

who continued to regard all national feelings, and especially Hungarian national feeling, as a threat to the integrity of the Monarchy. Flagrant proof of this was given by the prolonged resistance offered by them – which it took all Andrássy's personal influence with the monarch to overcome – to the dissolution of the Military Frontier. In the course of this controversy Francis Joseph also sanctioned the establishment of a secondline force, the *Honvédség*, in which Magyar was the language of command; but he refused absolutely to admit any language but German in the central army, and this the Hungarians regarded as another proof that in this field they were still regarded as mere subjects, and potentially rebellious ones at that.

A large measure of central control had survived also – partly, perhaps, because neither Deák nor Andrássy was well versed in the subject – in the finances of the Monarchy. There was only a single Bank of Issue, and Hungary had little control over its operations. In the numerous other questions which the Compromise left unclear, and over which Austria and Hungary soon clashed, it was not always the Hungarians who had the bigger grounds of complaint, but they had some grievances which were real.

Yet for all its imperfections, the Compromise still created a situation which was replete with possibilities for constructive work. Unfortunately, the political evolution of the country took from the outset a line which precluded the full utilisation of those possibilities by concentrating on the 'question of public law', i.e., the question whether the Compromise was to be accepted, altered, or completely overthrown.

It was on this question that the parties aligned themselves as soon as Hungary's parliamentary life proper began. Deák's followers, the men who had voted the Compromise and were now prepared to work on the basis of it, organised themselves in a party known by their leader's name. The view diametrically opposite to theirs was represented in parliament by a group known as the 'Party of '48', or 'Extreme Left', who rejected anything short of the position established by the April Laws. A third group, led by Kálmán Tisza and Kálmán Ghyczy, constituted itself under the name of the 'Left Centre'. Its programme, formulated in the so-called 'Bihar Points', emphasised its devotion to constitutional methods, but was tantamount to a complete repudiation of the Compromise, since it rejected any institutions which it described as incompatible with the nation's independence, as established in Law X of 1790, and consequently demanded an independent army and complete autarchy in the fields of finance and commercial policy.

This alignment was perhaps inevitable at the time, in view not only of the natural difficulty experienced by the national spirit, accustomed as it was by long habit to see politics exclusively in the terms of the struggle against 'Austrian' oppression, now to adapt itself to a new outlook, but also when the composition of the parliament itself is remembered; for new elections were not held when the Compromise was made law, so that the parliament of 1867 was, in membership, simply the Diet of 1865, whose sole *raison d'être* had been the settlement of the question of public law, and the two main parties were merely the successors of the groups which had formed in the course of the earlier discussions. But what were initially natural interests hardened afterwards into obsessional fixations. The evolution was fatally facilitated by the withdrawal of the Crown from its traditional role of protector of national and social minorities, and by failure to redress the grave social-political imbalance thus created, by introducing a franchise wide enough to enable those classes to speak for themselves. Sheltered by a franchise which was already narrow, and which an amendment which became law in 1874 restricted still further,[1]

[1] This reduced the number of voters from 6·7 per cent of the

the two great groups into which the 'political nation' fell simply ignored, by tacit agreement, social and (once the Law of 1868 was passed) national questions; or if these did raise their heads, combined to repress them; concentrating instead on barren constitutional issues in which prestige all too often played a larger part than real interest.

The Deák Party got off to a good start. It negotiated successfully the *Nagodba* and the Nationalities Law, and enacted a number of Laws consequent on the Compromise and a whole number more bringing the administrative, judicial, confessional and economic system of the country up to date. It was able, moreover, to sun itself in an air of prosperity. The harvests were good, and the big land-owners flourished. Foreign capital scented opportunities, and poured into the country. There was a banking and business boom in which speculators made quick fortunes, and a big programme of railway construction, most of it financed by foreign capital on which the state guaranteed the interest, was undertaken.

For all that, the position of the party was never easy. It kept its position owing to its good organisation, the support of the Transylvanians, and, in no small measure, the great personal prestige enjoyed by its leaders. But it never had more than a minority of the country behind it. The Nagodba had been got through the Sabor only by packing that body with the help of an electoral Law especially de-vised for the occasion, and Croat public opinion was un-mistakably against it. The nationalities of Inner Hungary were equally discontented. When the Law had first been discussed in draft in 1861, the Slovak, Serb and Roumanian representatives had opposed even the idea of a politically

population (1870) to 5·9 per cent by raising the property qualification. It is true that this change was not aimed against the proletariat or the non-Magyars, most of whom were already excluded under the earlier franchise, but against the Magyar opponents of the Compro-mise.

32. *A Kossuth bond to raise liberation funds in U.S.A.*

33. *Ferencz Deák: ref. p. 140*

unitary state, however great the freedom enjoyed in it by
a member of a national minority. The Slovaks had wanted
an autonomous 'Slovak Territory of Upper Hungary', the
Serbs, a near-independent Voivodina, and the Roumanians,
at least the maintenance of Transylvanian autonomy, with
corporate rights in it for themselves. In 1868 they had repeated these demands, and alternatively had proposed that
Hungary should be constituted as a multinational state with
six official languages, and corresponding administrative and
electoral divisions. The Law had been imposed on them by
force majeure, and its enactment had been followed by widespread unrest in several districts.

But the defenders of the Compromise were also under
constant fire from the other flank. Kossuth, still the most
popular Hungarian, had from his exile addressed to Deák
an impassioned 'Cassandra Letter', prophesying woe to the
instrument and accusing its author of having sacrificed the
honour and vital interests of the country to a short-lived
and illusory expediency. Few Hungarians at that time were
prepared to follow Kossuth the whole way; even the
Extreme Left, which went no further than 1848, could
muster only seven representatives in the 1867 Parliament.
But the feeling that Hungary had not made a good enough
bargain was widespread. The Left Centre had a large
parliamentary representation, and much popular support.
A free vote in the Magyar districts would probably have
gone heavily against the Compromise. As it was, when
elections were held in 1869 they brought the 'national
Opposition' considerable gains, and that although the
government had resorted to a good deal of pressure.

The Deák Party, however, still commanded a comfortable majority, and for another year or two things still went
well. Andrássy, in particular, was able on two notable
occasions both to demonstrate in striking fashion the
strength of Hungary's position, and to reinforce it. In
1870, while still Hungarian Minister President, he was

yet able to veto a plan, strongly urged by the Austrian war party, to intervene in the Franco-Prussian War in the hope of recovering for Austria the hegemony in Germany. In 1871, when Austro-Hungarian Foreign Minister, he thwarted a plan for reorganising the western half of the Monarchy on a federalist basis more favourable to Czech wishes.

But already matters were taking a turn for the worse. The personal composition of the Party deteriorated. Deák grew old and ill; Eötvös died; Andrássy moved to the Ballhausplatz. The government found that it had over-reached itself financially, especially on the railways programme; there were big budgetary deficits, and ugly rumours of personal corruption. The 1872 elections brought both the Left Centre and the Extreme Left large gains, while the Deák Party lost further members to a new Conservative Party. Then came the great financial crash of 1873, which pricked the bubble of the boom and swept away many insecurely-founded fortunes.

People were talking hopelessly of 'collapse' when the situation was transformed by a volte-face on the part of Tisza (Ghyczy had already crossed the floor), who announced himself ready to put the Bihar Points into cold storage until a more favourable moment; pending the arrival of this he would, in order to avert complete collapse, work on the basis of the existing Compromise. His motives were, of course, much discussed, and he was widely accused of having sold his principles for the sake of office, but the truth seems to be that he had come to realise that Hungary was simply not strong enough to challenge the Crown and the nationalities simultaneously, and had decided that the only practicable course was to suspend hostilities on the one front while consolidating the other. However this may be, he fused his followers with the remnants of Deák's in a new 'Liberal Party', pledged to the maintenance of the Compromise, and that Party thereafter remained continuously in office for thirty years, during sixteen of which (1875–1890) Tisza himself held the Minister Presidency.

The strength of the Left Centre had lain in the Magyar squires and squireens of the Alföld. When Tisza changed sides, many of these men followed their leader, so that, taking them together with the old Deákists, the Liberal Party now included a substantial proportion of Hungary's propertied classes. It still, however, had against it not only those factors in the country, such as the non-Magyars, who were against the Compromise for giving Hungary too much independence, but also those stalwarts who continued to oppose it for giving too little. The Magyar farmers and *civites* of the Alföld towns persisted in swearing by Kossuth and '48, and in rallying behind those who claimed to represent these magic traditions. Against both these forces the Liberal Party maintained itself by a brilliant internal organisation and by electoral devices. As the Magyar masses were difficult to dragoon, Tisza in 1879 carried through a redistribution of constituencies, the effect of which was that the Magyar districts of the Alföld elected only one deputy to several thousand constituents. In the non-Magyar districts, the educational qualifications confined the number of voters to what was sometimes no more than a handful, and they were quite simply coerced by administrative pressure into returning the government's nominees. By these means the party regularly secured comfortable parliamentary majorities, but its rule was simply that of a clique, and it was the achievements, good and ill, of that clique, not the free interplay of social and national forces, which made Hungary what it was at the end of the nineteenth century.

It is impossible to deny that those achievements were impressive in many fields. By the end of the period, financial order had been restored and although the national debt was still heavy, the most exorbitant loans had been paid off or funded on better terms. Budgets were balanced and the national credit was good. Foreign, as well as Austrian, capital had continued to find the country an attractive field of investment. With this help the grandiose programme of railway construction had been completed, the main rivers had been made navigable, and roads improved. This all-important first step had made possible further modernisation in almost every field. Agriculture still employed over 65 per cent of the population, but other occupations were gaining on it. The nascent industry of the first years had been set back by the crash of 1873, which ruined a great number of enterprises, and the customs union with Austria had retarded its rebirth; but after about 1890 the state had begun to encourage it by loans, subsidies, government contracts and similar devices, and by 1900 nearly a million men and 200,000 women (13 per cent of the gainfully employed population) were employed in mining and industry; the proportion in central and northern Hungary was considerably higher. The vast majority of the 'industrial enterprises' were, indeed, still tiny establishments of the village blacksmith or suburban cobbler class, but the larger establishments of 'factory' status were growing fast in number and size. The most firmly based were those which utilised the local natural resources: flour-mills, breweries, sugar refineries, sawmills, tanneries, but there was a growing metallurgical industry, and the mining of both coal and iron employed a considerable number of workers. Trade, too, had expanded largely, and the growing complexity of the new society had brought with it a big expansion of both the administrative and the professional classes. The 1900 census gave over 200,000 persons gainfully employed in the public services (excluding the army) and the professions.

Agriculture itself had made big advances: methods had been improved and yields raised. The area both under cereals and under intensive crops had risen sharply, and the national production of agricultural products had nearly doubled between 1870 and 1890.

The growth of the non-agricultural occupations had brought with it that of the towns. A quarter of the population still lived in scattered farms or small hamlets and only some 20 per cent in 'towns', but the latter figure was rising year by year. Budapest (now a single city) alone had a population of nearly 800,000, having doubled since 1880. Szeged had 102,000, Szabadka over 80,000, Debrecen 75,000, and a dozen more towns were on or near the 50,000 mark. The civic pride of many of these was attested by imposing public buildings. Thought and money had been lavished on the endeavour to make Budapest, in particular, a capital worthy of a great, and independent country and the peer of Vienna. Besides the famous Suspension Bridge, the child of Széchenyi's inspiration, four more bridges for road traffic and one for rail now spanned the Danube. An immense new royal palace crowned one end of Buda Hill; the other was laid out as a public garden, behind cunningly reconstructed bastions. From its walls the eye looked across the great river on to the 'corso' on which society strolled in front of a long row of fashionable hotels and cafés; behind these were the luxury shopping streets, and a forest of roofs above which there rose the great contours of the National Museum, the University, the Opera House, the Court Theatre, the Palace of the Academy. Upstream the waters washed the feet of the vast Gothic Parliament, architecturally inspired by that of Westminster; beyond it again, the green pleasure-gardens of the Margaret Island. Behind all this stretched huge quarters of humbler buildings, and away to the south, a forest of chimneys indicated Csepel Island, the site of Hungary's most important heavy industry.

In 1900 Inner Hungary had two universities, and Croatia one. Besides these there was a big polytechnic, afterwards promoted to university status, and a large number of colleges of law, theology, agriculture, mining, etc. Intellectual life was active. The contribution made by Hungary during this age to European civilisation was more than respectable: the names of the great physicist, Lorand Eötvös, and of Ignaz Semmelweiss, alone suffice to attest this. The generation which succeeded it tends to rank its achievements in the creative arts, qualitatively, below those of its predecessor and its successors: it is true that the men who first made Hungary glorious in these fields – Vörösmarty, Petöfi, Arany, Madách, Jókai, Liszt, Erkel – were either dead before the era opened, or had their best work behind them, and Bartók, Kodály, Ady were yet to come. But quantitatively, its production both in literature and in music was very big, and Hungary also produced exponents of the visual arts who achieved world fame.

Yet pride in these achievements – and the celebrations of its millennium in which the nation indulged in 1896 were the occasion of extraordinary self-congratulation – could not alter the truth that the era had failed to solve a whole series of problems inherited from the past, and had even seen the creation (not always through its own fault) of new ones. Its proud structure concealed weaknesses which were destined, only a few years later, to bring everything which it had built up, indeed, the whole edifice of Historic Hungary itself, toppling to the ground.

Among these unsolved problems, the most conspicuous were those of the non-Magyar nationalities, and of Croatia.

The history of Hungary's relations with the nationalities after 1867 is the same dismal hen-and-egg story as before 1848, embittered on both sides by the memories of the intervening years. As we have said, the nationalities had accepted the Law of 1868 only under *force majeure*, and few of them thereafter showed any wish to make a success of it; the majority continued to hope openly for a situation to arise in which at least their old programmes could be revived.

But neither had many Magyars accepted in their hearts the notion that the primacy which the Law allowed the Magyar language was simply a pragmatic concession to administrative convenience, and that Hungary was no more the Magyars' state than that of the Ruthenes or Roumanians. For them, the Magyar national character of the state was axiomatic, and the conduct of the nationalities in and after 1848, and the attitude of Vienna towards them, had only confirmed their conviction that the very survival of the Hungarian state depended on the maintenance of its Magyar character.

While Deák and Eötvös were still there to exercise a restraining influence, the Law was still, up to a point, observed, but even then the national character of the administration was complete; that is to say, the officials might deal with the public in the local language – and indeed, local administration was so conducted up to the last, of necessity and not, as a rule, reluctantly – but they did so as the representatives of a state which identified itself with Magyardom, and were seldom admitted to the service of the state unless they accepted the identification. Any cultural aspirations on the part of the nationalities, above the humblest level, even where permitted, were eyed with suspicion. The advent of the Liberal regime brought a further change for the worse. Now the whole public atmosphere at the centre of affairs (it is fair to make this qualification, for there were many localities which took their own multi-lingual character as natural and harmless; it was a case of the higher, the worse) became charged with poison. Parliamentary demagogues, and the national press which aped their tone, treated as treasonable even protests against non-fulfilment of the Law itself, and those daring so to protest were overwhelmed with the most intemperate abuse.

The Magyarisation of the educational system, of which so much has been written, was at first justified by its

authors, as it had been in the 1830s, as the necessary
means of producing a Magyar administrative class, but the
target was soon enlarged as, by a natural transition, it
came to be assumed that all members of society above the
peasant-worker level should at least speak and understand
Magyar, and before long chauvinists were again dreaming
of a day when the whole population should be Magyar.
When the era opened, the hands of the state were tied by
the fact that nearly all primary and secondary education
was then in the hands of the churches, whose autonomy
the Nationalities Law expressly recognised. In fact, the
only measures of Magyarisation imposed by law on the
churches, for many years, were that in 1879 the teaching
of the Magyar language, as a subject, during a number of
hours to be prescribed by the minister of cults and education, was made compulsory in primary schools, whose
teachers had to be qualified to give this instruction, and
that in 1883 Magyar language and literature were made
compulsory subjects in the two top forms of secondary
schools. These provisions did not greatly alter the nature
of the instruction given in the schools maintained by the
two Orthodox churches (Serbian and Roumanian) or by
the Transylvanian Saxons; the less so, as they remained
largely on paper. The Serbs and Roumanians, however,
possessed few establishments above the primary level, and
permission to add to their number was regularly refused.
The higher direction of the Roman Catholic and Greek
catholic churches; and the Lutheran outside Transylvania,
not to mention the Calvinist (which was purely Magyar in
any case) was Magyar even where the congregations belonged to another people, and their own authorities saw
to it that all secondary education in their schools, with
trivial exceptions, should be in Magyar, and Magyar was
also represented far above its due even in their primary
schools. The schools which the state began to found itself
in the '70s – originally, and ostensibly, where the local

church or commune was too poor to look after its own needs – were from the first deliberately used as instruments of Magyarisation, and although most of them were founded in non-Magyar districts, the language of instruction in them was almost always exclusively Magyar. The Hungarian Statistical Annual for 1906/7 listed 16,618 elementary schools in Inner Hungary, of which 2,153 were state, 1,460 communal, 12,705 confessional and 300 private. The language of instruction in 12,223 of these, including all the state schools, was Magyar; in 492 it was German, in 737 Slovak, in 2,760 Roumanian, in 107 Ruthene, in 276 Serb or Croat, in 10 Italian, and in 19 another. In the 400 burgher schools, the languages were: Magyar 386, German 5, Roumanian 4, Serb 3, Italian 2; in the 205 secondary schools, Magyar 189, German 8, Roumanian 6, Italian 1; one was mixed Magyar-Roumanian. The Slovaks had none at all: one of Tisza's first acts had been to close the three secondary schools which they had founded in the 1860s, under the pretext that they had been teaching Pan-Slavism, and they had been refused permission to open another. Their cultural association, the Slovenská Matica, suffered the same fate.

Among other measures of Magyarisation may be mentioned the Kindergarten Act of 1891 – instruction here, again, was almost exclusively in Magyar – and two other Laws which perhaps served to give more of the appearance than the reality of Magyarisation. One bestowed on every place in Hungary an official Magyar name; the other made it cheap and easy for the bearers of non-Magyar names to exchange them for Magyar ones. Officials were strongly urged to avail themselves of the facility.

It cannot be said that all this was waste labour. By the end of the century the state apparatus throughout the whole of Hungary was exclusively Magyar in feeling, and practically so in speech. Professional and business life on the higher levels had followed suit. Figures of the joint-stock companies in 1915, based on the language used by the boards or 'the names of the leading men' showed that 97·4% of them, with 99·5% of their total assets, were in the hands of Magyar-speaking persons. The Magyarisation of the towns had proceeded at an astounding rate. Budapest, three quarters German-speaking in 1848, was 79·8% Magyar in 1900 (when its population was three times the size). Pécs had changed from three quarters German to almost purely Magyar, and the same process had taken place in nearly all the formerly German towns of central Hungary, in the mixed towns along the ethnic frontiers, and in some of those lying deep in the 'nationalities' districts. During this process, moreover, the greater part of the German intelligentsia (outside the Saxons) and of the Slovak and Ruthene, had joined the ranks of Magyardom, simultaneously enriching it and leaving their own nationalities the poorer. The rural districts had not kept pace with the towns; nevertheless, the proportion of the population of Inner Hungary giving Magyar as its mother-tongue had risen from 46·6% in 1880 to 51·4% in 1900, the rise in absolute figures being about 2,200,000. The proportions of all the non-Magyar languages (except those grouped under the rubric 'others') had sunk, and their increase in absolute figures had been relatively small.

But these figures, impressive as they were, did not mean that the danger to Hungary from her multinational composition had been banished, or even seriously diminished. The increase in Magyardom had taken place chiefly in central Hungary, above all, in Budapest and its surroundings, the contributors to it coming from three main sources: the old German burgher population of the towns, plus a considerable contingent from the well-to-do German peasantry, who usually contrived to save enough to 'make a gentleman' of at least one of their sons: the Jews, who were arriving in the capital in increasing numbers – in 1900 they already formed nearly a quarter of its whole

population – and finally, the overspill from the congested
districts of the periphery, especially the north, who came
to central Hungary in search of work in the factories. But
central Hungary was Magyar by majority already.

The effect of all the efforts on the ethnic map of Hungary,
regarded in broad terms, was practically nil. It is doubtful
whether the Magyarisation of the·schools changed the ethnic character of a single village. The little Slovak or Ruthene who spent his schooldays painfully acquiring a few
scraps of Magyar (and often acquiring precious little else)
forgot them happily and completely as soon as the school
doors closed behind him. Where changes did occur, it was
as the result of some special cause: large-scale emigration,
or the establishment of a factory; and those changes were
by no means always favourable to the Magyar element. A
writer who investigated the question in 1902 reported that
during the Liberal period the Magyars had actually lost 465
communes to the nationalities while gaining only 261 from
them. Their chief gains had been from the Slovaks (chiefly
in central Hungary), their chief losses to the Roumanians
and Germans. Of all the nationalities of Hungary, the Ruthenes had been the biggest losers (chiefly to the Slovaks),
then the Magyars, then the Serbs (chiefly by emigration to
Serbia). The biggest gainers on balance had been the Roumanians, then the Slovaks, then the Germans.

Broadly, the ethnic frontiers in the west, north and east
remained stationary on almost the exact lines on which they
had been stabilised at the end of the *impopulatio*. Only in a
few, exceptional cases, of which Kassa is the best example,
did the growth of a Magyar-speaking town in a non-Magyar
environment alter the local balance. Behind the main lines,
the losses suffered by the Magyar element at least balanced
its gains.

The Hungarians had thus been unable to obliterate the
multinational character of the ethnic map of their country.
They had failed, partly by their own intolerant insistence

on complete Magyarisation, to create what alone should have been able to save the integrity of their state in 1918 (although as things turned out, it would not have done so), a substantial body of non-Magyar, but activist, feeling among any of the nationalities. Neither had they eliminated discontent and irredentist feeling. The degree of acuteness of the nationality question varied with conditions inside the Monarchy, and around it. A certain lull had set in after 1870, when it became obvious that the Compromise was there to stay for a long time. The secret treaties concluded by the Monarchy with Serbia and Roumania, in 1881 and 1883 respectively, had a considerable effect in damping down irredentist agitation by those countries. For a while, the Slovak national movement dwindled into insignificance, and the Serbian was seriously weakened. But neither quite disappeared; if the Slovaks' enthusiasm for Pan-Slavism had grown dim, the idea of Czecho-Slovak unity gained strength. The Roumanian national movement was always active. Here a large proportion of the people, particularly among those belonging to the Orthodox church, were more or less openly disaffected and their leaders, even at this date, were dreaming of union with their brothers across the Carpathians.

The development of the Croat situation was very similar. Croat nationalist opinion remained bitterly resentful, not only of several of the specific provisions in the *Nagodba*, but above all, of the fact that it relegated Croatia to a mediate position. This, of course, was irremediable, and it is hard to see what would have happened if a Sabor had repudiated the Nagodba, as its extreme nationalists were always urging it to do; as it was, the position was kept from reversal chiefly by the narrowness of the franchise, which gave an artificial weight to the officials, many of whom were Magyars.

It was the intemperate folly of the Croat national extremists themselves which proved Hungary's best ally. Their most prominent figure, Ante Starčević, leader of the so-called Party of Right', behaved towards the Serbs of Slavonia, who, after the incorporation of the Military Frontier, formed a full quarter of the total population, with such gross intolerance that when a new Ban, Count Khuen-Hedérváry, was appointed in 1883, they sought his protection, and their support enabled him to maintain what was essentially a dictatorship, and even a measure of order, until the end of the century. But it goes without saying that his rule did not satisfy the Croats – a people which has, indeed, developed the habit of opposition for opposition's sake further than any in Europe. After Starčević died in 1897, most articulate Croat opinion still followed one or the other of two parties, whose differences of principle were little larger than the difference in their titles (one kept the old name, Party of Right; the other, led by J. Frank, called itself the Party of Pure Right), both being extreme nationalist. The genuine supporters of the Union had dwindled to a handful.

An aspect of the Magyarisation campaign which was little considered at the time – or if questions concerning it were raised, they were brushed aside impatiently – was what effect this great addition to their ranks was having on the Magyar people itself. Had the new recruits become Magyars at all, in any real sense, when they entered their names in the rubric as Magyar by mother-tongue? Could the earlier stock assimilate so large an influx, and if it did achieve the feat without manifest symptoms of indigestion, had it thereby altered, for better or worse, its own nature?

The poor upland peasant turned factory worker in a suburb of Pest melted into his environment imperceptibly enough; his habits, his religion, probably even his family tree, if traced far enough back, differed little from those of his 'Magyar' mates; when his children grew up speaking Magyar, that mere fact made them Magyars, just like any others. The Magyarisation of the Germans had more important sociological consequences, for nearly all these recruits went into the expanding middle classes, in which they soon came to constitute a component of the first importance. They flocked into the new ministries, in some of which, especially the technical and financial services, they came to outnumber the Magyars themselves. They were strongly represented in the church, and even more strongly in the army, a service which the true Magyars tended to shun, on both sentimental and linguistic grounds. They did not venture much into big business, for which they were perhaps too cautious, or had absorbed too much of the national psychology, but they comprised a large proportion of the small shopkeeper, artisan and skilled labour classes. At one period they almost dominated some of the professions: nearly all the architects who built the new Budapest were of local German origin, and so were many of the period's leading figures in literature, painting and academic life.

The Magyarisation of these elements, too, seemed both to themselves and to others complete and sincere, and the Magyar people of the day neither regretted this accession, nor had cause to do so. The recruits filled gaps in the nation's social and economic structure which must otherwise have remained unfilled for at least two more generations, and if the dilution impoverished the original product by a little of its slap-dash charm, perhaps by a touch of its brilliancy, this was more than compensated by the diligence, sobriety and common sense which it brought with it.

The Jews presented a more difficult problem. Their numbers had been increasing rapidly ever since the annexation to Austria of Galicia, and the removal by Joseph II of the restrictions which had previously hampered their movements. From a mere 12,000 (0.1% of the total population) in 1720, they had already increased to 83,000 (1.0%) in 1787, 247,000 (2.2%) in 1840, 366,000 (3.2%) in 1850 and 542,000 (4.0%) in 1869. In 1880 they numbered 625,000 (4.6%), and in 1900, 830,000 (4.9%). Their numerical increase was now slowing down, but the importance of their role in the national life had become enormous. They had become an almost exclusively urban and middle-class element. In the towns of north-eastern Hungary, which lay on their main immigration route, they formed a proportion which was often as high as 35 or 40 per cent, and in Budapest itself there were in 1900 nearly 170,000 Jews, a little under a quarter of its total population.

The capitalist development of the new Hungary, in so far as it had been carried out by 'native' resources at all, had been almost entirely of their making, and the results of it were to an overwhelming extent in their hands. The occupational statistics for 1910 show that 12·5% of the 'self-employed industrialists' and 21·8% of the salaried employees in industry, 54% of the self-employed traders and 62·1% of their employees, 85% of the self-employed persons in finance and banking (283 out of 333) and 42% of their employees, were Jewish; and these figures, which do not distinguish between enterprises by their size and importance, ranking the head of a great business equally with a village cobbler or shopkeeper as a self-employed man, give but a faint idea of the real position. This was that practically all banking and finance, and the great majority of trade and industry above the humblest level, was run and staffed by Jews, into whose pockets also went most of the money so earned, whether in the form of direct profits, of dividends or of salaries. Even among the larger categories of landowners the Jews were now strongly represented: they owned 19·9% of the properties of 1,000 *hold*+ and 19% of those between 1,000 and 200 *hold* and constituted 73% of the lessees in the former bracket and 62% of those in the latter.

Their position in the intellectual life of the country was almost as strong. They were rare in the ministries and even rarer in the army, and were naturally confined to their proportionate numbers in the churches and the church schools, but 11·5% of the teachers in the burgher schools were Jewish, and a substantial number of the university professors. 26·2% of the persons entered under the rubric 'literature and the arts', including 42·4% of the journalists, were Jewish, 45·2% of the advocates and 48·9% of the doctors. Hungary owed to her Jews a considerable proportion of her most boasted achievements in the fields of science and the humanities.

The Jews were not yet entering parliament on a large scale, although all the later Liberal parliaments contained some Jewish members, but their predominance in the Press gave them an important influence over public opinion, and the leadership of both the Social Democrat Party and the various radical groups which were emerging at the turn of the century was largely in their hands.

The Jewish recruits to the new Hungarian society had thus achieved a position far stronger than the German, and even one which in many fields was stronger than that of the Magyars themselves. It was, however, undeniable that their integration into the nation had remained incomplete. Many of them were still newcomers of the first or second generation, for if their increase had slowed down, this was not because the immigration had slackened, but because it was now being partly balanced by emigration westward. The emigrants, of whom 110,000 left Hungary between 1870 and 1910, were precisely those who had acquired European characteristics – and, usually, some wealth – while the new-comers entered with their national characteristics undiminished.

Not all the Jews themselves wanted to Magyarise; of the two great bodies into which most of Hungarian Jewry divided, the Orthodox and the Neologs, the former opposed assimilation on principle and the latter discouraged changes of religion, which were, in fact, rare: between 1896 and 1907 only 5,000 conversions took place. The 'Magyarisation' of those whose spiritual allegiance belonged

34. *The Emperor Francis Joseph*

to their ancestral faith could clearly never be complete, however enthusiastically it was expressed in some directions, and it was not easy for the Magyars themselves to feel that their new brothers in statistics were brothers indeed. An anti-Semitic party, founded by a certain Istóczy, which returned seventeen members to the 1884 Parliament, was crushed out of existence, but even after this, and despite all official disapproval, many Magyars felt uneasily that the situation was dangerous which placed so many of the country's power-positions in the hands of an element which still appeared to them alien.

The social and economic picture, too, was far from healthy. The contrast drawn by so many writers between the wealth and luxury prevailing at one end of the social scale, and the destitution at the other, is fallacious in this sense, that it gives far too favourable a picture of the conditions of the rich. Some big fortunes were made in Hungary during the period, but many of them were made by foreign entrepreneurs – much of the new industry was in the hands of holding banks, which were themselves subsidiaries of Viennese or other non-Hungarian concerns; most of the others by the new industrialists. The great landed magnates formed an apparent exception; indeed, the quick and relatively generous compensation received by them after 1848 for such of their acres as they had lost, had enabled them to take advantage of the difficulties of their weaker brethren, so that the share of the mammoth and big estates in Hungary's soil hardly diminished. In 1895 over 12 million *hold*, nearly one third of the entire area of the country, was owned by under 4,000 proprietors (not all of them, it is true, private individuals)[1]. The 128 largest estates covered between them more than half of

---

[1] Some of the largest estates belonged to the Church – so the See of Nagyvárad owned 330,000 *hold*, that of Esztergom, over 170,000, etc. Some of the municipalities of the Alföld owned estates almost as large. These were mostly let, at low rents, to the local citizens.

this. In the first decades of the Compromise their estates brought the great agrarian interests real wealth, but when the competition of overseas wheat made itself felt, they got into great difficulties, and by the end of the century, many of them were mortgaged up to the ears. The 'gentry' class, as a whole, never recovered from the disastrous years after the reform, and the agricultural depression was another blow. Many of them were then saved only by the action of the state in taking them over into its new services. Here they carried on in new forms their traditional role of governing the country, and enjoyed sufficient social prestige, but their lives, although decent, were far from luxurious.

A few medium landowners, of course, weathered the storm, and there was a reasonably large class of smaller farms which afforded their cultivators a comfortable existence. But below these again, an alarming situation had developed. Population increased, very fast after the cholera decade of the sixties, and industrialisation was proceeding far too slowly to take up the surplus; nor did the Magyar peasant take kindly to the idea of leaving the land. The current usage among the Magyars was that when the head of a family died, his holding was divided equally between all his children, and this process was repeated until in 1895, when the last pre-war agricultural survey was taken, over two million of the 2,800,000 holdings in the country were of 10 *holds* or less, three quarters of these being under 5 *hold* and 600,000 of them under one. Many of these last were, indeed, vineyards or market gardens, or belonged to persons whose main occupation was not agriculture; but against these must be set the smaller holdings in the 5-10 *hold* group. The minimum on which a family could exist was generally put at 8 *hold*, so that it appears that nearly half the landowning population of the country was existing on plots insufficient to meet their necessities.

The lower brackets of the dwarf-holders merged into the still more unfortunate class of the true agricultural pro-

letariat, the men who had neither land of their own nor
regular employment on that of others. Such a class had,
of course, always existed in Hungary, as in every country,
and the statistics, such as they are, show that it had been
growing with some rapidity during the first half of the
nineteenth century. By 1848 the class ranking as 'peasants'
(i.e., villein holders of a quarter *sessio* or more) certainly comprised less than half the total rural population.
The other half, however, equally certainly contained many
persons not entirely destitute, and the residue were in any
case not so numerous as to force themselves on the attention either of the Hungarian reformers of 1848 or of their
Austrian successors. Even for several years after the Compromise there was a large demand for labour on the construction of the railways and the regulation of the Tisza,
and wages for those who remained on the land were comparatively high. But after the public works ended, wages
sank rapidly and many could find no work at all. Emigration began in the '70s, soon reaching a figure of 50,000 a
year, most of them from the congested rural districts.
Nevertheless, in 1890 the totally landless agrarian population numbered about 1,700,000 (wage-earners), over 48
per cent of the total agrarian population and over a quarter
of the gainfully employed population of Hungary. Of these,
about one third were in regular employment as farm-hands;
most of the rest lived from seasonal or casual labour. The
seasonal labourers literally existed during half the year in
a state of semi-starvation, or worse; there were several
epidemics of pellagra and hunger typhus, and cases of mad-
ness induced by starvation were not unknown.

The crisis of this class reached its peak in the 1890s,
when there was severe unrest, especially on the Tisza,
where a strange prophet named Várkonyi appeared, preach-
ing a kind of agrarian socialism. In 1897 the labourers in
several counties struck just before the harvest.

The authorities put down the movement with troops

and gendarmerie, and a draconic Law was enacted which dissolved all existing combinations among agrarian workers and made it a penal offence to address, or even attend, a meeting called for the purpose of founding a new one. It was also made a penal offence for an agricultural worker to default on his contract without reasonable cause; if he did so, he could be escorted back to his work by gendarmes. This Law naturally did not remedy the discontent, nor even quite put an end to strikes, but emigration, which in the peak year of 1907 exceeded 200,000, and the increased tempo of industrialisation, now began at least to retard the advance of the rural congestion. Wages rose slightly, and the state, while seeing to it that the agricultural workers remained without any organisation of their own, or any possibility of creating one, began itself to show some modest interest in their welfare. Even a few settlements were founded, but all of them on state land. The expedient of turning over parts of the big, extensively cultivated private estates to peasant colonists was never attempted.

Industrial labour fared little better than agricultural. The lateness of her industrialisation and its modest scale saved Hungary from the most extreme of the horrors of the industrial revolution in England, but the philosophy of the day allowed her capitalists as free a hand as their English counterparts enjoyed, and they were quite as greedy. Moreover, the state agreed that only low costs of production would enable Hungarian industry to compete against Austrian within the customs union, while the landlords opposed high wages in industry which tempted labour off the land. Their scarcity value often enabled the skilled craftsmen to command relatively good terms, but the mass of unskilled workers, refugees from the congested rural districts, were at the mercy of whoever offered them employment. Wages were always low, and protective legislation, which was generally copied from German or Aus-

trian models, lagged behind its originals. In 1900 28% of
all male industrial workers were earning between 14 and
20 crowns[1] a week, 48% between 6 and 14 and 15%
under 6. Women's and children's wages were proportionately lower. While some limitation had been placed in the
exploitation of child and juvenile labour, the adult was
practically unprotected. The commonest factory working
day was 12 hours, including breaks; the usual working
week ranged between 60 and 66 hours. Housing conditions
in Budapest were said to be worse than in any other large
city of Europe.

Political pressure on the workers was always heavy. In-
flammatory speeches made at the time of the Paris Commune engendered in the authorities a panic fear which led
to exaggerated repressive measures. A Law enacted in 1872
and re-enacted in 1884 legalised association and even
strikes, but incitement to strike was a punishable offence,
and any form of association had to be strictly non-political.
Nevertheless, a political movement gradually developed,
and in 1890 a Social Democratic Congress was held, which
adopted bodily the Hainfeld Programme drawn up by the
Austrian Social Democrats in the preceding year. The forbidden link with the Trade Unions was maintained by a
surreptitious device and was in fact very close, and after
this the industrial unions made considerable progress, although the authorities were able to prevent either the Party
or the unions from expanding outside industry. Even so,
the workers' movement now became a perceptible political force. It was, however, still regarded with extreme
aversion by the 'national' politicians, partly out of the
usual economic motives and partly because of its Marxian
tenets and its almost wholly non-Magyar leadership (the
Trade Union leaders were mostly German and the intellectuals Jewish), which earned it the repute of an 'international' and even an anti-national force.

[1] 24 crowns = £1 sterling.

Finally, it had not proved possible to induce in Hungarian national opinion itself sincere acceptance of the Compromise as the answer to its aspirations. The idea of 1848 maintained its popularity among the Magyar masses, and all governmental pressure was unable to prevent the regular return to parliament of a number of representatives of the extreme Left, whose programme, as reformulated in 1874 (when the name of 'Party of Independence' was adopted) and 1884 would have reduced the link with Austria to the purely personal one of the common Monarch. But even among those who accepted the necessity of common institutions, there were always many who thought the terms of the Compromise unsatisfactory. When the economic clauses came up for revision in 1876, Tisza himself pressed for a number of concessions, and obtained some of them, but had to renounce others, including the independent National Bank, and after this several groups of deputies seceded from the Liberals to form a 'United Opposition' (the name was changed in 1891 to 'National Party') with a programme of revision of the Compromise by constitutional methods in the direction of more independence, especially in the financial and economic fields.

To the eye of Vienna, the programme of the National Party was little more compatible with the spirit of the Compromise than that of the Party of Independence itself; and in fact, the developments of the situation drove the two parties increasingly into one camp. Revision of the economic clauses of the Compromise was a legitimate demand, within the terms of the Compromise itself, although each discussion revealed differences of interest between the Austrian and Hungarian parties which left them mutually irritated. But in the 1880's nationalist opinion, provoked by some acts of supreme tactlessness on the part of the central military authorities, began to concentrate its resentment against the joint army. Even the moderate Opposition,

although not asking for a fully independent army, joined
the agitation for 'national' concessions in this field. This
touched Francis Joseph on the raw, and his refusal to
make any concessions in the field left public opinion, in
its turn, more convinced that the Compromise was incompatible with true national independence.

It was the outcry raised by the Opposition against an
army Bill introduced in 1889, which strengthened (although only very slightly) the centralist features of the
army, that was the real cause of Tisza's resignation (although he only tendered it a few months later), and this
can probably be taken as the turning-point after which
the monarch and the 'political nation' alike recognised the
impossibility of complete and sincere reconciliation. The
Liberal Party continued in office, indeed, for another fifteen years, during the first part of which public attention
was partially diverted from the 'question of public law'
by social and religious problems (which produced the
phenomenon of the foundation of a major party – the
Christian People's Party – on a social basis) and by the
millenary celebrations. Meanwhile the revision of the
economic clauses of the Compromise in 1887 had gone
through without too great difficulty, and that of 1897
brought Hungary the great concession of equal partnership
in what was now the Austro-Hungarian Bank.

But in 1903 another army Bill evoked such unbridled
agitation and parliamentary filibustering that in the end
the Minister President of the day (Kálmán Tisza's son,
Count István Tisza) appealed to the country, and was
heavily defeated by a coalition mainly composed of the
Party of Independence and 'national' sympathisers.

Francis Joseph, indeed, dealt with the situation easily
enough. He appointed a cabinet of officials, under the
minister of defence, General Fejérváry, which threatened
to introduce universal suffrage. The Coalition capitulated
and agreed, in return for office, to renounce all its more

far-reaching demands and itself to introduce a suffrage Bill. After it had spent four inglorious years doing little but evade the latter promise (it did produce a Bill, but weighted the voting by complicated devices to maintain Magyar supremacy), Tisza reorganised his followers in a new party, known as the Party of Work, and duly recovered the parliamentary majority in the elections of 1910. But there was no concealing that by now the Compromise had lost all its popularity; those who, like Tisza, supported it, did so because, in their view, although objectionable, it yet offered protection against worse dangers.

And those dangers were mounting visibly. The twentieth century had seen a steady growth in Hungary itself of the forces which challenged the class-national supremacy which was the common basis of the '67 and the '48 parties alike. The agrarian crisis had been repressed rather than resolved. The industrial workers' movement had visibly gathered strength. A Trade Union Congress had been instituted in 1904. When the Fejérváry government raised their hopes, and again later, the workers had staged big demonstrations in favour of universal suffrage. The nationalities had emerged from their relative passivity. In the 1905 elections they had got ten deputies into parliament and in those of 1906 (held by the Coalition after it had agreed with the Crown) no less than twenty-six, who had formed an alliance between themselves and with the deputies from Croatia. There, in 1905, a Dalmatian politician named Supilo had succeeded in persuading a number of the Croat and Serb parties to form a coalition. This had at first offered to support the Hungarian Coalition against Austria, but had soon swung round to bitter opposition to Budapest. In the 1908 elections for the Sabor, the Coalition had secured 57 seats, the Party of Pure Right 24, the Unionists none at all. The new Ban, Baron Rauch, was reduced to ruling without a Sabor.

The danger of these developments was immensely enhanced by the developments which were taking place in the Monarchy itself, outside Hungary, and in Europe at large. The real basis on which the Compromise should have rested in the Monarchy had been swept away long since when the German centralists, whose supremacy west of the Leitha should have been the counterpart to that of the '67 parties east of it, had proved·unable to maintain their position. Since then, Austrian Governments had balanced uneasily between Germans and Slavs, who had never re- nounced their hopes of remodelling the Monarchy. While Francis Joseph lived, this, at least, would not happen, but he was growing old, and it was notorious that the heir pre- sumptive, the Archduke Francis Ferdinand, meant on his succession to carry through radical changes. In military and economic respects, the Monarchy was to be strictly unitary, but, politically, it was to be reorganised either as a trialist state (by forming a third component out of its Southern Slav areas) or as a more complex federation of national units. Either solution would have meant the end, not only of Dualism, but even, in practice, of Historic Hungary. The Archduke was in close contact with the nationality leaders in Hungary, and also with the new forces among the Austrian Germans, notably the Christian Socials, who were also bitterly hostile to Hungary.

Outside the Monarchy, Russia was in alliance with France, had reached a *modus vivendi* with Britain and since 1906 had again redirected its expansionist drive south- westward. Russian agents were at work in Galicia and even among the Hungarian Ruthenes, and in touch with the neo-Slavs in Prague. Above all, Russia had developed an intimate understanding with Serbia, where the replace- ment of the Obrenović dynasty by that of Karageorgević in 1903 had soon been followed by the emergence of an anti-Austrian feeling which almost reached hysteria when the Monarchy annexed Bosnia-Herzegovina in 1908. Rou- mania was still technically allied to the Monarchy, but its

most popular politicians were openly proclaiming the annexation of Transylvania as the supreme objective of the
nation's policy.

Tisza may have been too optimistic in thinking that in
this situation any policy at all could ensure the survival of
a Hungary recognisable to him as such. He was at any rate
convinced that if it could be saved at all, this could only
be by close adherence to the Austrian connection and to
the German alliance, and by keeping political power out
of the hands of the centrifugal forces in Hungary. Under
pressure from the Crown itself, the Party of Work
passed a franchise act, but it was as restrictive as the Coalition's had been. When the murder of Francis Ferdinand,
on 28 June 1914, brought the European crisis to a head,
Tisza, who had returned to the Minister Presidency a year
before, was personally against war with Serbia, which he
thought could only bring harm to Hungary, whether it
were won or lost. But his logic bound him to submit to,
and publicly to espouse, the decision of the Crown Council
which declared for war, and Hungary thus found herself
involved, as a part of the Monarchy and as Germany's ally,
in a conflict with the Entente, and presently also with the
U.S.A., on whose side stood also Serbia, after 1916 Roumania, and in 1918 a shadow Czecho-Slovakia. As this
international alignment took shape, it became increasingly
probable that if Hungary lost the war, she would be dis-
membered in the name of national self-determination; and
various secret treaties and agreements to this effect were
in fact made in the course of the war. The details of these
were not always known to the Hungarians but their existence was either known to them, or could be inferred,
and they came to realise that their only hope lay in victory.
Tisza held the country unswervingly on her course so long
as Francis Joseph lived, and when the old monarch died,
on 21 November 1916, prevailed on his successor, Charles,
to accept immediate coronation, thereby making it im-

possible for Charles to realise the intention with which he
was credited, of offering the Slavs and Roumanians of the
Monarchy concessions à la Francis Ferdinand at the expense
of its Germans and Magyars. All Charles could do was to
insist on further franchise reform, and Tisza's refusal to
sponsor this brought his resignation, but the tragi-comedy
of the Coalition period repeated itself; his successors
evaded fulfilling the condition, and haggled over 'national'
concessions at the expense of Austria, while the military
situation deteriorated, war-weariness and social unrest
grew, and disaffection spread among the nationalities and
in Croatia.

The effective end of Historic Hungary, when it came,
did so swiftly, although another eighteen months passed
before the treaty which legalised its demise was signed.
As the situation grew worse, one prominent Hungarian
politician, Count Mihály Károlyi, who had recently succeeded to the leadership of a fraction of the Party of Independence, came forward with the proposal that Hungary
should sever her connection with Austria and Germany,
conclude a separate peace, and at the same time introduce
social and political reforms, and concessions to the nationalities. In this way, he argued, the nationalities would be
reconciled to Hungary and the victors be deprived of any
reason to attack her integrity; the other reforms were desirable *per se*. The popular appeal of this programme grew
apace as conditions deteriorated, and on 25 October 1918,
when it was plain that the end was imminent, Károlyi's
own Party followers, the Social Democrats, and a group of
bourgeois Radicals set up a National Council in Budapest.
On 31 October Budapest was in a state of dangerous tur-
moil, and Charles, to save bloodshed, appointed Károlyi
Minister President. The National Council transformed itself into a cabinet. Károlyi opened negotiations with the
nationalities and went to Belgrade to ask the French commander, General Franchet d'Espérey, for a separate armis-

tice. Unhappily for his theories, most of the nationalities had by now lost the wish to stay in Hungary on any terms, and where the willingness did exist, it was irrelevant in view of the wishes of Hungary's neighbours, and the Allies' commitments to them. Croatia had already proclaimed her independence and union with Serbia in a new state; a meeting of the Roumanians of Transylvania declared for union with the Regat, and a meeting of Slovaks, for union with the Czechs. The demarcation line drawn by Franchet d'Espérey allowed Serb and Roumanian troops to occupy all south and east Hungary, and immediately thereafter, Czech forces entered northern Hungary and occupied it up to a line which, in most of its extent, corresponded to the full claims of the Czecho-Slovak provisional government. The *de facto* dismemberment of Hungary was already near-complete, and was brought nearer in the next weeks, as the Roumanian troops edged their way westward.

On 13 November Charles 'renounced participation' in the affairs of state, declaring that he recognised in advance whatever decision Hungary might take regarding its future form of state. On the 16th the National Council dissolved parliament and proclaimed a republic, with Károlyi as provisional President. The separation from Austria was popular, as was the prospect of peace, but the chief basis of Károlyi's appeal was destroyed and his programme discredited by the complete failure of either the nationalities or the Allies to behave as he had promised. Meanwhile, complete confusion reigned at home. There was mass unemployment in the factories and near-starvation in Budapest. Károlyi prepared to introduce a land reform and a democratic franchise, but did not get beyond preparations. Extremist agitation increased; the bourgeois elements in the government were pushed back by the Social Democrats, who were themselves outbid by the agitation spread by Béla Kun, a communist agent of Hungaro-Jewish origin whom Lenin had entrusted with the mission of bolshevising Hungary, and all central Europe.

On 20 March 1919, the representative of the Allies in Budapest handed Károlyi a Note ordering him to evacuate a further area of central Hungary for the benefit of the Roumanians. Károlyi understood that the new line was to constitute a political frontier, and resigned; as did the bourgeois members of the cabinet. Kun, on the other hand, promised Russian help, and the next day the Social Democrats fused with the Communists and proclaimed a dictatorship of the proletariat. A red regime under Kun now followed Károlyi's pink one, but it only re-enacted its predecessor's faults, in aggravated form, with none of its redeeming virtues. Kun turned the entire peasantry against him by announcing that the land was not to be distributed, but nationalised. He set the urban population, including the industrial workers, against him in innumerable ways, and inaugurated a red terror under the vile Szamuelly. Withal, he proved as unable to defend Hungary against her enemies as Károlyi had been. He undertook an offensive against the Czechs in Slovakia, but the Entente stepped in and vetoed it. The Russians never produced the promised help against the Roumanians, and when Kun nevertheless attacked the latter, his armies melted away. On 4 August he fled, with most of his associates, to Vienna; two days later, the Roumanian troops entered Budapest.

The draft peace terms were ready by this time; indeed, except in the west, where Austria put in a belated claim for the German-speaking fringe across the Leitha, most of the new frontiers had been in existence, *de facto*, since soon after the armistice. The Allies had, however, been unwilling to recognise Kun, and the presentation of the Treaty had therefore been deferred. There was now another delay until a new Hungarian regime was formed which the Allies were prepared to treat as stable; then a few weeks more, for discussion of the terms. It was thus only on 14 June that the Treaty was signed at Trianon which constituted the death certificate of Historic Hungary.

This was hard indeed. The Allies had entirely accepted the view that the 'principle of self-determination' called for the 'liberation' from Hungary, so far as this was practicable, of all its non-Magyars. Thus the Slovak, Roumanian and all Southern Slav areas had to go; and satisfaction was given also to Austria's claim.

Furthermore, it was not genuine self-determination that was applied at all, but a sort of national determinism which assumed that all peoples in Hungary of the same or kindred stock as their neighbours ought to be transferred; their wishes were taken for granted. More, it was assumed that any non-Magyar should, where at all possible, be taken away from Hungary, even if the state to which he was transferred had no ethnic claim on him. Thus the Ruthenes of the north-east were attached to Czecho-Slovakia although they were neither Czechs nor Slovaks, simply because they were not Magyars, and in the mixed districts of the south the Germans – not to mention the Bunyevci and Sokci – were counted to show that the local majority was non-Magyar, whereas another calculation, which would have accorded far better with the wishes of these peoples, would have given the answer that the majority was non-Serb.

Finally, even where the claimants could produce no sort of ethnic case, the frontiers of all of them, except Austria, were extended to satisfy economic or strategic claims, often of very exaggerated nature. The final result was that of the 325,411 sq. km. which had comprised the area of the Lands of the Holy Crown, Hungary was left with only 92,963. Roumania alone had received 103,093; Czecho-Slovakia 61,633; Yugoslavia the 42,541 sq. km. of Croatia-Slavonia and 20,551 of Inner Hungary; Austria 4,020; and even Poland and Italy small fragments. Of the population of 20,886,487 (1910 census), Hungary was left with 7,615,117. Roumania received 5,257,467, Czecho-Slovakia 3,517,568, Yugoslavia 4,131,249 (2,621,954+ 1,509,295), and Austria 291,618. Of the 10,050,575 persons of Magyar mother-tongue, according to the 1910 census, no less than 3,219,579 were allotted to the Successor States: 1,704,851 of them to Roumania, 1,063,020 to Czecho-Slovakia, 105,948 + 441,787 to Yugoslavia and 26,183 to Austria. While the homes of some of these, e.g., the Szekels, had been in the remotest corners of Historic Hungary, many of them were living in compact blocs immediately across the frontier.

In addition, the Treaty required Hungary to pay in reparations an unspecified sum, which was to be 'the first charge upon all her assets and resources', and limited her armed forces to a long-service force of 35,000 (officers and men), to be used exclusively on the maintainance of internal order, and on frontier defence.

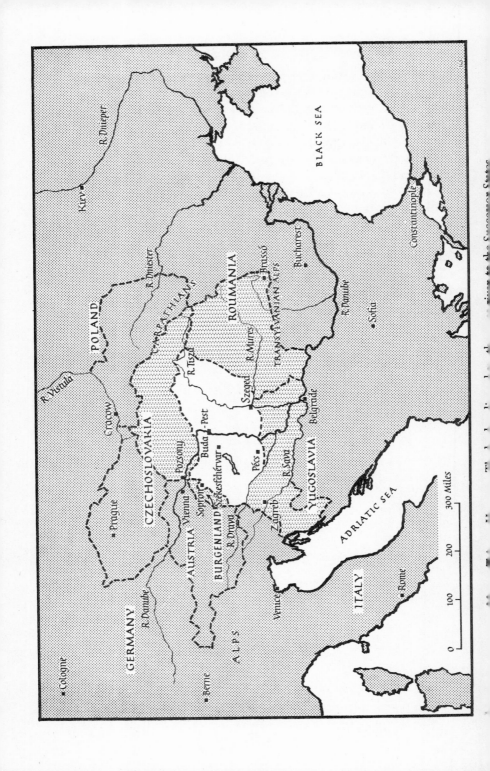

BLACK SEA

POLAND

R.Dnieper

Kiev

R.Vistula

R.Danube

GERMANY

Cologne

Berne

Prague

Cracow

CZECHOSLOVAKIA

R.Dniester

CARPATHIANS

Vienna

AUSTRIA

Sopron

Pozsony

BURGENLAND

Buda

Pest

R.Tisza

Szeged

R.Maros

ROUMANIA

Brasso

TRANSYLVANIAN ALPS

Bucharest

R.Danube

Sofia

ALPS

Szekesfehervar

R.Drava

Pecs

R.Sava

Belgrade

Constantinople

Venice

Zagreb

YUGOSLAVIA

ADRIATIC SEA

ITALY

Rome

0   100   200   300 Miles

9

TRIANON HUNGARY

IF the real demise of Historic Hungary had thus preceded by some eighteen months the formal recognition of the fact, so its diminished successor, Trianon Hungary, had of necessity largely taken shape before the same treaty legalised its existence. In the spring of 1919 a group of leading politicians of the old regime had formed an 'Anti-Bolshevik Committee' in Vienna; others had set up a counter-revolutionary government, situated first in Arad, then in Szeged, and had raised a small 'national army' under the command of Admiral Miklós Horthy, sometime Commander in Chief of the Imperial and Royal Adriatic Fleet.

On the fall of Kun the two groups had joined forces and asked the Allies to recognise them as the legal government of Hungary. The Allies had hesitated to hand over the country to a regime so pronouncedly counter-revolutionary in outlook, and had insisted on the formation of a provisional government including democratic elements, to hold elections on a wide, secret suffrage. The Roumanians having with some difficulty been induced to retire across the Tisza, this government was formed, under the Presidency of K. Huszár, in November 1919, and the elections (for a single House) held in January 1920. The successful candidates then met in what was *de facto* the first parliament of Trianon Hungary.

It met in a situation of extraordinary difficulty. Overhanging the whole picture was that shadow of the impending Treaty; and it may be said at this point that resentment against and determination to reverse what almost the whole nation, with little distinction of class, regarded as an intolerable injustice, was the dominating motif in the entire history of the diminished state until the extinction of its own real independence. But the situation in the spring of 1920 was also replete with immediate problems. Four years of exhausting war, in which the nation had suffered very heavy casualties, two revolutions and a predatory foreign occupation (the Roumanians had looted the country with great thoroughness, carrying off, in particular, much of its rolling-stock) would have been hard enough to repair within intact frontiers; but on top of all this had come the further blows inflicted by the dismemberment of the country and the disintegration of the Monarchy. The whole national economy had been disrupted by the disappearance behind new barriers, abruptly erected and jealously guarded, of accustomed sources of supply and markets, and the surviving national resources were being further taxed by a great influx of refugees from the Successor States.

Industrial unemployment had soared to unprecedented heights. Capital had fled headlong before the threat of Bolshevism; the national capital, estimated in 1910 at £51,794,000 foundation capital and £25,623,000 reserve capital, had dwindled by 1921 to £1,824,000 foundation and £1,153,000 reserve. The currency was following that of Austria, with which it was still linked, in a dizzy downward spiral of inflation. Shortage of labour during the war, exhaustion of stocks and deterioration of machinery had impaired even agricultural production.

There was extreme social cleavage and unrest. Both the industrial and the rural proletariats had seen their hopes raised high during the two revolutions, and were by no means willing to return to their previous condition of political impotence and social degradation. The same revolutions, on the other hand, had greatly embittered the former possessing classes (including all but the very poorest of the peasants, and some even of them), who ascribed to them

the blame for all Hungary's misfortunes. Feeling ran particularly high against the Jews, who had played a dis-
proportionately large part in both revolutions, especially
Kun's; but the Social Democrats had also compromised
themselves by their alliance with Communism, and even
Liberal democracy was tainted by its associations with
Jewry and its share in Károlyi's regime.

Already in the preceding autumn these resentments had
erupted into violence. While the Allies were still labori-
ously negotiating the formation of a government to allow
adequate representation to the workers and Liberal elements, bands of 'White Terrorists', most of them detachments of the 'National Army', were already ranging the
country, wreaking indiscriminate vengeance on persons
whom they associated with the revolutions. Huszár's
government itself had turned so sharply on the Social
Democrats and the Trade Unions, imprisoning hundreds
and interning thousands of alleged revolutionaries, that the
Social Democrats had withdrawn their representative from
the government and boycotted the elections. Thus even
this first parliament, the liberal franchise notwithstanding,
was not at all representative of the nation as a whole. It
was composed – apart from numerous 'independents' and
representatives of dwarf parties – of two main parties,
each hurriedly drummed together: the 'Christian National
Union' and the 'United Agrarians' and Smallholders'
Party'. Of these, the 'Christian Nationals' were Conservatives pure and simple, on the social issue. The core of the
second party was constituted by a 'Smallholders' Party'
formed shortly before the War by a peasant tribune, István
Szabó of Nagytád, and stood for the interests of the small
peasants, and above all, for land reform, but even it contained hardly any representatives of the agricultural proletariat, so that it was true to say that labour of any class was
unrepresented in the parliament.

Nor were impoverishment and embitterment confined

to the working classes. The inflation was quickly reducing a large part of the fixed income middle classes, especially those who had patriotically invested their savings in Austro-Hungarian War Loan, to great poverty. Worse situated still were the families who had fled or been expelled – a distinction which was often without a difference – from the Successor States, leaving their all behind them. By the end of 1920 nearer 400,000 than 300,000 of these unfortunates, nearly all from middle-class families, had found refuge in Rump Hungary, where many of them were existing under lamentable conditions, camped in old railway carriages and supported by the scanty relief which was all that the government could provide for them.

If the financial condition of the members of this class was far worse than that of the workman in full employment, their outlook was traditionalist and above all, nationalist. They were even more embittered than the representatives of property against the revolutions and their authors, whom they regarded as responsible for their misfortunes. Thus in the clash between Left and Right they had sided with the Right; they had, indeed, been the chief executants of the White Terror. But they regarded the crushing of Marxism as the indispensable first step towards political recovery, but only as a first step. They were of the Right, but they were 'Right Radicals', and their aspirations included fairly drastic changes in the national structure at the expense of the great landlords, banks and industrial cartels.

Finally, the nation was split from top to bottom on the dynastic question. While hardly anyone, unless among the proscribed Reds, wanted a republic, the nation was acutely divided over the question whether Charles was still the lawful King of Hungary, or whether his declaration of 13 November 1918 entitled the nation to fill the throne by 'free election'. This question took a precedence in the politics of the day that is only comprehensible in the light

of the national history, and in fact, as will be seen, ended
by determining, albeit indirectly, the course taken by the
national development in other fields.

It was the 'question of public law' with which the
parliament necessarily dealt first. Its first act was to declare
null and void all measures enacted by either Károlyi's or
Kun's governments. The institution of the monarchy was
thus restored, and in recognition of the new situation outside Hungary, the House also annulled the legislation em-
bodying the 1867 Compromise. In view of the division of
opinion among its own members, it left in abeyance the
question of the legal relationship between the nation and
the monarch, but decided to elect as provisional Head of
the State a Regent holding the essential political powers
normally exercised by the Crown. Admiral Horthy was
elected to this office on 1 March. The Huszár government
then resigned, and as the two main parties emerging from
the elections were approximately equal in strength (the
Smallholders being slightly, but only slightly, the larger), a
coalition government was formed out of these two parties,
under the presidency of A. Simonyi-Semadam.

At this time the national policy towards industrial labour
was still one of simple repression, but the demand for land
reform was too strong to be ignored: it was strongly
pressed by Szabó and his followers, and the necessity for
some concession was not denied even by some of the land-
owners themselves. Discussions began in May, and on 10
August (by which time the Simonyi-Semadam Government
had given place to a new one under Count Pál Teleki) an
Act was passed under which 1·2 million *hold* (about 7·5
per cent of the total area of the country) were to be taken
from the largest estates for distribution. This was a modest
figure indeed, especially when compared with the land
reforms being enacted by Hungary's neighbours; but Szabó
had been persuaded that a larger figure would be financially
impracticable at that stage, and had accepted it on the

understanding that it was to be followed by a second instalment when times improved.

But in 1921 the Habsburg question erupted. In March, and again in October, Charles returned to claim his throne. Both times he was forced to withdraw, the command coming from the Allies, on the insistence of Hungary's neighbours; but the anti-Legitimists in Hungary were no less determined to have none of him. The question cut across the parties, for it had not been made an issue at the elections, but while the Legitimists had in the main voted for the Christian Nationals, the great majority of the Smallholders' coalition were vehemently anti-Legitimist; indeed, many of them had joined the party for no other reason, being uninterested in, or even opposed to, land reform. The Right Radicals had voted for it to a man, for in their eyes Habsburg rule was identical with the dominance of big vested interests. This gave his opportunity to the man who for the next ten years was to dominate Hungarian politics and to shape the structure in the image of his own wishes: Count István Bethlen.

A man less Right Radical than Bethlen never stepped. On every social issue he was an arch-conservative, so obviously so that, although Hungary's most experienced politician, who had played the leading part in the Anti-Bolshevik Committee in Vienna, in Hungary he had had to content himself, in 1920, with a place behind the scenes. But in March 1921, when the government (several of whose members were Legitimists) resigned, Bethlen accepted the succession, and while not pronouncing formally (except in admitted lip-service to the Entente[1]) against the king's claims, consented to cover a policy which in fact excluded his return. In return for this, the Smallholders agreed to fuse with the non-Legitimists of the Christians in a new

[1] On the Allies' orders, the Hungarian Parliament passed a law dethroning the Habsburgs, but not even Hungary's own anti-Legitimists ever took this as morally binding.

party under Bethlen's leadership and to support him in a complicated manoeuvre, the result of which was that the franchise enacted before the War, which again restricted the number of voters and restored the open vote outside towns possessing municipal charters,[1] was declared to be still legally in force. This carried (against the frenzied opposition of precisely the highest Conservatives), Bethlen held new elections (May 1922), which naturally gave a large majority to his new 'Party of Unity'; in other words, since the structure of the Party itself made it a mere rubber stamp for endorsing the will of its leader, they gave Bethlen a free hand.

Bethlen was a very long-sighted man, and a man who put first things first. If asked to name in a phrase the supreme goal of his policy, he would probably have answered, like all his class and most Hungarians, total revision of the Treaty of Trianon. But he saw that as the situation then was, with the Allies, led by France, supreme in Europe, Hungary's chief neighbours banded together in the 'Little Entente' and Hungary herself weak and isolated, revision was not, for the time, practical politics; it could only become so when Hungary had recovered her internal strength, and had also acquired influential friends abroad. Thus, if only as the indispensable preliminary to revision, but also for its own sake, the first step must be internal 'consolidation', political and social, and this again, as he saw it, depended on financial reconstruction. The fount of capital was the west, and in particular Geneva, and it was therefore necessary, as a beginning, to renounce any actions which would block Hungary's access to those waters. He refused, indeed, to undertake any obligations towards Hungary's neighbours which, in his eyes or his country's, would have implied a moral renunciation of any revisionist claim; but he discountenanced any open policy of adven-

[1] Even in these a candidate's nomination papers had to be signed by a large number of sponsors, whose signatures were open.

ture (although conniving at certain surreptitious and sometimes scandalous devices) and applied for membership of the League of Nations. This was granted (not without difficulty) in September 1922. Bethlen then applied for a reconstruction loan, similar to that which had just been granted to Austria, and when the Little Entente (fearing that the money would be used for illegitimate purposes) made difficulties, authorised the acceptance of a declaration that Hungary voluntarily accepted, and undertook to carry out strictly and loyally, the obligations of the Treaty of Trianon. The only other political treaty concluded by him was a Treaty of Friendship with Italy, signed in 1927; and this, while it proved useful afterwards as a starting-point for a more active policy, did not signify very much at the time, since Italy in the mid-twenties was concluding Treaties of Friendship with practically every Central European State.

Bethlen's political opponents accused him of having betrayed the nation's cause for gold, but if the correctness of his order of priorities is conceded, then it must also be granted that his policy was most abundantly justified by its results. The protocols of the League loan, which were signed on 24 March 1924, included also the renunciation by the Allies of the lien held by them under the Treaty on 'all Hungary's assets and resources', and the substitution of a fixed total to be paid by her in reparations; and once this agreement had been reached, an almost magical change came over the whole financial picture. Money poured into the country – not only the League loan, but private capital from abroad seeking quick and large returns, while the fugitive domestic capital also returned home.

The inflation was stopped, and a new, gold-based currency, the pengö, introduced, which proved to be among the most stable in Europe. The budgets began to close with surpluses. Agriculture still formed the backbone of the national economy, but in 1926 a new autonomous tariff was introduced, and behind its shelter a considerable amount of industrialisation was carried through; official statistics showed that the number of establishments ranking as factories increased by two thirds between 1920 and 1929, the number of workers employed in them by a little more, and the value of their production by nearly 300 per cent. A greatly increased proportion of the national imports now consisted of industrial raw materials or half-finished products, which were worked up in the national factories. The bulk of the exports still consisted of agricultural products, raw or processed, but markets for these had been found, and prices were good. The total value of foreign trade doubled, and the calculated national income rose by 20 per cent.

Parallel with the financial rehabilitation of Hungary had gone its social and political reconstruction. Bethlen was not himself greedy for money, nor interested in squeezing the poor, and he was too intelligent not to recognise that new times brought new social forces which could not be simply repressed out of existence. But his associations with the landowning class on the one hand, and his conviction of the necessity of meeting the wishes of international capital on the other, biased his outlook strongly in favour of property; and in any case, the idea of allowing the poorer classes an effective voice in the government of the country was entirely foreign to him. His concessions to modernity were thus kept to the minimum which his great tactical ability could contrive. The keystone of his political system was the 1922 franchise, with the help of which he was always able to command a sufficient parliamentary majority for his decisions; the re-construction, in 1926, of an Upper House did not in practice weaken his position, for in a crisis, the Lower House could always impose its will on the Upper. The open franchise, combined with the complete authority exercised by him over the party machine, enabled him to eliminate foreign bodies from the

Government Party (as it was always known) by the simple process of dropping their representatives from the list of candidates, and to prevent their entering parliament in inconveniently large numbers on an Opposition ticket. With the help of these weapons, he was soon finished with the rural poor. The genuine peasant element in the Smallholders' Party had already been greatly weakened in 1921 by a grave financial scandal, in which Szabó himself was involved; and after the 1922 elections the survivors were soon quietly excreted. A close ban on any combination among the agricultural workers prevented them from making their voices heard by direct action. Nothing more was heard after this of the second instalment of the land reform, and the application of the 1920 Act itself was half-hearted. The big landlords whose estates were trimmed for the purpose were allowed to choose what land they would surrender, and naturally parted with the least fertile and most inaccessible corners of their estates. In the event, less than half of the 1·2 million *hold* was distributed to landless men or dwarf-holders, of whom 298,000 beneficiaries received an average of 1·6 *hold* apiece. The rest was retained by the state as unsuitable for distribution, and devoted to communal grazing-grounds, state farms, etc., or distributed to the 'Order of Heroes' (Vitézi Rend), a picked body of men selected for their loyalty to the regime.

The industrial workers were not muzzled quite so tightly; as early as December 1921 Bethlen had concluded a formal treaty with the Social Democrat leaders under which they had been granted an amnesty, the cessation of various forms of persecution, and the same right of association as was enjoyed by other parties, and the Trade Unions had had their confiscated funds restored to them with recognition of their right to pursue their legal activities. As, moreover, the franchise was not open in the towns, the workers' spokesmen were always able to send a quota of representatives to parliament. But these could never con-

stitute more than a minority, and in return for these concessions the Socialists had had to promise to abstain from
anti-national propaganda, to adopt an 'expressly Hungarian
attitude' on foreign political questions, to abstain from
political strikes, to confine the activities of the Unions to
the strictly non-political field, and not to extend their agitation to the agricultural workers.

It would be an over-simplification to describe Bethlen's
operations as simply putting the poor in their places, for
they also included the political neutralisation of a considerable opposition – Legitimists on the one hand, Right
Radicals on the other – among the ruling classes themselves. Towards these, Bethlen employed, indeed, gentler
methods. Whereas apprehended Communist agents were
punished with great severity, offenders of the Right were
usually treated very leniently, 'patriotic motives' being accepted as a sufficient defence, or at least as a powerful miti-
gating circumstance, in their cases. But the iron hand was
there under the velvet glove. The White Terror was liquidated quietly, but effectively, and it became not much
easier (although much less hazardous) to preach active anti-
Semitism than Marxian revolution.

It must be admitted that, judged by his own standards,
Bethlen's political and social consolidation was very successful. The Right Radicals were found jobs in a government service which was expanded, far beyond the national
needs, to receive them, and settled down happily enough
in what seemed to be a new security. The Legitimist question in any case lost its acuteness when Charles died in
1922, for although he left heirs, a new claimant to the
throne could not command the devotion which attached
to the crowned king. Even among the workers, of either
category, there was little active unrest.

Withal, only a moderate amount of pressure was needed
to keep this structure intact. Bethlen was an authoritarian,
but not totalitarian, nor tyrannical. Personal and political

freedoms were far more restricted than in the real demo-
cracies of the day, but generous compared with conditions
prevailing in Russia, or even Italy.

Nevertheless, Bethlen's Hungary was emphatically a class
state, and in a Europe which then believed itself to be advancing towards democracy, it was a conspicuous laggard;
and its handsome façade, like that of Kálmán Tisza's Hungary, covered grievous unsolved social problems. Some
not inconsiderable improvements were introduced in the
working conditions of industrial labour in the '20s, when
real wages also rose perceptibly, but neither wages nor
conditions could be called satisfactory. The condition of
the rural poor was worse still. Fortunately for them, their
birthrate was falling rapidly, and industrialisation was now
proceeding fast enough to absorb most of the surplus. On
the other hand, the American legislation had closed the
main outlet of emigration, so that if the rural congestion
did not increase, neither did it much diminish. The agrarian census of 1935 showed that nearly three million
people – 30 per cent of the total national population and
60 per cent of that employed in agriculture – was either
totally landless or occupying holdings insufficient to support life in decency. Real wages in agriculture were below
even the pre-war level. Even the poorer members of the
middle classes – and true wealth was concentrated in a
very few hands indeed – existed precariously enough, and
the universities were beginning to produce a large new
potential intellectual proletariat.

Many of these evils might ultimately have vanished if
prosperity had continued, but the whole structure of
Bethlen's system rested on two pillars: the maintenance of
international credit, until such time as Hungary no longer
needed to borrow, and the continuance of high prices on
the world market for her exports, particularly wheat. In
1929 both of these were shaken by the collapse of world
wheat prices, started by over-production in Canada, and

by the Stock Exchange crash on Wall Street. In 1930 the Government had already to support the price of wheat, but the consequences for Hungary did not become really serious until the collapse of the Austrian *Creditanstalt* in May 1931. Even this did not shake Bethlen's position; a month after it, he held elections which returned the Government Party to power with the usual large majority. But in the next weeks the full impact of the financial blizzard hit the country. Unable to meet the demands of her foreign creditors, who were trying hurriedly to withdraw their funds, she had to appeal to the League of Nations, which prescribed a policy of ruthless financial orthodoxy, including the balancing of her budget by increasing revenue by heavier taxation and reducing expenditure by salary cuts and dismissals in the public services, and the balancing of her balance of payments by the throttling of imports. Meanwhile the cascading agricultural prices had left her entire producing agricultural class practically penniless and heavily indebted to the banks to boot, while the disappearance of the purchasing power of this class, coupled with the dwindling of exports (since other countries were in the same plight) and even of imported raw materials, sent industrial unemployment rocketing sky-high.

The fantastic severity of the depression not only wiped out the economic gains of the previous decade, but also threatened the political and social consolidation. Bethlen himself resigned in August 1931. His successor, Count Gyula Károlyi, was another great aristocrat, of unbending conservatism and irreproachable probity, who set himself with determination to carry out the League's recommendations. But as one severe measure followed another, unrest grew. There were strikes and demonstrations among the workers, but more dangerous to the system was the revolt of the medium and small farmers, crushed under the weight of their indebtedness to the banks, the axed civil servants and the officers, and the jobless young university graduates. This discontent took the form of a revived Right Radicalism, directed especially against the Jews, who were the creditor class in Hungary and whose entrenched positions in trade and industry barred employment to a class for which the state was now forbidden to provide.

In September 1932 Károlyi declared himself unable to fight any more against the clamour of the malcontents, and on 1 October the Regent yielded, and appointed to the Minister Presidency the acknowledged leader of the Right Radicals, Captain (as he then was) Gyula Gömbös.

Gömbös and Bethlen are the two anti-poles of inter-war Hungarian politics. Even their personalities form an extraordinary contrast: the Transylvanian aristocrat, in whose veins mingled the blood of half Hungary's historic families, and the up-and-coming product of west Hungarian yeoman stock, at least half Swabian; the suave grand seigneur, the theatrical poseur; the calculating and long-sighted threader and contriver of mazes, the bull-headed charger of fences. Gömbös' political creed was centred round two main tenets, both of them, indeed, the products of the same primary emotion, a passionate nationalism: a fanatical anti-Habsburgism and an equally fanatical racialism, which found its chief vent in a *bruyant* (although not sadistic) anti-Semitism. Round these two poles he had draped a sincere, although not closely reasoned, Fascism, which found room for a genuine wish to improve the social conditions of his people, whom he regarded as the exploited victims of Jewish financiers and Habsburg-tainted landlords.

His foreign political programme had no place for Bethlen's patient *ménagement* of existing forces. Early in his career he had conceived a vision of an 'Axis' (the term, in this connotation, was of his minting) which was to consist of the new Hungary, Fascist Italy and Nazi Germany; in this edition, Germany was to annexe Austria (except for the Burgenland, which she would restore to Hungary), allaying Italy's fears by guaranteeing the Brenner frontier.

These three states, linked by kindred ideologies, were to help each other to realise their national objectives (in Hungary's case, her historic frontiers) and thereafter to exercise a sort of joint leadership of Europe, a better Europe, purged of Bolshevism and its shadows.

The appointment of such a man to the Minister Presidency should have brought with it a revolution in Hungarian policy, both internal and foreign. In fact, it brought no more than a half turn. During his first three years of office Gömbös in any case enjoyed little of the reality of power. In the old days he had been Horthy's favourite, but the Regent had grown more sedate with the passing years, and Gömbös' radical tenets, good and bad, were now alike repugnant to him. He censored his list of ministers, and also refused him permission to hold new elections, so that he had to govern with a parliament mainly composed of Bethlen's adherents. On top of this, he found himself no more able than his predecessors to defy the then generally accepted rule that the creditor calls the tune, and his time was largely spent in trying to lift Hungary out of the depression by entirely orthodox methods. Finally, it was borne in on him that the said rule was not only international in its application. He consequently astounded Hungary by announcing that he had 'revised his views on the Jewish question'; and his internal political activities were as non-subversive, in this respect, as his dealings with international capital.

He made one important move in foreign policy. When he came into office, one member of the proposed Axis was in any case lacking, for Hitler was not yet in power in Germany. But Mussolini was there, and Gömbös took an early opportunity of visiting Rome, when he elicited from the Duce a public expression of sympathy for Hungarian revision. This, far more than the 1924 Treaty, really committed Hungary to an Italian orientation, for no Hungarian government could thereafter possibly disavow the only Power of stature approximating to greatness which had said a word in favour of revision. But it did not bring the Axis nearer, for when Hitler did come into power, the only early move which he made in eastern Europe was to start an agitation in Austria. As Mussolini by no means accepted Gömbös' original Axis doctrine, but regarded Austrian independence as a vital interest of Italy's, the first result of Gömbös' policy was that Hungary was drawn into a bloc, composed of Italy, Hungary and Austria, the chief *raison d'être* of which was precisely to thwart Hitler's ambitions. Gömbös tried to keep an open door towards Germany, struck up a warm personal friendship with Göring, and wheedled a very advantageous commercial treaty out of Hitler himself, but the documents show the Germans, at this time, as highly suspicious and resentful of Hungarian policy. If, in the negotiations which began at the end of 1934 between Italy and France, France had been able to persuade her allies of the Little Entente to make any concessions of substance to Hungary, Hungary might yet have found herself a member of a new European combination directed against Germany.

The Franco-Italian negotiations, of course, failed, and were followed in due course by Mussolini's quarrel with the West and, eventually, his announcement of the formation of the 'Rome-Berlin Axis'. By this time Hitler had occupied the Rhineland and it was clear that Germany would soon be able, if she were willing, to perform the role which Gömbös had assigned to her. Further, Horthy had at last allowed Gömbös to dissolve parliament, and as a result of the elections 'made' by him in May 1935 he had brought a strong contingent of his own followers into parliament and had placed others in many key political and military posts.

But by now it was clear that the situation created by Germany's emergence was nothing like so simple as Gömbös, in his early enthusiasm, had imagined. Hitler

35. *Miklós Horthy, Regent of Hungary*

36 and 37. *The old and the new Hungary*

soon made it plain that he had no intention of simply restoring Hungary's historic frontiers for her. He told Gömbös himself, as early as 1934, that while Hungary might, if she would, take her share in the partition of Czechoslovakia, she was to keep her hands off Yugoslavia and Roumania.

Even this fraction-loaf was something which no Hungarian would refuse if it could be received safely. But Hungary was still practically unarmed, and in no case to defend herself against attack, much less attack anyone else. She needed assurances and protection. Germany might give them, but presumably, only at the price of a contractual obligation. And then, what if Germany's policies resulted in a general war? No fate could be worse for Hungary than a second time to enter a great war on Germany's side, and a second time to share her defeat.

Neither – it was now plain – could the new Germany be regarded simply in the light of a potential liberator. It was a ruthless, self-centred Power, which might well not even leave Hungary's own independence unimpaired, but seek, if not actually to annexe Hungary, to reduce it to satellite status, dominating its economy and intervening in its internal conditions. And at this point the German problem became inextricably bound up with that of Hungary's own internal politics, by reason of the ideological character of the Nazi regime, and in particular, its anti-Semitism. Those elements in Hungary which had most to fear from an extension of German-Nazi influence – the Legitimists, the Socialists, and above all the Jews – naturally saw most clearly the dangerous aspects of the situation, including – since every man's calculations are largely the children of his wishes – the international danger which association with Germany might bring, while the sympathisers with Hitler's ideology took the dangers lightly, or where they did admit them, used them as an argument in favour of their own domestic programme. The way to make sure of

Hitler's good will, they contended, was to copy his doings, while to refuse to do so was to invite his hostility. Was Hungary not merely to renounce revision, but to jeopardise her own independence for the sake of a system and an element which in their view were *per se* undesirable?

Hungarian political opinion thus split along a new line of cleavage in which the Right Radicals were faced, on the domestic issue, by a curious shadow Opposition Front, stretching all the way from the Legitimists through the traditionalist 'Liberal Conservatives' right to the Socialists; these two groups also, in the main, personifying respectively the party of caution on the international issue, and the forward party which advocated the closest possible co-operation with Germany. And even Gömbös' victory at the polls by no means meant that the forward policy was going to have a free course, for the last word in politics rested with the Regent, and the Regent's sympathies were with the traditionalists in domestic politics, while on the international issue he was strongly on the side of the party of caution, his naval past having implanted in him a strong conviction that great wars were always won by the side holding the command of the seas.

The Right was further weakened by the death of Gömbös in October 1936. None of his closer adherents enjoyed such prestige as to compel his appointment, and the Regent appointed as his successor Kálmán Darányi, who was much more of a conservative than a radical on domestic issues. In fact, the domestic legislation enacted during his term of office, which included a Franchise Act introducing the secret ballot in the rural districts, was non-contentious, and most of it had been agreed with the Opposition. In any case, Hungarian internal politics, from this date until 1944, had become little more than a function of foreign politics, and the history of Hungary during the same years is little more than that of her relations with Germany; that is to say, endeavours to pluck for herself the fruits which Germany's growing power brought within her reach, while escaping the dangers. It was, as the following years showed, a hopeless attempt. It brought, indeed, temporary gains – the restoration of about half of what Hungary had lost at Trianon – but it ended in a fresh disaster which wiped out all those gains and left Hungary saddled with precisely the odium which she had hoped to escape. Nor is the story free from blots on Hungary's own record. Yet in the main it appears above all as a tragedy, in which good actions could do no more to arrest, than bad to precipitate, a doom dictated by forces far exceeding Hungary's own.

The Germans chose to greet Dáranyi's appointment with hostility, and his first year of office was enlivened by brisk disputes with them on Hungary's treatment of her German minority. These were smoothed over when Darányi, with Kánya, the foreign minister, visited Berlin in November 1937, on which occasion Hitler again intimated to his guests that Hungary could have Slovakia-Ruthenia when he acted against Czechoslovakia. The Hungarian General Staff now began pressing for co-ordinated agreements with Germany, but the politicians remained cautious. Close contact was made with Poland and a campaign initiated to convince Britain of the justice of Hungary's cause. A little later, when Darányi tried to reach a working agreement with the most important of the extremist parties of the Right, Ferencz Szálasi's Arrow Cross, Horthy dismissed him in favour of Béla Imrédy. It is true that Imrédy introduced (as part of a complex of legislation which included a programme of rearmament, to which Hungary now declared herself entitled) a law limiting the participation of Jews in certain callings to 20 per cent; but this measure (which had been prepared before Darányi's fall) had been approved by the Jewish leaders themselves as a prudent and not excessive sop to Cerberus. For the rest, the chief reason for Imrédy's appointment, which was made on Bethlen's advice, was precisely that he possessed good connections with the West.

Another recruit to the cabinet was Count Pál Teleki, the distinguished geographer (thus returning to ministerial office after eighteen years), who shared to the full Horthy's belief in the invincibility of the West, while Kánya, who remained foreign minister, was the very embodiment of caution. When the Regent, accompanied by Imrédy and Kánya, paid a state visit to Kiel in August, the Hungarians, pleading their unarmed condition, declared themselves unable to take part in a military operation, and when the Munich crisis broke in September, they made almost passionate endeavours to get their claims realised on their own merits, limiting their demands, in that cause, to the ethnic frontier which they thought Britain would approve, and thereby, if unintentionally, nearly wrecking Hitler's plans.

This was their first great disappointment. Mr Chamberlain ignored them completely, and it was left to Hitler, after all (who was infuriated with them, but needed their collaboration, with that of the Poles and Slovaks, if his own gains were not to be limited to the Sudeten areas), to put their case for them. Ultimately it was referred to direct negotiation between the parties, with the proviso that if they failed to agree, it should be referred back to the Munich Powers. Naturally, they failed, whereupon Britain and France disinterested themselves, and Hungary was left alone (except for platonic and not in practice very helpful support from Italy and Poland) to face an irritated Hitler, who now showed an inclination to support the Czechs and Slovaks (who had abjured democracy and flung themselves into his arms) on the disputed issues. Yugoslavia was already very nearly in the Axis camp, Roumania moving towards it. In these circumstances, the argument that Hungary could not afford to antagonise Hitler was convincing indeed. Placatory offers were made, and although no bargain was struck at the time – the arbitral award, rendered by Germany and Italy on 2 November, gave Hungary only the Magyar-inhabited southern fringe of Slovakia-Ruthenia, which she would probably have received in any case, while denying her Ruthenia – a new course was set immediately after it. Kánya was dropped in favour of Count István Csáky, a young man who announced his policy to be 'quite simply, that of the Rome-Berlin Axis all along the line', and at a subsequent meeting with Hitler, gave him far-reaching, albeit indefinite, promises of support.

Meanwhile Imrédy, who had been profoundly dis-illusioned by his experiences at Munich, announced a near-Fascist internal programme, including a second Jewish Law, more drastic than its predecessor (the quota was to be reduced to 6 per cent and the definition of a Jew tightened up). This, indeed, provoked a revolt. His enemies unearthed documents which purported to show a Jewish strain in Imrédy's own ancestry. He resigned (February 1939), and the Regent appointed Teleki, whose devoted determination not to let Hungary become in-volved in a conflict with the West was unquestionable. But Teleki himself thought it impossible to do more than stabilise Hungary's position on the lower level to which Imrédy and Csáky had brought it. He kept Csáky at the foreign ministry, and on a visit to Berlin agreed that in a world conflict Hungary would 'take up her position by the side of the Axis Powers', only stipulating that she would not act against Poland. Similarly, he steered the Second Jewish Law through parliament. Incidentally, when, in June, he held elections on the new suffrage, with the secret ballot, all the parties of the Left-wing Opposition lost heavily, while the Arrow Cross and its allies appeared as the second largest party.

Early in Teleki's period of office came the completion of the dismemberment of Czechoslovakia, as a by-product whereof Hungary in March 1939 re-acquired Ruthenia.

Here Teleki was lucky, for although Hitler had sanctioned the operation, the West did not take it ill. He was lucky, too, when the Second World War broke out, for Germany did not ask for Hungary's participation, and for nearly a year more Hungary could still hope that the end of the conflict would leave her uncompromised. But the next developments showed how inextricable was the tangle in which she was involved. She had promised both groups of belligerents (both of whom, remarkably, wanted the same thing in this respect) not to 'disturb the peace in South-Eastern Europe' by pressing her claims against Roumania unless others took action likely to prejudice the peaceful realisation of those claims after the war. But in June 1940 the U.S.S.R. occupied Bessarabia, and Hungary now told the Axis Powers that she must receive satisfaction of her claims. By threatening to march, she forced them to render the 'Second Vienna Award', of 30 August, which gave her about two fifths of the disputed territory. But the result of her action (with Russia's and Bulgaria's) was that Roumania swung right round, repudiated the guarantee of the Western Powers, accepted one from Germany, and in a trice had become Germany's favourite client in south-eastern Europe.

Roumania as Germany's client was, in the situation of the day, far more dangerous than Roumania as her enemy, for, much more than in the parallel but less acute case of Slovakia, the situation produced a race for Germany's favour, for which Roumania bid in the hope of securing the reversal of the Award, and Hungary to ensure its maintenance. This rivalry led to Hungary's signing the Tripartite Pact, in November 1940, and the next development drew the toils closer still. A party among the Hungarians, to which Teleki belonged, had long urged reconciliation with Yugoslavia – originally, indeed, with the purpose of detaching her from the Little Entente. This consideration no longer applied, but Teleki favoured pursuing the policy, with the idea that the two countries should help each other to resist excessive pressure from Germany. Yet Hitler, although doubtless aware of Teleki's thoughts, favoured the rapprochement as making it easier for Yugoslavia to enter the 'Axis orbit'; and that she should do so was an obvious, and understood, condition of the whole move, for close contractual relations between the two countries would have been impossible if they had been on opposite sides in the world alignment. A Hungaro-Yugoslav Treaty, called with unfortunate grandiloquence a 'Pact of Eternal Friendship', was duly signed on 12 December, and the Yugoslav Government then in fact took step after step towards the Axis. But Hitler pressed them too hard; the Opposition revolted, and on 26 March, deposed its government. Hitler in fury prepared to invade Yugoslavia and called on Hungary to join him. The Hungarians, caught in a situation which they had not at all envisaged, did not join in the attack, but did not try to stop the transit of German troops across their territory into Roumania, whence part of Hitler's attack was launched, and on 11 April, after Croatia had proclaimed itself independent, Hungary occupied the ex-Hungarian parts of Inner Hungary, claiming that Yugoslavia no longer existed.

Britain had threatened to declare war if Hungary joined the attack, and on 2 April, when it seemed likely that his policy – undertaken with such different intentions – was involving Hungary in that conflict with the West which it had been his supreme aim to avoid, Teleki had taken his own life. In the event, Britain contented herself with breaking off diplomatic relations, but a few weeks later Teleki's successor, Bárdossy, took the step which was technically decisive. The occasion was Hitler's attack on the U.S.S.R. In his preparations he had not assigned Hungary a role in the campaign, but the Hungarian generals had pressed their German colleagues to let Hungary participate, so that she should not be left behind in the race for favour (and arms) by Roumania, which had been invited. No one calculated that Russia would hold out for more than a few weeks, nor expected complications with the West to arise.

After the attack had begun, messages from the O.K.W. and a queer incident, still unexplained – the bombing of Kassa, in north Hungary, by aircraft bearing Axis markings – convinced Bárdossy, who had hitherto resisted the representations of the generals, that Germany really wanted Hungary's participation, and would exact it in the long run; and arguing that willing compliance would be cheaper than reluctant submission to pressure, he adopted the General Staff's version that the unidentified aircraft had been Russian aeroplanes disguised, and sent an expeditionary force, conceived as a token, across the Carpathians.

This step soon brought its nemesis, for whatever the outcome might have been if the calculation of Russia's weakness had proved correct, when the resistance proved prolonged, Hungary found herself pushed fatally down the path of no return. In January 1942 the Germans arrived with a demand that she should mobilise practically her whole available manpower and send it up to the line. Meanwhile Mr Churchill had identified the cause of the West with that of Russia. In December 1941 Britain had declared war on Hungary and a few days later Hungary in her turn declared war on the U.S.A. Further, Britain had recognised the Czechoslovak Government in exile and had withdrawn recognition of the First Vienna Award; the U.S.S.R. even formally recognised Czechoslovakia's 1937 frontiers. The re-creation (in shadow form) of the Little Entente was practically complete.

Many Hungarians now thought that the only course was to fight on in the hope that the Axis would win the war. Horthy saw the situation differently. He was quite convinced that the war would end in an Allied victory, but he also believed that the West did not want the bolshevisation of Europe, and that Hungary could regain its favour while continuing the fight in the East. In March 1942 he therefore dismissed Bárdossy in favour of Miklós Kállay, who shared these hopes, and one more attempt was made to recover the lost ground. For two years Kállay conducted a remarkable policy. He afforded to Hungary's Jews a protection then unparalleled on the Continent; allowed almost complete freedom to all anti-Hitlerite and non-Communist elements, whom he allowed to build up an 'Independence Front' which openly speculated on an Allied victory, and opened secret conversations with the Western Powers, with whom, in August 1943, he actually concluded a secret agreement to surrender to them unconditionally when their troops should reach the frontiers of Hungary. The active prosecution of the campaign in the East was, meanwhile, brought to an end by the catastrophe of Voronezh, in January 1943, in which Hungary lost half her armed forces and nearly all her equipment.

Kállay's balancing feat at least gave Hungary's traditional institutions, and also the anti-Hitlerite elements in the country, two years of life; but such hope as might ever have existed for his policy vanished when the inter-Allied strategy assigned south-eastern Europe to the Soviet armies. Further, when those armies approached the Carpathians, Hitler (to whom most of Kállay's activities were an open book) decided that he could no longer afford to leave his vital communications with the East at the mercy of a regime in whose loyalty he could not trust. In March 1944 he summoned Horthy and offered him the choice between full co-operation in Germany's war effort, under close German supervision, or undisguised occupation and the treatment afforded to a conquered enemy country. Horthy chose the former course, and appointed a collaborationist government under General Sztójay, but for some three months thereafter the Germans in practice did as they would in Hungary, the government seldom resisting and often abetting them. All anti-Nazi parties and organisations were dissolved, and their leaders arrested or driven into hiding. Above all, the Jews suffered one of the greatest tragedies in the history of Israel. They were herded into camps and then deported, chiefly to Ausschwitz, where all but an able-bodied minority were sent to the gas-chambers. All the Jews outside Budapest, some 450,000 in number, suffered deportation, and of these not more than 120,000 survived. Meanwhile, another army, comprising almost Hungary's last reserves, had been sent to the Front.

After a while the pressure eased and Horthy recovered some freedom of action. He stopped the Jewish deportations before they had extended to the capital, and in August, after Roumania's surrender, appointed a new government on the loyalty of most of whose members, including the Minister President, General Lakatos, he could rely. Now he reopened secret communications with the West, but the answer was categoric: Hungary must address the U.S.S.R., whose armies were, indeed, now standing on, or across the frontier. So it was Bolshevik Russia, after all, that entered Hungary as its conqueror, although there was one more short scene before the curtain fell. A mission sent by Horthy to Moscow duly concluded a 'preliminary armistice', but when, on 15 October, Horthy announced the negotiations on the wireless, the Germans, whose forces round Budapest far outnumbered the Hungarian, seized him, forced him to recant and to abdicate and allowed Szálasi, with whom they had long been in touch, to take over the Government. The great majority of the Hungarian army itself preferred to fight on, and it was only slowly, and at the cost of bitter fighting, that the Germans and their Hungarian allies were driven westward. The last of these forces crossed the Austrian frontier on 4 April, following or preceding a great host of civilian refugees.

Meanwhile the birth of a new order had again preceded the passing of the old. Under Soviet auspices, a 'Provisional government of Democratic Hungary' had been assembled and 'appointed' on 23 December 1944, by a 'Provisional National Assembly' brought together in Debrecen by pragmatic methods. This government then signed an armistice, under which the new Hungary renounced all territorial acquisitions made since 1938. The Peace Treaty, signed on 10 February 1947, formally restored the Trianon frontiers, further aggravated by a small but strategically important frontier rectification in favour of Czechoslovakia.

10

THE PEOPLE'S REPUBLIC

THE end of the Second World War left Hungary facing even greater material difficulties than had its predecessor. This time the country itself had been a theatre of war, and the fighting had left a trail of devastation across it: cities – notably Buda, which had been stubbornly defended – in ruins, fields scorched, communications wrecked; in particular, all the vital bridges between Buda and Pest had been blown up. The retreating Germans had taken with them what even they could of the country's portable wealth. On their heels had followed huge and disorderly Soviet armies, living off the land, and a big force of these remained encamped in the country after the fighting had ended. Already under the armistice Hungary had been assessed to pay reparations to the value of 300 million dollars. As the U.S.S.R. took its share in kind, putting its own valuation of the objects seized, Hungary was in fact stripped of property worth far more than the stipulated sum, on this pretext alone.

But as in 1919, the material difficulties were overshadowed by the political problem: this time, the vital question whether Hungary was to belong to the West or the East. And while the next three or four years saw the healing, with gratifying rapidity, of the worst of the material damage, they saw also the steady advance of the East into what seemed to be an impregnable position.

The Soviets opened their operations with a caution imposed in part by the international situation, in part by the almost complete absence of native sympathisers with them; for effective agents they had at first to depend almost exclusively on a handful of ex-émigrés, popularly known as 'Muscovites', who had returned in the rear of the armies. They announced that the new Hungary was to be a democracy, resting on the will of all its genuinely democratic elements, and they allowed this quality to the non-Communist parties of the Left which had belonged to the 'Independence Front' during the war: the Social Democrats, the Smallholders, the National Peasants[1] and even a group calling itself the 'Progressive Bourgeoisie'. The Provisional Government contained only two Communists (both Muscovites), and was composed for the rest of representatives of these four parties, and even of four figures closely associated with Horthy; and its programme, as read out at Debrecen, while envisaging sweeping social changes, including a drastic land reform and the nationalisation of the mines and heavy industry, promised guarantees of democratic rights and freedoms, respect of private property as such, and the encouragement of private initiative in trade and small industry.

The first elections, held in November 1945, were really free, although only the parties of the coalition were allowed to contest them, and although the Communists had by now gathered a certain number of adherents, sincere and otherwise, and had further induced the Social Democrats to form an alliance with them, they gave an absolute majority to the Smallholders. Now, however, came the first disillusionment, for the head of the Soviet Mission insisted that the coalition form of government must continue, and backed by pressure from him, the Communists obtained the ministry of the interior, with the control of the police. The Smallholders were allowed to retain the Minister Presidency, but were forced by 'salami tactics' of pressure and blackmail to expel successively their more

[1] A tiny group, at that time a headquarters staff without an army, which had formed itself during the war and claimed to represent the interests of the agricultural proletariat.

courageous elements as 'Fascists', and the next elections, held in August 1947, reduced their vote to 15 per cent. Although this time fraud and pressure had been exerted, the vote for the 'Workers' Bloc' (Communist and Social Democrats) had not gone up very greatly, for this time Opposition parties had been allowed to stand, and had polled 35 per cent of the total votes. But the Communists were now strong enough to deal with these without much circumlocution, and now they turned on their own Social Democrat allies. In June 1948 these were coerced into fusing with the Communists in a single 'Workers' Party', those who refused to do so being expelled. The next elections, in May 1949, were farcical. The voters were presented with a single list, on which 'Smallholders' and 'National Peasants' still figured, but the persons using these names were simply stooges. A new Constitution was now introduced, a copy, in all relevant respects, of that of the U.S.S.R. This proclaimed Hungary a 'People's Republic'[1] and although the President of the Republic and, for a while, the Minister President were still nominal Smallholders, all real power was now in the hands of the Party, which in its turn was controlled by its Secretary-General, Mátyás Rákosi, now, under Moscow, the complete boss of the country. The last act in the struggle for power was now fought out between the two wings of the Communists themselves, the 'Muscovites' or Soviet agents pure and simple, and the 'national Communists', who had spent their lives in their own country and retained some affection for it. In October 1949 the leader of the latter group, László Rajk, was executed on a trumped-up charge. Several of his chief adherents shared his fate and hundreds more were imprisoned.

The civil service, judiciary and army had already been purged, and the Trade Unions reduced to the role of executants of party orders. After the fall of the parties, the

[1] It had already been proclaimed a republic in January 1946.

chief surviving ideological opposition to communism had been in the churches. On these the regime had begun its attack in 1948. Much of the spiritual strength of the churches lay in the large control which they still exercised over education, and this was now also economically their Achilles' heel, since they had lost their endowments under the land reform. The Calvinist and Lutheran churches accepted, without much difficulty, a composition under which the state took over their schools and paid the teachers' salaries, two hours religious instruction weekly being allowed, although the rest of the curriculum was laicised. The roman catholic church, under its obstinate and courageous leader, the Cardinal-Primate Mindszenty, stood out. In December 1948 he was arrested and condemned to life imprisonment on trumped-up charges. The catholic schools were then forcibly laicised and the bulk of the catholic Orders dissolved.

All these campaigns had been carried out with Asiatic brutality. A series of mock trials of 'war criminals' (including, of course, some real criminals, but many whose only offence had been patriotism) had been followed by mass judicial murders, imprisonments or internment under wretched conditions, often accompanied by vile torture, of the opponents of the new order.

Meanwhile, the Sovietisation of the economic system, outside the land, had been practically completed. Industry, foreign and wholesale trade and banking were early nationalised. The nationalisation was linked with Plans for the redevelopment of the national economy. The first of these, introduced in August 1947, consisted chiefly of immediacy measures for repairing war damage. It was declared completed, seven months ahead of schedule, on 31 December 1949, when a more ambitious Five Years' Plan was introduced. The declared intention of this was to turn Hungary into a predominantly industrial country. This meant that the production of consumer goods was starved, while large sums were invested in heavy industry. Much industrialisation was carried through, some of it beneficial, but the new industries were often planned without regard to Hungary's own resources, and with even less regard to her own needs. Many of them produced, out of raw materials imported from Russia, goods (often munitions) needed by Russia, which overcharged for the materials and underpaid for the products. Thus while industrial production increased very largely, the benefit of the increase to Hungary was far smaller.

So long as the Communists had felt it advisable to share office with the Smallholders, the peasants had been left in peace. But in 1948 Rákosi announced the collectivisation of agriculture to be his policy. Three forms were envisaged. the collective pure and simple, and a closer and a looser form of co-operative. While there was no legal compulsion, very strong pressure was applied, and peasants owning holdings above a shrinking minimum were persecuted in innumerable ways. Owing, however, to the very stubborn resistance of the peasants, collectivisation made slow progress.

From 1949 to 1953 Rákosi was nearly all-powerful, except in this one field, and except that the roman catholic church had still not submitted unconditionally. After Stalin's death a period of fluctuations set in. In July 1953 Rákosi, who since 1952 had presided over the government as well as the Party, was deposed from the former office in favour of Imre Nagy, who was, indeed, a Muscovite, but unlike any of the rest of that group, discernibly a Magyar in his mental and even his physical characteristics, and consequently enjoyed some popularity, even among non-Communists. Nagy promised a new course: the forced development of heavy industry should cease, more consumer goods be produced, the peasants no longer forced into the collectives, and even allowed to leave them, more tolerance be shown in political life, especially towards the

38. *Budapest*, 1945

39. *The Danube Steel works, 1958*

intelligentsia and the churches, political prisoners be released and the internment camps closed. Many of these reforms were really introduced, and were warmly welcomed by the country and even by a considerable fraction of the Party itself. The new course was, however, bitterly opposed by the Old Guard of Stalinists, led by Rákosi, who had retained his position at the head of the Workers' Party. It seemed that Rákosi still had Moscow's ear, for in the spring of 1955 Nagy was dismissed from his office and even expelled from the Party.

Supreme again – for the new Minister President was a nonentity – Rákosi whipped the country back onto its old course, economic and political; but this was another short-lived episode, for in July 1956 he was again dismissed, this time from all his offices, and in disgrace. Again reforms were promised, but this time the hopes which they evoked received a chilling blast. Kruschev had sacrificed Rákosi merely to appease Tito, whose personal enmity the Hungarian had occurred, and his successor as Party Secretary was E. Gerö, a man as fanatical and as detested as himself, who announced that there were to be no concessions on matters of principle, and none to Nagy and his group. Disappointment at this, embittered by grievances both old and new against the Russians, led to the event which once more coupled the name of Hungary with that of freedom. Nagy's new course had set stirring in the country a new life, especially among the writers and students, which the reaction of 1955 had stimulated rather than repressed, and Rákosi's second fall had given it more confidence still. On 23 October the students of Budapest staged a grand demonstration in favour of political, social and national freedom. The population flocked out to join them. An unwise and truculent speech by Gerö, followed by shooting into the unarmed crowd by the hated political police, turned into revolution what had begun as a peaceable demonstration. Army depots and munition factories opened their stores; the people armed themselves and turned on their tyrants. Soviet troops hastily summoned by the regime were driven from Budapest, and in the following days a series of kaleidoscopic political changes took place, at the end of which Nagy, for whom the people had first called, found himself heading a genuine coalition cabinet drawn from representatives of the Smallholder, Social Democrat and National Peasant parties, which, with a 'Catholic Alliance', had reconstituted themselves as by magic. The doors of the prisons were opened to the political prisoners, and a cheering crowd brought Cardinal Mindszenty to the capital. Throughout the country local Councils sprang up, the communist bureaucracy melting away before them.

The revolution was as complete as it had been spontaneous, but it clearly could not stand up against the Soviets if they determined to crush it, and if no friend intervened. A leading popular demand was that the Soviet army of occupation should evacuate the country, and the Soviet government promised to 'negotiate' on this. But while spinning out the conversations they had been calling up reinforcements, and on 30 October these began to enter the country, fanning out to surround Budapest and the other chief centres. On this, Nagy appealed for help to the United Nations, announcing Hungary's withdrawal from the 'Warsaw Pact'[1] and asking that she be recognised as a neutral state under the protection of the Great Powers. But the West, fatally preoccupied with Suez, did not even acknowledge the appeal. The Soviets simply waited until their deployment was complete; then, at dawn on 4 November, they attacked. Simultaneously, an ex-national Communist named János Kádár announced from behind their lines the formation of a new 'revolutionary peasant-worker government' to save Hungary from 'Fascist counter revolution'.

[1] A Treaty of mutual defence and military co-operation, concluded in May 1955 between the U.S.S.R. and the Satellites.

This time the fighting was embittered, and even after the last shots had been fired, the workers and miners maintained a long and obstinate General Strike. But in view of the odds, only one end was possible, and by the end of the year 'order' had been restored, leaving Hungary the poorer by thousands of dead, thousands more deported to Russia, nearly 200,000 refugees who had escaped into the free world, and much material damage; the richer by another glorious name on her tattered battle-colours.

It is too early to write in any detail on what followed. In the first weeks, before it was clear that nothing more than platonic disapproval would come from the West, Kádár made many promises of reform. It is true that his regime lacked the sadism of Rákosi's. Personal freedoms were larger, more contact with the West allowed, more production of consumer goods permitted and the economic exchanges with the U.S.S.R. made less inequitable. But no concession was made on fundamentals, and the Hungarian people remained the prisoners of that East on which they had turned their backs when Árpád led them across the Carpathians, more than 1,000 years ago.

INDEX

H. denotes Hungary or Hungarian

245

Pázmány, Cardinal, 83-4
peasants: in mediaeval kingdom,
30, 45-6, 50, 61-3; in Turkish
H., 68-9; in Royal H., 113-4;
in 18th C., 101, 102, 113-6,
123; proposals for reform,
136, 139, 149; emancipation
(1848), 156, 158-9; under
absolutism, 164; in Dualist
Era, 194-5; Kun and, 205;
in Trianon H., 213; under
Communism, 240; Revolts,
50, 62-3, 135, 195
Pesti Hirlap, 147-8
Petchenegs, 8, 21, 31
Peter, King of H., 18, 19, 20
Petöfi, S., 141, 182
Piarists, 109
Pilgrim of Passau, 11
Plan Carpini, 33
Podiebrad, George, 54, 56, 58
Poland: 12, 14, 41, 43, 46, 47,
52, 79, 85; and Trianon
H., 206, 227, 228
land ceded to, 206
population: of Danube Basin
before Conquest, 4-5; after
Conquest, 9-10; in national
kingdom, 21-2, 23, 33, 43;
reduction under Turks, 70-2;
after Wars of Liberation, 88-
9; growth in 18th C., 98, 119;
lost to H., after Trianon,
206-7
porcelain, Herend, 107
porta, 41-2, 45-6, 50, 58, 114
Portia, 86
Pragmatic Santion, 94
preliminary sanction, 171
press, 139, 147-8, 153, 156
Progressive Bourgeoisie, 237
Progressive Conservatives, 151-2

Protestantism: Reformation in
H., 76-7; in Transylvania, 78,
81; protection of, 80-2, 84,
85, 93; persecution of, 84,
86-7, 89-90, 92; disabilities,
109-10; accorded equal rights,
122-3, 124, 133; Patent of
Toleration, 122-3, 124
Public Law, question of, 174-5,
198-9, 212-3, 214

Radetsky, Field-Marshal, 161
raids, H., into Europe, 10-11
Rajk, László, 238
Rákóczi, György I, 82
Rákóczi, György II, 85, 92
Rákóczi, Ferencz, II, 92, 93, 96
Rákosi, Mátyás, 238, 240, 241,
243
Ratio educationis, 100, 112
Rauch, Baron L., 200
rearmament, 227
reconstruction loan, 216, 221
Red Terror, 205
Reformation: in H., 76-7; in
Transylvania, 78-9, 81-2, 83,
84
Reform Era, In H., 122-54; in
Croatia, 141-3; in Transyl-
vania, 151-2
refugees, 210, 212, 243
Regency, establishment of, 213
Regnum Marianum, 110
Reichsrat; reinforced, 166; re-
stricted, 167
religion: under Crown control,
101; Patent of Toleration,
122-3, 124; Habsburg policy
towards, 76-84, 89-90, 92,
109-10, 122-3, 124, 133;
Transylvanian settlement, 78-
9; established, 78; tolerated,
78

succession (*contd.*)
hereditary, 18, 75, 89; problems of, 18-20, 36, 38-9, 40, 47, 51-2, 53-4, 59-60, 65-6; principle of legitimacy, 38; female, 47, 94; vested in Habsburgs, 89, 94, 212-3; conditions of, 89, 94
Suleiman the Magnificent, 63, 65, 66-7, 77
Supilo, F., 200
Supplex libellus Valachorum, 125
Sviatopluk, Duke of Moravia, 4, 8
Swabians, 117-8, 145
Swabian Turkey, 118
Sylvester II, Pope, 12-3
Syrmium, 20, 22
Szabó, István, 211, 213-4, 218
Szálasi, Ferencz, 227, 234
Szamuelly, T., 205
Szatmár, Peace of: settlement, 93-5, 96; effects of, 96-103; religious settlement, 108-10
Széchenyi, Count István; character, 135-6; Kossuth and, 138, 139, 140, 148; political philosophy, 135-6; writings, 135, 136, 137; view on nationalities question, 148; part in Ministry, 156, 181
Szekels, 5, 9, 10, 23, 31, 50, 207
Székely, Moses, 79
Szelepcsényi, Cardinal Primate, 86
Szepes (Zips), 31, 41
Szilágyi, Mihály, 54, 56
Sztójay, General D., Minister-President, 233-4

Taksony, 11
tariffs: applied against H., 108, 123; abolition of, 148-9, 153,

164, 168; customs union, 148-9, 168, 173, 180, 196; under the Compromise, 168, 173; autonomous, 216-7
Tatars, 32-3, 68
taxation: exemption of nobles from, 15, 16, 28-9, 102, 108, 113, 114-5, 123, 124, 136, 139, 148, 152, 153; in mediaeval H., 16, 41-2, 48, 50, 57-8, 60-1; under Habsburgs, 102, 108, 123; in April laws, 156; growth under absolutism, 165; in Trianon H., 221
Teleki, Count Pál: first Minister-Presidency, 213; part in Imrédy government, 228; second Minister-Presidency, 229-31
Teutonic Order, 86, 90
Thesauriat, 103
Thirty Years' War, 81-2, 83
Thököly, Imre, 87, 91, 92
Timur, 51
Tisza, Count István, Minister-President, 199, 200, 202-3
Count Kálmán, Minister-President; leader of Left Centre, 175; founds Liberal Party, 178-9; policy, 178-9, 185, 198; resignation, 199
tithes, 15, 45-6, 156
Toleration, Patent of, 122-3, 124
towns: growth of, 25, 33-4, 43, 48, 57, 62; free boroughs, 29, 43, 83, 105; market, 43, 57; village towns of Alfold, 69-70; in Croatia, 133; in 19th C., 181; Magyarisation of, 186
Toxun, 11
trade unions, 197, 200, 211, 218-9, 238; Congress, 200
trade, international, 43, 48, 81, 217, 239; internal, 106-7,

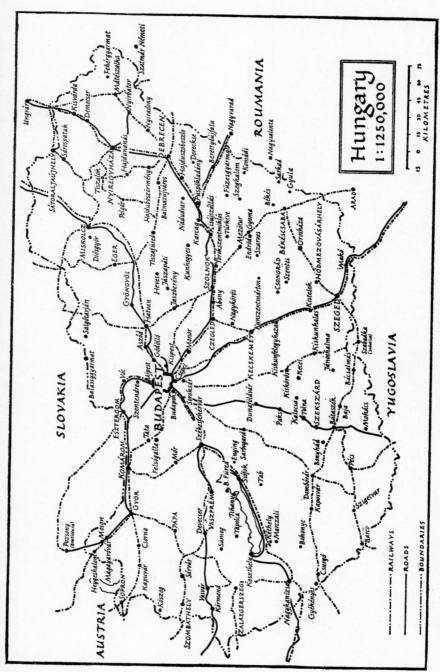

Map 6. Hungary since 1919